A HANDSOME GUY

BY

PHILLIP R. DOLAN

PublishAmerica
Baltimore

First printing

ISBN: 1-4137-2637-2
PUBLISHED BY PUBLISHAMERICA, LLLP
www.publishamerica.com
Baltimore

Printed in the United States of America

DEDICATION

This book is dedicated to Jack and Roberta Dolan.

ACKNOWLEDGMENTS

Frank Moody filled in the details of combat on Okinawa and is quoted often.

Contents

CHAPTER ONE
JACK GETS INTO THE MARINE CORPS

At the forty-acre farm of Jack and Roberta Dolan, Northern Missouri, August 24, 1996. Jack Dolan, "One fellow, I never knew his name, a handsome guy. We got orders to retreat one day. A sniper, evidently, had shot him. He was a handsome fellow. He was lying across the path. I never will forget how scared or how rude people could be that was stepping on him. Right on his face. I will never forget his face. I never even knew his name. I pulled him off the path and covered him up. I couldn't understand the guys ahead of me not doing something. You know? There he lay, face up, looking you right in the eye, dead, and they stepped on him. They didn't even hesitate. You have to be awfully damned scared that you wouldn't even slow down to pick up one of your own buddies and lay him off the path and cover him up. I never will forget his face. Fifty-six years hasn't dimmed his face. I see his face every night."

Roberta Dolan, "Jack has nightmares every night since he came home from the war. He prowls the house eating cheese. We have to make sure that there is always cheese in the refrigerator."

By the spring of 1945, all of the Japanese Island strongholds had fallen in bloody combat or had been bypassed by the Allied forces, except one; Okinawa. It still lay between the American forces and the Home Islands of the Japanese nation. To end the war with Japan, it would have to be taken, and it was the largest and heaviest defended of all the Islands. More than one hundred thousand ten defenders waited and all of the Japanese leaders knew that their position was hopeless. Their plan was simple. It was to kill so many soldiers, Marines and sailors and to sink so many ships that the American people would lose the will to continue the war. Peace could then be worked out that would save the Japanese the unthinkable, an invasion of their homeland. It made no difference at all to the Japanese how many of their people died defending Okinawa, they meant to save their remaining honor. Again, they underestimated the American will. An invasion was being planned and would have taken place if the Japanese had not surrendered after the two atomic bombs struck their homeland.

Just ten months before the battle of Okinawa began, Jack Dolan was still wanting to get into the service. He was a young Missouri farm boy who would, in a very short period of time, be turned into a Marine who would fight in the battle for Okinawa. The fighting began on April 1, 1945 and did not end until June 21, 1945. Jack fought every day until he was wounded three days before it ended. He would experience fighting that took the lives of one hundred thousand seventy-one Japanese defenders, one hundred thousand to two hundred thousand Okinawan civilians, and twelve thousand five hundred twenty United States soldiers, Marines and sailors. In addition to the deaths of nearly three hundred thousand people on this small piece of land, Jack would be among the thirty-six thousand six hundred wounded. America's military would also send twenty-six thousand non battle casualties home. The price for Okinawa was high.

Battle casualty figures can be very misleading and they are in the case of the battle for Okinawa. For example, the Marines landed two divisions on the island that contained more than forty thousand men. Out of this number, slightly more than twenty thousand would become casualties, which is a lot, considering the total number in each division. There is another consideration that makes the numbers seem much worse. A division of Marines contains only three infantry regiments made up of about nine thousand men. These regiments receive the bulk of the casualties in combat. The rifle companies in Jack's regiment averaged casualty rates of 150 percent during their three months on Okinawa with Jack being one of them. He would be back in the United States only seven months after leaving it, but he would be back badly wounded with two Purple Hearts and The Bronze Star Medal with the "V" for valor. He would be back with a "bad" leg, limited vision in his right eye, and no hearing in his right ear. He would be back with the faces of dead comrades and other horrors in his mind. The latter would be his *". . . a lot of glory,"* for the rest of his life.

The Dolan family had finally settled on a large farm fifteen miles northwest of Trenton, Missouri by 1944. Jack had finished high school and was working for A T & T and helping his dad and his oldest brother with the farm work. Missouri farm work in 1944 was long, hard, hot and dirty. By this time, the Dolans had one tractor, but most of the work was done with horses and by hand. Jack was the youngest of four brothers and his next oldest brother, Junie, had been drafted in 1942 and was somewhere in the South Pacific with the Army. Because of censorship, no one knew exactly where he was or what he was really doing. Everyone worried a lot about Junie. The fourth brother, Francis was married, had two small children and also worked for A T & T. Francis and his family lived in Chillicothe, Missouri which was in the next county from where Jack lived. Royal Staly, the head of the family was adamantly opposed to anyone else joining the service. He felt one son sent to war was enough. By 1944 the services would not accept enlistments from men Jack's age (22) anyway. The government had decided that the best way to control manpower was to use the draft to provide the services with all the men they needed. Jack could have volunteered for the draft and gotten in that way except that the Grundy County Draft Board had him listed with an occupation (farmer) that was draft exempt at the time. He wanted to go very badly.

"I was young and thought it would be the thing to do. Everyone else was going and I thought I'd gain a lot of glory."

Francis Dolan received his draft notice in January of 1944. This became Jack's opportunity to join the service. Francis felt that he was too old for war and further believed his wife and two young children needed him more than his country. So he moved his family to Grundy County and his dad, Royal Staly, had him listed with the draft board as a farmer. Jack saw his chance and changed his address to Francis' former county and volunteered for the draft. By doing this, he was placed first on the draft list. This, then, had the effect of Jack taking his brother's place.

"Dad, was so mad that he threw me out of the house. I had to go live with a friend till I left."

Jack asked for the Marine Corps and was sworn into the Marine Corps Reserve, even though he was too short and light to meet the Corps' requirements. Men were badly needed by the Marine Corps and lots of eligibility requirements were being overlooked by the medical examiners. Soon he was shipped to San Diego for basic training.

The Marine Corps was first formed in 1775 during the American

Revolution. The Corps was modeled after the British Marines who were originally organized in 1664. The mission was for them to serve aboard capital warships. They kept order aboard the vessels. During sea battles, they climbed into the rigging to bring musket fire on the enemy crews. They also served as landing parties when the need arose. After the revolution, the Marine Corps was disbanded, except for a brief recall in 1794. In 1798 congress established a "Marine Corps". The assignment was basically the same as the earlier organization, but it evolved into an elite amphibious force that would fight all over the globe. Many attempts have been made over the decades to disband the Corps and turn their duties over to the army. Some attempts were closer than close but they have survived up to now and will likely continue as long as America has a military force.

By World War II the Marine Corps had evolved into experts in amphibious warfare. The Navy who "owned," in a way, the Corps gave them free rein to develop training standards that would turn young civilians into Marine riflemen. The training far exceeded that of the other services and instilled a pride and *esprit de corps* unknown to the Army and Navy. The Marines had become legends. They were highly respected by the other services but not envied. Most people who went into, or were drafted into, the service during the war tried to avoid the Marine Corps because of the difficult training and the self-imposed misery. The Corps did attract the glory seekers, at least the tough ones, and it did attract Jack.

Boot camp was rough but easier for Jack than most others since he grew up working on a farm and had hunted and trapped for extra money. He was small, hard and lean going in, and the same coming out.

"That drill sergeant's verbal abuse just kind of bounced off of me. I was used to working with men that was harsh."

There were men in the Missouri "forks of the river country" who could have made the Marine drill instructors weep with envy, so their abuse just rolled off his back. Basic training had been shortened from twelve weeks to eight weeks, by this time in the war, to enable the rapid deployment of men overseas where they were badly needed.

"I don't know anything that was amusing about boot camp, but I met a lot of people from all around the United States, everything from Cajuns in the South to Finns in the North."

Upon graduation, Jack had enough money for a train ticket home and ten days leave. While on leave, his girlfriend and future wife, Roberta (Bertie) Baugher did what most young people in their situation do. It was 1944, we were at war, they were in love. They had less than ten days together. Then he was headed to the fighting, or so he hoped. He wanted to see combat. Leave ended and he went back to Camp Pendleton for assignment. Of all the things to happen to a new and very proud Marine, the train was a few hours late and Jack lost his Pfc. stripe. He had earned it early and only had it for a few days. While at Camp Pendleton, the Marine Corps offered him a volunteer assignment that would put his stripe back on and purge his record of the Company Punishment that had taken the stripe. He was assigned to a newly organized outfit called Marine Intelligence and sent off to the scout and sniper school located at Camp Quiamaka, in the San Bernardino Mountains of California. The Marine Corps had decided to stop having to rely on the Navy for battlefield intelligence and do it themselves. They selected Jack, among twenty-four others, because he had shot "Expert," was small and had a hunting/farming/outdoor background.

"Well, we learned to creep, crawl and sneak."

In addition, the school taught the young Marines scouting, map making and other intelligence skills in addition to sniper shooting techniques. Creeping, crawling and sneaking seems to be a standard form of mobility but the Marine Corps Scout and Sniper School made it practically an art form. The main test to pass, however, was to hit a twelve-inch silhouette target at a thousand yards with special sport produced sniper rifles.

"We was issued 0-3 scope rifles, Stargaze. It's a special model, a sporting model, which you didn't see in the military, with an eight power scope and a twenty power spotting scope."

The students' emotions and mind sets were monitored daily. If it could be determined that a Marine might hesitate to kill or feel remorse, then he was cut from the school. It proved out later that the scout/snipers functioned much better, even mentally, in the hell of combat than did many other Marines and soldiers. They were taught to not hate the enemy and that sniping was just a job specialty. They developed an above normal compassion for their fellow Marines. This attitude caused most scout/snipers to continuously volunteer to go "in harms way" to pick up wounded and dead Marines.

"The first time I shot somebody it didn't bother me because it was with a sniper rifle and you are never up close so you don't see what happens except through the scope."

Frank Moody, Grangeville, Utah, Scout/Sniper. "I met Jack in sniper school. After that we went back to Pendleton and went overseas together.

Jack became about the best friend I ever had. When we got overseas, the gunny sergeant wouldn't let us serve in the same squad together. We was put in different platoons but in the same company so Jack and I saw each other a lot over there. He was crazy. He would do about anything. He was always volunteering to do something."

After eight weeks of this intense training, they reported back to Pendleton at the replacement depot for assignment. Jack was hoping for shipment overseas to a combat unit. After a few days of hanging around and waiting and waiting, the homeless replacements were called into formation and volunteers were sought for an elite outfit. The only information offered to the potential volunteers was that it was dangerous. They weren't even told where they were to be sent.

"Well, every time somebody said go, I went. I liked to go so when they said stand up, I stood up. I went overseas to the 1st Marine Division that was scheduled to invade Okinawa."

Jack felt that he had been well trained to do dangerous work, and that was what he wanted to do. The volunteers were assigned to the first Marine Division and because their skills were wanted there as soon as possible, they were put aboard a ship that was leaving the next day. All of the replacements aboard were selected for the 1st Marine Division, so the vessel was not scheduled for any stops other than their final destination. They considered themselves lucky that they didn't have to travel in one of the standard troop ships. All of them had heard the horror stories of troop ship life. Their vessel was the USS *Wharton* (AP-7), a converted passenger-cargo liner built for the Manson Steamship Line in September of 1927. The Navy had acquired the liner in 1939 and began using her to transport service personnel and their families until war time duties required her to begin troop transport trips from the States to the South Pacific. Her construction, outfitting and prewar use made her a comfortable home for the Marines. It was a comfortable ride, but the trip still took nearly a month because the vessel's top speed was only 16 knots. Complete boredom set in after the first few days at sea. Jack was placed in charge of a small group and a Marine officer managed to saddle him with an oddball named Dodge on the trip. Dodge had been AWOL but was caught just before they left and quartered in the brig. The officer wanted to be rid of him and required only that Jack get Dodge to clean his filthy rifle. In order to get him out of the brig, he had to be convinced to do that one little thing. Just clean his filthy rifle. He agreed, but cleaned it by taking it to the ship engineers and having them sand blast the weapon. It was as clean as any rifle could ever be, but was as shinny as stainless steel and exposed to the salt air. Jack, although unauthorized, managed to exchange the rifle for a new one from the ship's crew issue before Dodge was thrown back into the brig. No one ever knew what the sailors thought about that blue-less rifle that had appeared in their gun locker. Jack managed to hang onto Dodge through most of the Okinawa campaign.

The ship arrived at a small island in the Russell Islands named Pavava in mid-November of 1944. There is no clear answer as to why the 1st Marine Division was quartered on this small island. It had to be one of the strangest rest, retraining and staging areas ever chosen for any division in World War II. The 1st Marine Division had been reactivated in 1941, some months before the war began and had fought for four months in late 1943 for Guadalcanal. (Except for its 7th Regiment. It was posted to Samoa to oppose any attempted invasion there.) They were then transported to Australia for rest and refitting before being sent back into action at Cape Gloucester in four months. Cape Gloucester was a jungle hell that sapped, rotted and diseased the non casualties into an exhausted stupor. The Marines were dreaming of returning to Australia to heal. They dreamed of heaps of civilian food, that cold Australian beer and the friendly blond girls. What they got was Pavava!

CHAPTER TWO
PAVAVA AND OKINAWA

Pavava was a ten mile long by six mile wide island in the tiny Russell Islands chain sixty miles northwest of Guadalcanal. Before the war, the English had operated a coconut plantation with the help of two hundred natives. The English had abandoned the island before the war and the natives had long returned to a contented life of fishing and food gathering. A Marine Raider unit had conducted a through search of the island in 1943 and had not found any evidence of any Japanese presence. The natives found the search amusing since they knew that no one other than the English had ever been on the island. Finding nothing to do, the Marines left. Marines would be back though, lots of them.

The Division did not want their Marines to go back to Australia. It was felt that they had grown soft while they were there before Cape Gloucester. Morale dropped to a dangerous low when the Division left and they had trouble with men who had become attached to Australian girls. It was also believed that the soft life had contributed to the dissipation of the men during the Cape Gloucester campaign. A new rest area was needed, but where? The decision was up to the III Amphibious Corps commander, a general named Geiger. He did not want the Marines as far away as Australia nor did he want them on Guadalcanal. The "Canal" had now been built up into a huge military complex that was supporting the Army campaign in New Guinea and was serving as a training base for the 3rd Marine Division who was training for the invasion of Guam. Geiger was informed about Pavava and he flew there with some of his staff, to see for himself if it would serve as a base for the weary and sick 1st Division. He saw beaches and groves of palm trees. He did not land and did not notice the jungles and swamps just past the old coconut plantation. He approved the site and ordered the division, which then was being loaded aboard ships at Cape Gloucester to their new home, Pavava. General Geiger's decision would surely have been different if he had consulted the Raiders and learned that of the entire island, only about 600 acres were usable. When nearly thirty thousand men were jammed onto Pavava by the end of the year, it seemed crowded, to say the least. In early May, the Marines landed at their new base. They found that they were to live in a swamp where it rained every day. The heat and humidity were worse than the green hell of Cape Gloucester from which they had just come. The smell of rot and especially that of the rotting coconuts was overwhelming. There were no tents, no roads, no showers, there was nothing. Food was C rations augmented with powered eggs, dehydrated potatoes and Spam. Men and clothes were washed in the rain. Instead of rest, the Marines were turned out to clean up Pavava. They worked from early May, until they left for the invasion of Peleliu in early September, to try to clean up Pavava. They knew the place could never be made livable. They quickly found that was not possible, but perhaps it could be turned into a place where everyone would not just lay down and die. Some Marines did that very thing. The Marines never eliminated nor conquered the rotting coconuts, the armies of land crabs nor the large rats. The men were already sick with jungle rot and ring worm when another epidemic hit in the early weeks on Pavava. Widespread mental illness swept through the division. The Marines called it going "Asiatic" or "rock happy." There were enough medical evacuations and even suicide to concern the doctors, but most of the insanity was just accepted. Just plain depression and utter despair were about an average mental state for the veterans.

"We had a couple of guys that went kind of nuts. Some guys had been out there since the "Canal." A lot of guys had gotten pretty strange."

In July, four thousand plus replacements found themselves joining the division. The veterans finally began to actually get some rest in comparison to how they had been living for nearly three months. In addition to the misery of their living conditions, intense training was added and the 1st Division was shipped to Peleliu in early September of 1944 for one of the worst battles yet seen in the Pacific Theater. When the Division remnants returned to Pavava in mid-November, they found a completely different place than the cesspool they had left.

Jack and another four thousand replacements had arrived on Pavava just before the veterans of Peleliu returned in November. The replacements were almost in shock upon seeing their new home and could not understand why anyone would be made to live in the conditions of this place.

"It was a little island, five miles across, with just one little peak and that was about it. There was barely room for us to stand with about thirty thousand of us there. That was about it."

The first thought among the replacements was that the Division was being punished for something. What had they done to deserve Pavava! It was rumored that the brass was unhappy with the way the Marines had behaved in Australia. They had heard that too many men did not want to leave and many went AWOL. Too many men were completely out of shape, causing casualty rates to soar when they engaged the enemy. It was told that the Division had grown soft from the easy living and the exposure to the luxuries offered by the admiring Australian civilians. The Marine Corps felt there was a better way to keep the 1st Division battle ready so they came up with the idea of Pavava. The island was close to Guadalcanal and therefore lay within transport and supply routes. It was uninhabited and had the same climate and terrain as the islands that the Marines would be asked to fight on. It also had the same diseases, etc. that the men would have to face in future combat.

The returning Peleliu veterans had a different experience upon disembarking and moving back into their "hell hole." The "hell hole," at least, to these "old" veterans was gone! Replacements, though, still considered this as the worst place that ever existed. The swamp had been drained and there were new tents with plywood floors. Each company area had showers and laundries. Each a screened mess hall. There were electric lights and plentiful food. There was a beer ration and a post exchange. There was recreational equipment, movies and sometimes ice cream. There were roads and an airstrip. The Seabees and Marine engineers had been busy while the Division was fighting on Peleliu. One of the first orders of business for the veterans was to make the new replacements shut up and stop complaining about the Pavava living conditions! A Marine could actually live on Pavava now. The heat, humidity, rain, land crabs and rats were still there, however, and equipment still rusted by the minute. Cloth and leather were always in some stage of rot. The veterans still hated it, but after what they had been through, they found their living conditions tolerable. The replacements had never experienced such a horrible place and were puzzled at the veterans' acceptance of it. The replacement Marines found that the veterans were listless and hostile and they mostly refused the menial tasks that are always present wherever the military goes. Work and guard duty of any sort was assigned to the replacements and they marveled at the veterans ability to disappear at the mere thought of work. Most of the replacements respected what the veterans had done, but felt little respect for most of the veterans themselves.

"Well, my instructions was from stateside. It was to look to these old-timers, these old regulars. Boy, they're the guys! I found out they wasn't the guys. Look to the young guys that just got in. The old guys, about two-thirds of them was drunks and professional do nothings. They knew how to get out of work, not do any work. We figured when it got rough on the line, you wouldn't even be able to find them!"

The "old" veterans didn't care about such opinions and ignored the replacements for the most part. The new Marines would finally understand how wrong their assessment of the veterans was when they went into combat themselves in the coming spring. The veterans had learned a lot about the ways of staying alive in combat. Part of it was because the Marines' misery had quickly turned to rage at the Marine Corps and the United States Government. They were furious at their living conditions and shabby all around treatment. The Division turned into exactly what was hoped for. The men were in shape and used to shortages of food and everything else. They were as mad as hell. They had only the Japanese to vent their fury on and they did. The plan was a good one as long as you didn't have to be Jack or one of the other Marines who experienced it. The Pavava Marines laughed at, to them, the ridiculous complaints of servicemen stationed in other areas about the crummy living conditions they felt that they faced during the war. What could possibly have been worst than Pavava?

Pavava had still another serious shortcoming as a military base. It was too small to train the Division for the division's next invasion assignment. So the commanding general came up with the idea of sending strength units the sixty miles to Guadalcanal. There they could train on the large scale that would be needed on Okinawa. The Okinawa terrain was suitable for tank use and the coordination needed between the tanks and infantry was constantly worked on.

Jack was assigned, as a replacement, in 2nd Platoon, G Company, 2nd Battalion, 7th Marine Regiment, 1st Marine Division. Marine units were organized such that the close relationships that developed, (people who became buddies) were mostly confined to a person's squad of thirteen men. One might know several other Marines in a company, but his close support were the men in his own squad. Jack's circle was widened because of his scouting specialty and his missions for the company and battalion, but even for him, his squad was his "family." Operations were generally conducted by the battalion with assignments made to each company. Jack, as a scout had a fairly close relationship with the G Company Commander, a captain named Ed Norton. Captain Norton had been with the regiment when the 7th Marines had been detached from the division, and sent to Samoa in the early months of the war. He was a veteran of Guadalcanal, Cape Gloucester and Peleliu, as were Jack's platoon leader, Sergeant Robertson and his squad leader Sergeant Slitz.

"Captain Norton was a wonderful guy. Wouldn't ask you to do anything he wouldn't do himself. Cliff Slitz was a sergeant. He was my squad leader. He was crazy. Asiatic! You know a guy been there six years, wouldn't go home, had to be crazy."

The junior officers, serving as platoon leaders, had almost completely disappeared, thanks to the heavy casualty rates the rifle companies had suffered on Pelelui. The only times that Jack's 2nd Platoon would have an officer to lead them was late in the Okinawa campaign. One officer was a green replacement and didn't last long enough to even be much of an irritation to the veterans. The other was wounded only a day before the battle ended.

"Neither one of them had any experience and tried to go by the book, and you didn't go by the book with the Japanese. They learned the hard way."

When the replacements reported, the Division had just returned from the battle of Peleliu. Casualties had been heavy and the 7th Marines were badly depleted. The rifle companies were so under strength that enough replacements could not be found, before the next invasion, to bring the regiment to full strength.

"We would go down to the docks when replacements would come in and pick men for the different specialties. Flamethrower guys were real hard to find. No one wanted to do that."

The regiment's time was taken up for the next few months resting and training. On New Year's Eve, the division's officers held a party for themselves. They even brought nurses and Red Cross girls from the Naval facilities, located on a nearby island, to join them in the celebration. The excluded enlisted men had paid no attention to the upcoming officer's party. Plans had been formulated by the men to fire every weapon in the Division at midnight but the officers heard about it and orders were issued that no weapons would be fired. It seems that the Division commanders did not want the women at their party to be frightened. Many Marines were outraged and a small group who were never identified, blew-up a large latrine as a protest. They set larger charges than were necessary and parts of the latrine roof damaged the chow hall. The officers, whose party continued the next night, set guards to prevent any repeat.

"In our area, I had Sergeant of the Guard. They had set up more guards because somebody blew up the latrine. I was walking post when I seen what looked like an —M1 rifle leaning against a coconut tree. I shined my light around. I had a little light that didn't put out much light. I seen a Marine on the ground leaning against the tree, asleep. It turned out to be a guy that I knew from home, but he wasn't from my company. I was pretty rough on him and he was a good guy. There wasn't any Japanese on the island, but we were still in a war zone. If an officer had caught him asleep we would have both been court-martialed. So, I was pretty rough with him. He was in Fox Company and they went through some of the worst fighting they was. Dub made it all the way through till the end."

Mrs. Max "Dub" Miller, Missouri. "My husband said that although they didn't serve together, he ran into Jack sometimes over there. Dub always said, 'Don't ever mess with Jack Dolan, he is the meanest SOB you will ever see. For a while after they came home, they used to meet at the Hy-Power almost every day. They would drink coffee and swap war stories. Those boys had been through so much, they needed to do nothing for a while. They was so skinny. I don't think they ever got over what they had been through, over there. Dub wouldn't ever tell us what he did on Okinawa. When our daughters tried to ask him what he did in the war he would just say, 'We was just animals over there. I helped bury a lot of bodies.' He had the greatest respect for Jack Dolan. He always told me, 'You don't ever want to mess with Jack Dolan. He is the meanest SOB there ever was'."

Since Pavava was so close to the "Canal," Marines were sent there often for training and to dig out left over sniper holdouts. Jack only knew of one Marine who was ever hurt, but there was some sniper fire. He learned what it was like to come under fire and credits the Guadalcanal sniper hunts with lessening his fear of fire, later on Okinawa.

"We were shot at some but the shooting didn't scare me near as much as the first earthquake I had. We was following tanks and smoke had been thrown to provide some cover. We were trying a little Japanese stronghold and I was following a tank when I got fired on. I laid down in the tank track, the mud was about knee deep and it was 110 in the shade. I was laying in that tank track with full gear and I thought I was getting dizzy. I looked down the tank track and it was supposed to be straight, it was crawling like a snake. I took off my helmet and wiped my face and said, 'boy I'm dizzy'. Pretty soon I looked up, coconut trees was all swaying in union. Pretty soon here come all the coconuts. Well, I sat up and found out and finally realized I wasn't dizzy, it was an earthquake. We had a lot of them. I did get accustomed to some sniper fire, you would get a shot throwed at you every once in a while. Later on it was something you put up with every day. And if he got too bothersome, you went after him."

His two months on Pavava didn't affect Jack's feelings about the Japanese as much as it did the older veterans. They had spent much longer on their island hell hole. Jack spent much of his time on Guadalcanal training and chasing snipers. There had also been study of the Japanese culture in intelligence school. The scout/snipers were taught that hate could throw them off targets.

"I didn't know much about them except what they had taught us. I did know more about their weapons than I knew about my own, though. Some of them is ingenious, most of them crude, but of course they got a lot of stuff and copied it and some of it was made in Germany. They was good machine gunners. They had a little light machine gun, one man machine gun, was light, had a rate of about fourteen hundred rounds per minute, where ours dropped down to eleven or twelve and smoked and took a crew to handle it. One Jap could handle his. It was deadly and it was light."

Being in intelligence, Jack learned about the planned invasion of Okinawa before most people and helped make maps from aerial reconnaissance photos. They were well trained by the time they embarked for the invasion, planned for April 1, 1945. The veterans and replacements thought they would be fighting the elite of the Japanese since Okinawa was so close to the Home Islands. They knew that their enemy would fight to the death also, so they had trained hard and well by the time they embarked for the invasion.

"After Pavava, we heard that Eleanor Roosevelt said the 1st Marine Division was the fightingest outfit that she had ever seen, the cleanest bodies and the dirtiest minded, they'd have to rehabilitate them before they could bring them back to The United States. She was funny."

There were more than a few people in authoritative positions who believed that the Marines, after what they had done and what they had lived through, could not be brought home and released from active duty. It was felt that the public would be in danger from these hardened killers. The idea was to put the Marines in camps outside of the United States until they could be rehabilitated enough to release them to their homes. One place considered as a camp was Panama, because it was thought to be similar to where the Marines served and wouldn't be a shock to them if they had to live there for a few months. Eleanor Roosevelt subscribed to this silly theory and was vocal enough to make most Marines hate her. Fortunately, this plan never got beyond the talking phase.

Okinawa is sixty miles long and from two to sixteen miles wide. It lies three hundred miles south of the Japanese Home Islands. The island was an independent kingdom until the 14th century when it became a vassal of China. Then it was annexed and occupied by Japan. Most of the population, the capitol city and the coveted airfields lay in the southern third of the island. The northern part is mountainous, wooded, sparsely populated and has hardly any cultivated land. There were few roads and they hugged the coast line, staying away from the all but impassible interior. The south landscape consists of hills and limestone plateaus that are intensely farmed. The land here is broken up by ridges, scarps and ravines. Nearly all of the low-lying tillable land, planted in rice and sugar cane, is closely overlooked by high ground. Whoever holds the high ground in the south of Okinawa holds the whole island. The Japanese decided to defend the island by fortifying and defending the three east-west ridge systems. The ridges started just south of the invasion beaches and crossed the southern third of Okinawa. The ridge systems just south of the landing beaches were named Kakazu and Nishibaru. The next system, south, was the most formidable with sheer cliffs and deep draws. This system was anchored on the east, near the landing beaches, by Shuri Castle. Just above the southern extreme of the island lay the third defense system of Kunishi, Yuza-Dake and Yaeju-Dake.

The Japanese had years to plan and prepare their defenses. The ridges were mutually supporting with the reverse slopes established to provide fire on anyone attacking the forward slope of any other ridge. They were honeycombed with caves, both natural and man made, and connected with networks of tunnels. It was possible to concentrate troops in the ridge being attacked with supporting fire from the next ridge, and then withdrawing the entire force, to another ridge without exposing troops to enemy fire during the withdrawal. The Japanese General Mitsuru Ushijima had the defenses prepared using all the knowledge gained from all of the previous island battles. Places such as Iwo Jima, Tarawa, and Peleliu. He placed the one hundred ten thousand men of the Thirty-Second Army in the ridge system with the intent of killing enough American invaders to destroy the will of the American people to continue the already too long war. General Ushijima planned to hold what they called the Shuri defensive area to the death. Shuri contained the ancient royal castle, and the second largest city on the island with the current Capitol and the largest city, Naha, anchoring the defense on the western coast. The natural terrain and caves provided the defenders with a certain killing ground for any attacker and insulated the Japanese from American artillery, ship gunfire and even bombs.

The American Joint Chiefs of Staff decided in September of 1944 to invade Okinawa. Earlier that year the Allies had become aware that Japan would not surrender without an invasion of their Home Islands. Okinawa would provide a large staging area for the invasion and give the Allies air bases so close to Japan, that the air campaign could intensify to an incredible level. Once the decision was made in September of 1944, air attacks on Okinawa began. The U.S. Navy moved submarines into Okinawan waters which made supply and troop shipments very dangerous for the defenders. In March of 1945 the carrier task forces moved into the area and began air attacks on Okinawa, Tokyo and the Japanese southern home island of Kyushu. The mission was to eliminate the Kamikaze threat to the invasion fleet consisting of troop and supply ships. The Japanese, instead of waiting for the invasion fleet, immediately commenced Kamikaze attacks against the carriers, battleships, cruisers and destroyers. From March 19 until the end of the month, nine ships were hit by Kamikazes or were struck by mines. A destroyer and a minesweeper were sunk and the carrier *Franklin* was put out of action for the remainder of the war. Another carrier, the *Wasp*, was hit but survived. The Navy lost eighteen hundred officers and men during the March engagements. *Franklin*, alone, had seven hundred twenty-four killed and another two hundred sixty-five wounded.

A few years after the war started the Navy had been building a large ship repair facility in the Pacific rear area. It was located on an atoll named Ulithi in the Caroline Islands, north of Peleliu. This was where the battle damaged warships, fighting in the Pacific, were towed or made it under their own power for damage assessment and repairs. Some ships damaged too badly to repair were scuttled, while most ships were repaired enough so the crew could steam them to shipyards back in the States. A few were returned to action. Navy records abound with documentation of crews engaging in heroic efforts to save their badly damaged ships and get them to Ulithi.

The American invasion plan was for the landing force of the U.S. Army and Marine Corps to land on April 1, with the Army's 7th and 96th Divisions attacking and taking the Shuri Castle area and the Capitol to the south, Naha. The Marines, consisting of the 1st Marine Division and the 6th Marine Divisions, were tasked to cut the island in two pieces and then swing north and secure the northern part of Okinawa. The entire Marine and Army force would then reunite, head south and complete the total destruction of the Japanese forces and take of all of Okinawa.

2nd Battalion was transported to their assigned beach assault station aboard an LST (Landing Ship Tank) with the well deck loaded with amphibious tractors. The tractors were to be the transportation ashore. They were loaded aboard their LST on March 15 and sent to Ulithi where the attack fleet was being formed. They arrived on March 21 and left Ulithi in large convoys on March 27. The LST ride was miserable but at least they would not have to climb down a cargo net fully loaded with gear. Cargo net debarkation from the troop ships was always dreaded and chancy. The ship arrived on assault station the day before the assault, scheduled for April 1, which happened to be Easter that year.

"It took a long time to get to Okinawa. We had to run five miles every morning besides all our other work. Now we laid aboard a troopship without even enough room to move, for sixteen days. It was close, but I was made gunner on the ship's five inch gun so I had the lead place. I slept topside. The first hatch inside. The first bed was mine. Then we set up a tent around the gun and I lived in the tent a good share of the time."

"We rehearsed every day. We had amphibious tractors down in the well deck on the ship. We made ladders and we had barbed wire because we thought we were going over a seawall. When we got there, they would lower the bow ramp and we would take off to the beach aboard amphibious tractors. Their speed was only three mph so they was sitting ducks."

March 31, 1945. The troop ships pulled into their assigned slots in the assault assembly area. "Well, more or less, when we got there we held off out to sea. We was a surprise. The 2nd Marine Division went on the other side of the island and made a mock landing. The Japanese had pulled a lot of their heavy stuff to the other side of the island to defend it. Well, the next morning we was laying out to sea, out of sight. We came in and landed on the west side of the island and the 2nd Marine Division loaded up and went to Hawaii to a rest area!"

Jack has been ordered to go to the beach with a pre-assault team of Navy demolition experts and Marine scouts. His job was to scout the beach for the landing teams and help the Navy teams with destroying obstacles and any mines located in the area. There is a reef about a thousand yards from the beach so the men were loaded into PT boats and carried to the reef. From there they had to continue with inflatable rubber rafts.

"Because I was a scout, I went in on D minus one (the day before the scheduled landing date) the night before with the Navy UDTs (Underwater Demolition Team) who blew up anti boat barriers. We got some fire. We went in and I scouted the beach. The only thing that I could find was two submarine torpedoes. They was set to blow up when heavy equipment went over them. I put a forty-pound pack charge on them and blew them up. I found out that the Japanese had moved everything else off the beach area some days before. So all we would be facing would be small arms fire. We was to rendezvous back on the reef at 0200 and that was the most scared I had been yet, during the war. I wondered if they was going to get me picked up out there in the dark. We depended on PT boats to pick us up. They had put four of us in a life raft and pulled us in as close as they could to the reef and then we floated ashore. We finally got found by the boats and I got back to our ship and got ready to go in on the first wave, the next morning"

CHAPTER THREE
LANDING ON OKINAWA

April 1, 1945. Jack was in the amphibious assault force designated Combat Team Seven (CT-7). This unit was made up of the 7th Marine Regiment consisting of three battalions of nine hundred men in each battalion and attached companies from an engineer battalion, a heavy weapon's battalion, a medical battalion, a medium tank battalion and an ordinance battalion. The three rifle battalions and the attached companies were designated Landing Team seven (LT-7). Each, of the three battalions of 7th Marines was designated LT 1-7, LT 2-7, Jack's battalion, and LT 3-7. CT-7 was chosen to lead the assault waves on the 1st Division's landing beaches. The Marines were transported to the beach in amphibious assault tractors called Landing Vehicle Tracked (LVT).

At 0630 the Marines in LT-7 were loaded aboard the LVT's just as three Japanese Zero's appeared over head and were immediately shot down by Naval antiaircraft fire. Naval gunfire from ten battleships, nine cruisers and twenty-five destroyers began bombarding the landing beaches and up to a thousand yards inland. The firing was lifted just before the Marines landed. As the LVT's moved toward the beach in a line abreast, Navy fighters and Marine Corsairs came up from the LVT's rear and begin strafing the beach. Lots of the Marines saw the plane's empty shell casings hitting the water and thought the planes were strafing them. At 0843 LT-1 and LT-2 landed on Blue Beach One and Blue Beach Two. In Jack's LVT a Marine in the rear leaning against the ramp froze in terror. When the LVT landed part way up the seawall, something happened to the ramp and it would not open. The Marines wanted out as quickly as possible because they were sitting ducks in the LVT now stalled part way up the seawall. Two men grabbed the frozen Marine and threw him over the ramp because he was blocking the way out. The other Marines piled out of the vehicle and observed the thrown Marine sitting in two feet of water still frozen. The last two men out grabbed their buddy and dragged him ashore where he finally recovered his nerves. The Marines had expected to go over the wall with ladders and had carried them to shore. They felt lucky that the Army assault boats had crowded them further up the landing beach, where the seawall presented no impediment to them.

"It would have been funny if we wasn't so scared because we couldn't get out of the Amtrack. He had been put there to pull the thing that drops the ramp. Nobody could get to it without throwing him over the ramp. Later on we thought it was funny seeing him frozen in the water where he had landed, still holding his rifle. He got over it and he wasn't the only guy this happened to. The first thing I did when I got off the tractor was look for something to get behind but we didn't get no fire."

LT-3 was kept aboard their troop ship as a reserve battalion until 1103 when they, too, were landed. There was almost no resistance, at all. The landing battalions suffered only thirteen casualties of which seven were caused by accidents. Jack's squad advanced with LT-7 twenty eight-hundred yards inland, set up a perimeter at Yontan Airfield to protect the beachhead and dug in for the night. This ground was a clay-like soil instead of the coral and rocks the Marines were used digging in and they made their holes deep for the protection they thought they would need. They expected a massive artillery barrage followed by a large force counterattack. Neither one came.

"We was supposed to take Yontan about twelve hundred yards inland. We was expected to be at it for four days and have at least 33 percent casualties. We took it in fifteen minutes and one of our buddies shot another one."

In the late afternoon a Japanese airplane surprised everyone by landing at the airfield. The pilot parked his plane and began walking toward the administration buildings before he discovered his mistake. He turned to run but several Marines opened fire and he was killed. A search of the plane brought a pleasant surprise; in a case were the Japanese naval soundings for the entire island area.

"Our soundings wasn't too good. They was from the National Geographic and was made in 1927. Finding these soundings was a stroke of luck, because our Navy didn't have any good soundings. That fleet out there was a thousand ships so a lot more of them could have run aground than did. And they did run aground, a lot of them."

After the plane incident the Marines took to their holes to wait sleeplessly for the inevitable Japanese counterattack that never came. It was chilly and clear and they didn't have any food and little water. They had carried some water but not enough for the night and had carried no food at all. Their packs were filed with the gear for killing and no room was left for anything else. Naval gunfire and illumination shells fired all night helped keep the tense Marines from sleeping. The assault battalions had captured the small towns of Sobe and Irammiya and began sending civilians to the rear for processing and internment. The native population was considered hostile and orders were issued to treat them as such until the end of the campaign. In specific orders were issued to all of the assault forces about shooting civilians. Reports of some incidents had reached the commanders. There was, however, much compassion for the women and children and when they were taken to the rear, they were well-fed and received medical attention.

The 6th Division, on the left of the landing beaches, and the two Army divisions on the right also had an easy time. There had been only sporadic fire from a few Home Guard troops along the eight-mile front. The Navy and service support troops worked throughout the night to land the heavy guns, tanks, ammunition and other equipment needed by the assault troops to maintain the beachhead. Water and some food supplies began to come ashore early in the morning.

The American Fleet was attacked by a small number of suicide craft and planes. Transports *Hinsdale* and *Alpine*, the destroyer *Adams* and *LST-884* were hit and damaged. Two British ships, assisting in the invasion, were also hit.

The Marines first learned about the Japanese military when the first land combat began on Guadalcanal in mid 1942. Our military had been trained for the kind of conventional war that was being carried out in Europe. The American forces quickly learned that the Japanese tortured, mutilated and killed captured Americans. The Marines knew that they could not let themselves be captured under any circumstance. They developed a fear that would stay with them throughout the war. It was the fear of being wounded too badly to take their own life, allowing the Japanese to capture them. Experience had proven this to be a valid fear. Another tactic of the Japanese would be to send a soldier forward to surrender to the Marines, unarmed and with his hands in the air. He would be strapped with explosives under his clothes and detonate himself when he got close enough to kill the most Marines he possibly could. Wounded Japanese would hide a hand grenade knowing that compassionate corpsmen would treat their wounds after a battle. Several

Navy corpsmen and Army medics were killed or wounded before they learned not to go near Japanese battle casualties. The Marines learned to take no prisoners, to not go near wounded Japanese, to make sure dead Japanese soldiers were really dead and not to be taken as a prisoner. The Japanese combat tactics, especially those involving suicide attacks, were strange and even incomprehensible to the Marines, but they adjusted and used the tactics in their own training to make a Marine rifleman the most deadly of all weapons.

"I never shot no prisoners but I never took any neither, unless they was civilian or Home Guard. I never, exactly, saw anyone shoot a prisoner but I knew they was doing it and I didn't try to stop it neither. One time we had an idiot replacement lieutenant assigned as platoon leader. He went out on his own once and came back with eight Japanese prisoners. He was a by-the-book guy and really proud of himself. He ordered our sergeant Doherty to take the prisoners to the rear. He marched them off and as soon as he got out of sight, around a rock, we heard his Tommy gun. A few minutes later he showed up by himself. The lieutenant was fit to be tied. He was ready to really jump on the old sergeant but Captain Norton was sitting there. He just glared and pointed at the lieutenant and it was all over. He got killed later because he wouldn't stop, going by-the-book."

To die for the Emperor was every soldier's duty, desire and fulfillment, from the lowest private to the highest general. To err and bring shame on oneself was to shame the Emperor and called for immediate suicide as atonement. The *Bushido* code had governed and directed the militaristic Japanese for decades. This old code required these things and much, much, more. The code and its followers, which at the time of WW II was everyone, created a culture that required total obedience and discipline. Strict adherence was created through violence visited upon each pupil by each teacher throughout the society. It started with birth and ended with death. A group mentality developed over a number of decades that pain, suffering, misery and death were honorable conditions to be sought out and savored.

Japanese military basic training made Marine boot camp seem like a walk in the park. Recruits were trained with fear, intimidation, pain and even death as their motivating factors. The smallest infraction would bring sever beatings, sometimes the recruit would be beaten to death as an example to the other recruits. There didn't even have to be an infraction to cause a wrathful beating. The trainer could simply decide that he felt like beating someone. Soldiers went into battle believing that surrender was so disgraceful that is was simply not considered. Enemy troops who were captured were therefore viewed with utter contempt and treated as sub-humans with no right to any comfort or even life. Their battle plans were not based so much on the taking and holding of positions but on the killing of all of the enemy. The way they fought in battle, the brutality, rape, torture and murder of prisoners and civilians who fell under their control wasn't really inconceivable. It was their culture in action on a world stage.

The Japanese high command realized, in the middle of the war, that the American strategy would likely necessitate an invasion of Okinawa. It was a poor island with no value to any enemy except that it was located only three hundred fifty miles from Japan and could provide a close base for the invasion of Japan itself. Okinawa had to be held. It had to be held to the death and the highly respected Lt. General Mitsuru Ushijima was chosen to lead the Army tasked with the job of defense of the island.

The Japanese Imperial General Headquarters (IGHQ) activated the 32nd Army and began reinforcing Okinawa in March of 1944. A huge number of heavy guns, ammunition, and other war supplies were sent for General Ushijima's use. His Army consisted of one hundred ten thousand men made up of mostly combat hardened veterans of the China Campaign (China was invaded by Japan in 1931). It was augmented with trained conscripts of Okinawans and the Home Guard. They also raised civilian labor battalions to construct and arm their defenses. A few were paid but most were worked, by the Japanese, as slaves.

The IGHQ plagued General Ushijima with conflicting orders, troop movements and defense locations until shortly before the invasion. The General decided on his own that his defense would be at the southern quarter of the island. The main defense was on the "Shuri Line" with his secondary defense farther south in the rough escarpments at the south end of Okinawa. He sent one battalion into the north to mingle with scattered units there in order to confuse the invasion force as to where the defenses were actually located. This latter part of the plan kept the two Marine divisions tied up for a month. General Ushijima and his higher-ranking officers knew their jobs were suicide, so they knew they could only kill as many Americans as possible before they were all killed. The motto was "Ten Americans for every Japanese death."

The allied fleet used in the invasion force totaled nearly fourteen hundred ships. There were carriers loaded with planes, battleships, cruisers and destroyers to protect the carriers and provide gunfire support to the landing force. There were rocket ships, troop carriers, hospital ships, supply ships of all kinds and numerous other vessels with special tasks like mine sweeping, patrolling and so on. The landing force itself consisted of six highly trained divisions, four Army and two Marine. The land campaign was assigned to Lieutenant General Simon B. Buckner, USA. He broke the invasion into two parts. All forces would land on an assault beach that started about eight miles north of Naha and ran north for another eight miles. The Marines were to take the northern two-thirds of the island and the Army would take the southern section. The 6th Marine Division would land to the north side of the beach and proceed to the north to operate near the west coast. The 1st Marine Division would land to the right of the 6th, cut the island in two and proceed to the northern tip. The 2nd Marine Division was held in reserve and, except for one regiment and a landing faint, did not take part in the battle. This northern group was named the III Amphibious Corps and was under the command of a Marine Major General, R. S. Geiger, USMC. The Army landed its 7th Division to the right of the Marine 1st Division and the 96th Division anchored the south end of the assault beach. The 27th Division was held in reserve while the 77th Division was used to invade and secure some offshore smaller islands. The Army was designated the XXIV Army Corps and placed under the command of Major General J. R. Hodge, USA. The 7th Division was ordered to proceed to the center of the island and fight their way south. The 96th Division's job was to turn south on the west coast, capture Naha and continue to the extreme south end. The landing force totaled eighty-one thousand Marines and ninety thousand soldiers.

April 2, 1945. The American command was pleased and slightly stunned at the landing success but puzzled by not knowing where the Japanese forces might be. The veteran riflemen were relieved to be able to walk ashore. The feeling of relief was short lived, however. Each hour now filled them with more dread by what they were certain was bound to happen. The Marines were assembled and issued orders for the day and by 0730 the entire force jumped off behind their scouting teams to continue their mission. The Landing Team designations were dropped and Jack's unit went back to its official military title of 2nd Battalion, 7th Marine Regiment, 1st Marine Division. The riflemen had no food and very little water and neither would be available for them until later in the day. The Marines moved so fast through the month of April that supplies always lagged behind. Sometimes their supplies were so far behind that crisis' were created for them by the lack of ammo, water, medicine, etc. Jack and a party were sent ahead of the battalion to scout the area and hopefully find the Japanese defenses.

"My orders was to take some men and cut the island in two. There was a railroad. They wanted the train blew up and they wanted all the telephone wires cut. We didn't get any opposition until about 1000 the second day, and by the end of the second day we had made fifteen miles over the hump and we cut her in two! We didn't blow the train up. We couldn't find it so we blew the track up."

"About 1000, believe it or not, we was all asleep. Oh, I wouldn't say asleep but we was crapped out. We had got clear up on the hump. (A land formation running north to south down the center of Okinawa.) We went beyond our orders for that first day. We made probably five miles. We was up on the hump of the island where we could see down on both sides. We had started to move down on the other side. We was all crapped out around a little old hut or two in a little grassy valley. We was all lying down, not behind anything, and here come eight Japanese out of a hut and they all kneeled down. Four in the front and four behind, like you would see a formation in school, and started firing at us. They didn't hit us and they were close, thirty or forty yards. Close enough to see the expression on their faces. It didn't take me long to get behind something. We had a heavy machine gun crew but the gunner was on one side of the clearing and his equipment was on the other side. He didn't have his water can, he didn't have his bipod or anything so he just rolled her up on a hump and cut loose. She was loaded with incendiaries and tracers and they all ran back in their little shack and they never came out. They was enough fire from five or six men went through that building that they probably couldn't survive anyway, but they never came out. We burned the shack! It fell in. Wasn't nothing to see and our orders was to move. We felt kind of sheepish because we got caught flat-footed. Nobody could ever figure out why they done that."

"We went on to cut the island in two and wait for additional orders. We had crossed pretty hard terrain, there was ridges with cliffs and ravines everywhere. Later on in the day, I was scouting and I heard something coming and they was four men with ropes pulling a German 88 up the road. They was just coming back. They found they was on the wrong side of the hill. They had moved it over to withstand the 2nd Marine Division. (The 2nd Division made a faint landing in order to freeze the defenders in place and keep pressure off the real landing beaches.) They thought Marines were landing on the other side of the island, the day before, and they was pulling it back up the mountain with ropes, four men was. Trying to get it back facing where they ought to have been. We got them. We captured them and took their gun. They surrendered. They was Home Guards, not elite Japanese troops."

By nightfall, the rest of 2nd Battalion and their sister battalions had advanced two and a half miles inland and dug in on high ground only yards short of their goal for the day. Hundreds of civilians had been taken as prisoners and returned to the rear to the Division stockade. They were, as always would be the case, sorted through for disguised Japanese soldiers and/or Home Guard troops. Resistance consisted of only scattered small arms fire, but the regiment still suffered twenty-five casualties with seven killed in action (KIA).

The 6th Marine Division turned north off of their landing beach, and moved as quickly as the terrain allowed. They captured the town of Nagahama and two small defense positions by killing all of the two hundred fifty, mostly Home Guard, defenders.

The XXIV Corps (the two Army divisions) turned into their zone of operations which went from the west coast to the center on the island. They posed themselves to turn south and carry out their mission of taking the southern portion from the Japanese defenders.

The fleet continued offloading tanks, service troops and battle supplies. They carried out bombing missions on both Okinawa and on the southern coast of Japan. Only a few enemy planes were sent against the fleet but a lot of damage was done. *Achernar*, an attack cargo vessel, received heavy damage while three troop transports, *Telfair, Tyrell* and *Goodhue* were hit with only minor damage. Destroyers, *Borie* and *Franks* collided with each other and were damaged to the extent that both were withdrawn from combat. A ship named the *Dickerson* was damaged to the point where it was towed to sea and sunk. This rather unique vessel started life in 1919 as a destroyer and operated as such until August of 1943 when she was overhauled, converted and re-commissioned as a fast troop transport. She was sent to the Pacific and assigned various missions until the second day of the invasion of Okinawa. The *Dickerson* had discharged her troops and retired to the transport anchorage to await further assignment when the planes came. She was hit by two Kamikazes and damaged so badly that the crew was forced to abandon her.

April 3, 1945. The 7th Marines were assembled and then continued their advance across the island. Terrain became increasing steep, craggy and rocky in the center of the island. The high ground was criss-crossed with steep ridges and rocky ravines. Progress was difficult and slow and resistance increased. They began to encounter some mortar and machine gun fire which was quickly silenced by the weapons company's mortars. Both 1st and 2nd Battalions were ordered to dig in for the night while the 3rd passed through them to seize and occupy the town of Hizaonna. K Company became separated from the main body and strayed into the 5th Marines zone. They ran into an enemy outpost with an estimated one hundred soldiers and were pinned down for the rest of the afternoon and night by mortars, machine gun fire and grenades. By the end of the day the 3rd battalion had taken twenty-one casualties, mostly from K company. The battalion command post had a lot of service Marines doing various tasks. They were formed into a Headquarters Company that also provided riflemen for protection of the post. There were Japanese infiltrators every night and many times some of them made it into command post. Playing it "by the book" the Commanding Officer ordered that there was to be no firing in the Command Post. The Marines were to use only knives to protect themselves. The few men who tried this practice paid a price and the rest ignored the order and kept shooting when it was necessary. They just denied that they fired if questioned. The order finally just faded away.

"That was a dumb thing to do. It probably got guys killed or hurt. We was ordered not to fire unless it was necessary. They said firing give our positions away but the Japanese always knew exactly where our positions was. Some of us was always blazing away, even if they just heard a noise. They was a lot of trigger-happy guys. The brass was always ordering us to do something or not do something that didn't make no sense. If the orders was silly, we just didn't carry them out. They ordered us to stop eating the native's livestock and vegetables. They might be poisoned. The natives was eating them, so we did too. If we hadn't we would of starved to death. They ordered us not to drink the water either that even if it wasn't poisoned it had things in it that might kill you. They said don't even bathe in it or even wash your clothes in it. That was one order that we followed."

The 6th Marine Division continued north at a rapid pace and was now twelve days ahead of the schedule. They received orders lifting all restrictions on their movements and they accelerated their already blazing pace. Service troops to their rear were working at a fevered tempo to provide them with supplies and support, but the effort could not even hope to keep up with their speed. The division's scouts began detecting individual and small bands of the enemy heading toward the Motobu Peninsula, which is a large land mass jutting westward from the northern portion of the island. This was part of the division's area of operations and the Marines over the next several days begin "herding" the enemy troops onto Motobu. By April 7, the Peninsula was sealed off from the rest of Okinawa and attention was then directed to killing the forces trapped there.

The Army was making rapid advances to the south with little opposition but one unit did receive heavy casualties. The 77th Division was sitting aboard troopships in the reserve transport area when one of their ships, the *Henrico*, was hit by a Kamikaze bomber. Eighty-six men were hit with thirty being killed. Casualties included several high-ranking officers of the division. Moral was lowered throughout the Division before they could even get ashore.

The fleet, in a manner of speaking, was attacked by suicide boats but the attack was confined to the small naval vessels patrolling in Kim Bay. There were two suicide boat bases located on the bay at the eastern side of the island. They had been located, bombed and strafed by Marine planes the day before. The commander had three operational boats left out of fifty, and he sent them against part of the American fleet that was operating in Kim Bay. This was a problem for the Japanese suicide sailors. The American Navy thought the bay was mined and only permitted small gunboats to operate there. These were LCI's (Landing Craft-Infantry) converted to gunboats by adding gun mounts and additional crewmen. The three suicide boats managed to sink a gunboat thinking it was a destroyer.

Destroyers, *Pritchett*, *Bennet* and destroyer escort *Foreman* were hit with bombs forcing the Navy to withdraw the *Pritchett* and *Foreman*. A bomber scored a direct hit on the *Foreman*. The bomb hit the top side of the ship and passed all the way through the ship before it exploded underwater. The damage control efforts by her highly trained crew saved the ship and she returned to combat duty after permanent repairs were effected. A plane hit the aircraft carrier *Wake Island*, but caused little damage and no injuries. The *LST-599* was also hit by a Kamikaze that caused some moderate damage and wounded twenty-one of her crew.

April 4, 1945. Marine 7th Regiment's "lost" K Company had fought through the night and in the early morning hours 3rd Battalion sent forces to provide cover fire so that the trapped company could withdraw. After obtaining the safety of their own lines, it was learned that their separation from the Battalion had cost them twenty-seven casualties. The other two battalions proceeded east in a line abreast and destroyed small pockets of resistance as they proceeded. When they reached the east coast at 1130, they hooked up with Jack's scouting party and dug in to await their 3rd Battalion. The latter unit had been held up by heavy defensive fire and did not arrive until 1700 hours. All three battalions were in a level, somewhat marshy area, on the southern edge of Chimu Wan Bay. The entire regiment had out paced their supply lines and was in dire need of supplies, especially ammo and water. An air drop was necessary to resupply the Marines. This supply problem would plague the Division throughout the land battle. Fifty-two casualties were recorded in the regiment on this one day.

"At the first part, they had give us scout/snipers, those camouflage suits to wear but we got rid of them after the first few days. It wore out when you crawled around and was more trouble than it was worth. Everything wore out. When I was wounded, at the last, I was wearing a green Seabee shirt they give me. It even had *SEABEES* printed on it in the back. I had green Japanese pants on. Me and Frank had got them out of a storage box in a cave. At least they was the right color but I was the only one little enough to wear them. If they had fit, all of us would have been running around in Japanese pants. My other clothes just rotted off."

The 6th Marine Division continued north and had little contact with the enemy, but it was clear to the scouts that the division's movements were flushing small groups of enemy soldiers who headed directly to Mobotu Peninsula.

The Army divisions spent the first three days of April consolidating their beachhead and bringing supplies and large guns ashore. Now since the island had been cut in two by the Marines, the Army began a southward movement. The 96th Division headed down the western coast toward Naha. The 7th Division turned south on the other division's left flank, inland of the west coast. Both divisions begin running into small pockets of well fortified and camouflaged positions. They did not know it, but these positions were outposts of the main line of resistance and the defenders fought hard. Both divisions began to take casualties that continued over several days. This fighting would sap their strength by the time they hit the main defense works. No thought was given by the commanding generals of flanking movements. A landing south of the known Japanese strongholds would have cut them off from their main defense line and brought annihilation to all of the outlying strongholds. The generals rejected this strategy and attacked their targets head on. This allowed the Japanese to reinforce, at will, or to withdraw as they saw fit. American soldiers did not know from day to day whether the fighting would be deadlier than the day before or whether they were assaulting empty emplacements.

The fleet went about its missions knowing nothing about the massed air attack being assembled and readied to be launched against them in two days. A lone suicide boat did manage to find and attack the cargo vessel, *Carina*. Enough damage occurred to require sending *Carina* back to the Ulithi repair facilities with major damage and six wounded sailors. A gunboat was also damaged killing eight and wounding eleven.

April 5, 1945. The Battalions of the 7th Marines set up defensive positions and began to mop up the small pockets of resistance they had bypassed the day before. In the early afternoon, the Division (excepting the 3rd Battalion which was attached to the 5th Marines for a while) ordered the regiment into reserve and to occupy and defend the town of Ishikawa until further orders were issued. There were thirteen casualties on this day.

"I never did think that I would ever get killed. I figured we was a whole lot smarter than the Japanese. They could whip you at a distance but not up close. They always needed the element of surprise. I always think about the guys like Frank Moody. He grew up with a gun in his hand. He could shoot over his shoulder with a mirror. He could twirl a gun just like any movie cowboy done. He always bragged that he never shot a Japanese in the back, but boy was he ever deadly. If you tried to sneak up on Frank you was gonna be dead."

The 6th Division just simply raced north. They put a regiment on both coasts with tanks and engineers in the middle. All of the road bridges had been destroyed by American air attacks before the invasion. Now it fell to the Marine engineers and SeaBees to repair the roads and rebuild the bridges for the tanks and supply convoys.

The 7th Army Division ran into stronger outposts along its line of attack. Its 184th Regiment hit a position that the defenders had prepared well and received such heavy and accurate fire that by nightfall, they had to fall back from the hill they called the Pinnacle. The 96th Division ran into more resistance also. They approached a low hill they named Cactus Ridge and quickly lost four tanks. The firing caused the soldiers to withdraw several hundred yards for the night.

Air attacks of small groups and even single planes struck the fleet, causing only minor damage. The proud old battleship *Navada* was hit by a coastal battery shell that killed two and wounded sixteen of her crew. She had been sunk at Pearl Harbor but was re-floated and repaired. She served with distinction through to the end of the war. The Navy decommissioned her and sank her as a gunnery target to the dismay of the veterans who had served on her. A somewhat sad ending for a famous ship.

CHAPTER FOUR
THE MARINES SEARCH THE NORTH

April 6, 1945. At this time all of the objects of Phase I of the operations had been accomplished by the ground forces and Phase II began. 1st Division moved to and set up defensive positions around the coastal town of Ishikawa. Local patrols were sent out as a part of their defense of this area of valleys and ridges. In the afternoon the Division received assignment orders, setting up areas for patrolling to establish contact with the enemy and to mop up previously bypassed pockets. Each battalion was given a zone of responsibility so there would be no overlapping and wasting of time covering the same ground.

"While we was sweeping the north we didn't know where we would get the opposition. It wasn't heavily fortified. Our objective was to make contact and secure it. We done a lot of scouting and chasing up there. But meanwhile, they pulled out. We was spread pretty thin to start with and they infiltrated our lines and didn't bother to fight. They went south where they had heavy fortifications. Well, it was all fortified to a degree, but not like the mountains in the south. Those cliffs and escarpments, we called them, had been prepared for years"

The regiment had ten casualties on this day. Thus far, the majority of casualties were what the military called non battle casualties which meant accidents and psychiatric problems. The latter would pull men from the front lines in large numbers throughout the battle for Okinawa.

The 6th Marine Division halted its drive north at the town of Nago to regroup, resupply, rest the men and scout Motobu Peninsula for strongholds. They planned for the men not needed at Motobu to build up supplies and equipment for the drive to the tip of northern Okinawa. This was supposed to complete their part of the campaign. The division's regiment, operating on

40

the east coast, had overrun and captured two Japanese Navy suicide boat bases. Any operational boats had been expended in feeble attacks against American small craft patrolling Kim Bay in the first three days of the invasion. The Japanese Naval personnel had scattered throughout the north and fought as individuals or in small groups. A lot of these wanderers were shot down by Marine snipers. Some Marines even made a game of hunting them down.

"Even if I felt terrible sometimes, shooting someone, I kept doing it. It was either him or me. I wouldn't stop sniping either, because I was young and restless. To me, sniping was more or less a game. I hunted at home as a kid and the Japanese, he was fair game. If he had slanted eyes, he was fair game. For the first thirty days, I was shooting, mostly at long range, at Japanese snipers or transport trucks or other things like that. Put the fear of God in them. That was what I was supposed to do, no matter what else I done. Shooting up close? Well sometimes that felt terrible."

The 96th Division continued its assault on Cactus Ridge after air strikes and in a frontal attack like those of World War I, captured the entire area. Army regiments to the west of Cactus Ridge reached the Kakazu area which was part of the outer perimeter of the entire Japanese defense zone. Fighting turned so savage that the Army began to understand what they were up against and their casualty rates were beginning to stun the commanders.

The 7th Division attacked, for the second day, a coral mound known as the Pinnacle because it stood alone and was not connected to other ridges or fortifications. The target was flanked because of its lack of defensive support. American soldiers found themselves on top of the Pinnacle with the defenders underneath them in holes and caves. The Japanese were blasted and burned from their holes, with only a few managing to escape. The Pinnacle was secured with only one American losing his life. Capturing this high point permitted the Division to continue their advance toward Shuri.

Some days earlier the Japanese High Command had decided, after bitter debate, to send, their last battleship, the *Yamato* and a small escort force of two cruisers and seven destroyers to Okinawa. The idea was to scatter the American fleet so a coordinated air strike would have an easier time hitting individual targets. This was an important decision because everyone knew it was suicide to send such a force against the American fleet especially without air cover. The knowledgeable Naval commanders didn't object to a suicide mission, but they felt that the *Yamato* could not even get close enough to the Americans to inflict any damage. Also, they did not believe the American ships would scatter which would increase the threat to their pilots. To many senior officers, it was felt that the great ship would be better served at home to help protect against the coming invasion of Japan proper. The decision had been made, however, and the officers and crews went seeking death for the Emperor as the highest honor that could be obtained by a sailor.

The *Yamato* and her escort were spotted by air reconnaissance shortly after leaving port and tracked south by planes and submarines every inch of the way. Waiting for her were twelve carriers and hundreds of other American war ships.

In coordination with the intended attack by the *Yamada* the Japanese launched three hundred fifty-five Kamikaze and five hundred forty-five conventional planes against the American ships. In all, there were three hundred fifty-seven confirmed kills of the nine hundred planes they sent. The American forces suffered as well, with six destroyers and a minesweeper being hit but all were able to continue fighting. Kamikazes, bombers, and fighters sank the destroyers *Bush* and *Calhoun* and the ammunition carriers *Hobbs Victory* and *Logan Victory*. These latter two vessels were "Victory ships" crewed by members of the Merchant Marine and therefore, their casualties were not entered on the Navy's casualty roll. The *LST 447*; and the minesweeper *Emmons* were sunk. The *Emmoms* was built as a destroyer the year before the war began. She had a long combat career in the Atlantic Theater until December of 1944 when she was converted to a high speed minesweeper and sent to the Pacific. Five planes hit her in a three-hour period killing and wounding over 60 percent of her two hundred forty-six man complement. Damaged beyond repair were destroyers *Leutze, Morris, Newcomb* and *Witter*. These ships added another nine hundred forty-five sailors to the Navy's casualty list.

April 7, 1945. The 7th Marines carried out assigned patrols and worked to improve and strengthen their defensive position. Their patrols killed five Japanese soldiers and several caves were destroyed. Sometimes there were civilians and supplies in the caves. After the people came out, the cave entrances were closed with explosives to deny the enemy their use and to destroy food supplies.

"We had stopped shaving from the day we hit the beach till the end of Okinawa. We didn't have anything to shave with. A tooth brush was about the most valuable thing you could have. You didn't use it to brush your teeth, you used it to clean your rifle. You was always cleaning your weapon."

"In the rest areas they would bring up water in tanks and hang Lister bags up for us but you couldn't have more than a helmet full to wash with. That water tasted so bad you could hardly drink it. It was island water and it had hook worms or something in it so they treated it with something that tasted like iodine."

The 6th Division had been spread out over the north and their commander had decided from the small encounters with the enemy that there were no enemy strongholds at all in the north. The Division scouts, however, had reported that the Japanese were gathering in the Yae Take hills in the center of the Motobu Peninsula. The dominating hill was fifteen hundred feet high and the entire area was honeycombed with caves. By this day the Division had been gathered and was set to begin the search of the Peninsula for the Japanese defenses.

The Army's 7th Division had worked its way south and now hit the main Japanese defenses. The strongly fortified positions were called Red Hill, Tomb Hill and Triangulation Hill. Enemy artillery was heavy and the Japanese had perfected a way of destroying the American tank-infantry teams when artillery wasn't enough. They sent troops with explosives charging into individual tanks. These suicide bombers were very effective and the 7th Division lost a lot of tanks and crews to these effective and deadly tactics. Casualties in the Division began to mount quickly. The Division was destined to fight at this location for many days, failing in each attack they made. They finally realized that they could go no further without the 96th Division moving forward on their right flank. They needed a joint assault to make any forward progress possible. They dug in and waited, not knowing that their sister division was in even more trouble than they were in.

The 96th Division on the west flank was working its way slowly and cautiously southward taking out outposts as they went. Now they attacked Kakazu. The attack continued for five days without success and ground to a halt. A lot of Japanese were killed but the Army lost two thousand nine hundred men.

In the early afternoon, Admiral Ray Spruance, as commander of the entire fleet, gave the signal to attack the *Yamato*. In short order the first wave of two hundred fifty American planes jumped on the *Yamato* and her escort vessels. Three other waves followed for a total of three hundred eighty-six planes and the giant ship was sunk in an hour and a half with a loss of life of two thousand sixty-three officers and men. All of her escort vessels were sunk with the exception of three destroyers that made it back to their home port with a few survivors.

The Japanese High Command tried to keep the sinking of the *Yamata* a secret from the people so morale would not be affected. The secret didn't matter much because when word did leak out no one believed it. It was perceived as American propaganda because the Yamato, to the Japanese, was unsinkable. America lost twelve pilots in the one-sided battle, while there were four thousand two hundred fifty Japanese deaths recorded.

A gunboat and a dredge hit mines and sank while the destroyers *Bennet* and *Wesson*, the battleship *Maryland* and the aircraft carrier *Hancock* received hits from Kamikazes. The *Hancock* had only been in commission for a year and had been in combat for nearly all of that time. A Kamikaze making a run on the carrier was badly damaged but made it to the flight deck and cart wheeled into a number of parked planes. Damage to the flight deck and below decks was severe but the crew saved the ship. She was sent all the way to Hawaii for repairs and made it back into combat by July 17. The damaged ships had a total of one hundred eighty-seven casualties, mostly from the *Hancock*.

"They brought a destroyer in close there to provide gunfire support. She finished her mission and some of us was sitting there watching her. A plane came over and dropped his bombs at her but they missed. The plane circled around and come at her just above the waterline. He blew a big hole in her side. You could see fire coming out. They got the fire under control because they stayed there and did some more firing into shore. The next morning she was gone and there was a cruiser setting there. The Navy never quit their gunfire support no matter what the Japanese throwed at them."

April 8, 1944. The 7th Marines moved their three battalions around in an attempt to make contact with Japanese fortifications. They were sure they would find some any day now. They were now spread out on the coast and moving inland toward the north. No Japanese were found at all.

Motobu Peninsula was now the sole focus of the 6th Marine Division.

They didn't know exactly where the Japanese defenses began and ended but they knew it was somewhere in the rugged, mountainous, Yae Take region. This region provided high ground and natural defenses and was the obvious place to find the Japanese.

The 7th Army Division completed the capture of the three strongly defended hills it had faced. After the Division tried a flanking movement to the east that was totally repulsed, they realized they were now up against the Shuri Line. An attack would have to wait for the 96th Division to come up so a joint effort could be made against the Japanese perimeter. The 96th Division stumbled up against Kakazu Ridge. Without knowing it yet, this ridge position was an integral part of the main defense system and was as heavily fortified as any position ever could be. The Division was ordered to attack the next day.

Air attacks from Japan continued on the American fleet with the destroyers *Gregory* and *Badger* hit by Kamikazes. The attack cargo vessel *Starr* was struck by a suicide boat. Suicide boats getting through the protection against them were rare, but it did happen. *Starr* was at anchor with her landing craft moored alongside for the night. Not long before daylight, a huge explosion startled her already nervous crew. Fortunately the suicide boat crew crashed into a cluster of landing craft instead of the side of the ship. There was such little damage that the ship continued her duties without any delay.

April 9, 1945. 7th Regiment sent its1st Battalion to the village of Kim where they set up defensive positions and began patrols in their assigned sector. In the afternoon light contact was made by 2nd Battalion in the vicinity of Kin. Six Japanese Naval personnel were killed with the loss of seven wounded Marines. Jack's unit remained near Ishikawa where they carried out patrols but made no contact with the enemy.

The 6th Division did not know the disposition of the Japanese gathered on Motobu nor their numbers. The Japanese had assembled various units from all over the north including Naval personnel and Okinawan conscripts. They had adequate supplies, ammunition, plenty of artillery and were well dug in on high rugged ground. The Marines started to search for them by sending the 22nd Regiment into the Peninsula. The regiment's 1st Battalion set out down the center directly toward Yae Take with the 2nd Battalion moving along the north coast and the 3rd Battalion was sent up the south coast. Late in the day, 2nd Battalion took an abandoned PT boat and midget submarine base, but did not see any other action by the end of the day. The 3rd Battalion found nothing, but just before night fell, the 1st Battalion was hit by heavy fire and was forced to dig in for the night.

Two companies of the 1st Battalion of the 96th Division crossed the gorge in front of Kakazu Ridge, undetected by the defenders. During the night they had come to rest on the crest of the ridge.

Approximately twenty Japanese planes were sent against the fleet, but no serious damage occurred except to the destroyers *Badger*, *Sterett* and *Hopping*. They were hit respectively by a suicide boat, a Kamikaze and a shore battery. Two sailors were killed and twenty-seven were injured.

April 10, 1945. Patrols from the 7th Marines contacted small groups of enemy soldiers, mostly Home Guard, in defensive positions scattered throughout their assigned sectors. Enemy soldiers killed is unknown because most were in caves that were simply sealed off by the Marines. Defensive and supply installations were destroyed or captured with the supplies being sent to the rear with a number of Japanese documents included. After darkness fell, the enemy, using small arms and grenades, tried to infiltrate the Marine lines. Booby traps, set out by the Marines, killed and wounded many of the small groups making the attempt and survivors withdrew before the dawn came. There were no Marines killed in this action, but six were wounded and twelve were evacuated for other reasons.

Frank Moody. "I went out on patrol a lot. Jack didn't do that as much as I did. I would lead out two or three guys up to ten guys sometimes. One time thirty guys. I kind of took them out through the brush on patrol. Jack just went out on his own a lot, sniping. One day his shoes come apart. He couldn't go out for a few days while they ordered new ones for him. We was scouting a lot up north there and one day a guy named Clark went out in my place. He got killed. Jack heard about it and thought it was me. He had heard it was me. So when I saw him, he looked kind of funny at me. I asked him what the heck was wrong. He said he thought I had been killed because I always led the patrol. That was me, most of the time. He was just sitting there trying to decide what he should write to my folks. He looked so funny at me that I thought, 'What the heck is wrong with him.' He had a look that I had never

46

seen before or since for that matter. That was what it was like. Things like that happened to you."

The 6th Marines, on Motobu, kept their 1st Battalion in contact with the Japanese they had run into late on the previous day. The 2nd Battalion, who had gone down the north coast the day before, now turned inland and hit the Japanese defenses while trying to get to the rear of Ye Take. The 3rd Battalion on the south coast had not yet made any contact but they soon would.

Early in the morning, the Japanese finally saw the 96th Division's two companies on the crest of Kakazu Ridge and begin firing on them and on another company trying to cross the front gorge to reinforce the ridge crest. These three companies were so decimated that not even the few survivors were returned to duty. The rest of the Division attacked along the ridge but was thrown back with staggering losses.

Few planes went at the fleet and none of the ships were damaged

April 11, 1945. Marines of the 7th Regiment mopped up the area where they had made contact the day before and continued patrolling their assigned areas. A lot of native men of military age were rounded up and sent to the rear. Once there, they were interned and sorted for disguised Japanese and Home Guard troops trying to escape to the south.

"Captain Norton called me out. We was in fairly level country at the moment. He said, 'We got a fellow waving a white flag, he wants to palaver.' He said, 'You think it's a trap?' I said I didn't know. I said he was a long ways from anything that we could see. He had a western suit on and he was carrying his shoes in his hand and waving a white flag. So I said, why don't somebody cover me and we will go out and talk to him. If he speaks English. So the Captain said, 'If you got guts enough to go, I'll go with you.' We went out and captured him. He spoke better English than I do. He taught school, eighteen years, at Sacramento, California. He was captured by the Japanese. He had lost his wife in the Philippine invasion and he had a family of twin daughters and a single daughter. The twin daughters was married to Japanese soldiers and he had distinct knowledge of all of the island. He had worked on about all of the emplacements. He drew us a map and showed us where all the heavy opposition would be. The only thing about it he said was, 'There ain't no way you can do it!' He decided we was whipped and, of course, he listened to Tokyo Rose too, I reckoned. He was glad to surrender, because I asked him. I said, 'What did you miss most about the United States?' He said, 'Camel cigarettes and ham sandwiches.' He smoked pine needles and hadn't had a piece of ham in five years. He was a very gracious fellow. Him and his family was nice. But there wasn't no way we was going to win the war. The little fellow thought they was gonna win the war. I had a little telephone so I could hook into communications at night and they sometimes broadcast Tokyo Rose, over the wire. She said the first night of the invasion, 'Look out to sea, all of your ships is sunk. The 1st Marine Division is cut off. They are annihilated. You just as well surrender now.' All I could see was airplanes of ours in the air and about 700 ships between me and Japan. So, I didn't think Tokyo Rose was quite on the ball, but the old man he thought she was. We got a lot of information out of the old man that was invaluable later on. Because he knew, in detail, where everything was at. But that didn't mean, to him, that we could take it."

"Them Navy guys put the daughters to work making Japanese flags out of parachute silk and selling them to the air corps and service troops for booze and money. They was getting two hundred dollars a piece for them. "

The 6th Marines kept probing Yae Take to learn all they could about the Japanese defenses before launching an attack in force.

The Army attacked Kakazu again and made it to just below the crest of the ridge when the Japanese counterattacked in strength. After a few hours of close combat they drove the Americans back to their original positions. That night the American soldiers experienced a particularly heavy bombardment. Casualties in the two assault regiments were so heavy that some commanders thought the regiments might be finished as fighting units.

Attacks on the fleet were concentrated on the radar picket destroyers north of Okinawa. (One of the author's uncles, Jack Dollar, served aboard the destroyer *Kidd*. No one in his family ever knew his ship was badly damaged and that many of his friends were killed by a Kamikaze.) The destroyer *Kidd* was knocked out of the war when a kamikaze hit the ship and exploded in her forward boiler room. The entire crew of thirty-eight men stationed there were instantly killed. The battleship *Missouri* was struck as were the carriers *Enterprise* and *Essex*. Hit as well as the *Kidd* were the destroyers *Miles*, *Bullard, Hale, Trathen, Hank* and the destroyer escort *Manlove*. The famous carrier *Enterprise* known as "The Big E" had a lot of experience with damage from bombs and planes. In fact she was the first aircraft carrier to win a Presidential Unit Citation. She was forced to leave the battle a few days for repairs but was soon back in action.

April 12, 1945. 2nd Battalion's area was bombed by three Japanese planes early in the morning but no one was hit. By midmorning all of the companies, except George Company which was held in reserve, had sent out patrols including one with trucks to round up civilians. Easy Company ran into heavy action in their zone, including machine gun positions and lots of sniper fire. Some of George Company had to be sent forward as stretcher bearers. Smoke was fired so Easy could extract itself from the fight and to provide cover for the stretcher bearers. George Company carried out twenty-eight dead and wounded Marines, mostly from the 2nd Platoon. They had born the brunt of the fight and had only five men left standing. George was moved out shortly before dark, to the edge of Easy's battlefield to catch any infiltrators and to be ready to attack the Japanese positions the next morning.

Frank Moody. "We were up in northern Okinawa, oh, for at least a month. I spent my nineteenth birthday up there with the total company up in the mountains. Jack was up there somewhere, but I didn't see him too much. There was a fight, I think it was Easy Company and they sent my platoon up there to get some wounded guys out. Heck, we didn't even take our packs, blankets or anything. We was gonna come out that night, but we ended up staying up there for nine days! We just took some hand grenades and guns so we could get out fast. Our whole platoon went, thirty-eight or forty-one guys. We ended up having to stay up there all night away from everybody else. It was cold up there at night just like this country here (Utah). It was cold at night, we had no blankets just light clothes and we was used to the heat over there. We just about froze to death. You sat there with your teeth chattering and shaking so hard. We had sat down on the side of a little old mountain that night, there. We didn't have very many trees so you could see pretty well what was going on around us. We just about froze to death. We didn't have no blankets or ponchos. We had left everything down at camp where we were when we took off. That is the coldest I've ever been. It was just so cold because we weren't use to the cold at all. We come out of there nine days later but we were supposed to have been there part of one night to get wounded guys out. I didn't see Jack for all those days until we got back. I was really glad to see him and get out of those mountains."

By this time, spring had arrived on Okinawa and two types of flies emerged to pester the Marines. They couldn't even eat without swallowing a few of them. Also hatched, were hoards of mosquitos. It was too far north for the bugs to carry malaria, but they did pass dengue fever to the troops. The worst pests of all were the Okinawa fleas. Almost every Okinawan household kept livestock of some sort and the war had killed or driven away the domestic animals. So the fleas found Marines to be suitable hosts and thrived on their filthy bodies and unshaven faces. For the first time Marine commanders sent in an air strike to bomb their own people, but instead of bombs the planes carried insecticide. The Marines were greatful and rolled around trying to get as much of the spray on themselves as they could.

"Those fleas crawled all over me, but they didn't bite me. The crawling around was bad enough, but I was lucky that they didn't bite me. Think about laying out there in concealment waiting for some Japanese soldier to come along or trying to sneak up on some sniper with fleas crawling all over you. We was so hairy and filthy that the fleas just loved us. They liked to drove some of the guys crazy, so we was always glad when they sprayed us. We would run around and roll around in the spray trying to get it all over us."

The 6th Marine Division had finished their patrolling of the Motobu, Yae Take hills and now had a clear understanding of their target. The slopes of Yae Take were so steep that it appeared the attack would bring horrendous casualties. To try to lessen the casualty rate, the 6th Division's outstanding commander, General Shepherd, implemented a plan that split his division. He would assault Yae Take from two opposing sides. Before the attack, he put maximum heavy weapons fire in the center of the defenses by both attacking forces. Air strikes and Naval gunfire were added. This plan was made possible because the Japanese defenses, here, stood alone and could be surrounded. This would permit heavy fire on the Japanese from all directions. The enemy would not be able to use their tactic of firing mortars from the reverse slopes of their defenses. Thanks to General Shepherd's attack plan, the reverse slopes were exposed to his artillery and were really hammered.

The 7th Division was still waiting for the 96th Division to move forward. The latter committed more regiments and attacked all along Kakzu Ridge after a massive concentration of fire from ground artillery, air and gunfire support ships. The division gained the ridge, but was so broken that further advance was impossible in the face of enemy fire.

Some high level Japanese commanders could not stand defensive warfare any longer and finally convinced General Ushijima to launch a heavy attack this night. For several days the Japanese had been maneuvering troops into positions. The idea was to infiltrate units behind the American lines and then launch an all out attack from front and rear positions. They expected to kill large numbers of soldiers and regain defensive positions previously lost to the Americans. At approximately 2330 diversionary attacks hit all across the Army's lines. The result was nil except for a lot of Japanese casualties. Then the main attack began against the 27th Division at Kakazu. If things worked correctly, a wedge would be driven into the American line and the 27th Division could be enveloped and destroyed. The plan failed. The well dug-in 27th Division soldiers slaughtered the attackers. One battalion did manage to reach the rear of the American division, but they were too scattered and disorganized to cause much trouble. Most escaped back into their own lines while the others were hunted and killed.

The Japanese air attacks on the fleet at Okinawa continued with the destroyer *Abele* being sunk along with an infantry support craft. Serious damage was inflicted on thirteen other ships including six destroyers and a destroyer escort. The *Abele* was sunk by the Japanese new secret weapon, a piloted bomb. While on picket duty, she was hit by a Kamikaze that penetrated and exploded in her engine room. There was every likelihood that she was going to sink anyway when the "Baka" bomb hit her at the waterline with its two thousand six hundred pound warhead. Two other ships were hit by "Bakas", but the *Abele* was the only ship ever sunk by one. Admiral Nimitz called out B-29s to attack the airfields in southern Japan in an attempt to reduce the number of enemy planes. Regardless of the effort, two hundred eighty-six fighters bombers and Kamikazes would fly against the Americans on this day. The Navy and Marines lost twenty of their own planes while claiming to have shot down one hundred twenty-six of the enemy aircraft. The damaged and sunken ships reported another seven hundred casualties. The Navy was becoming very concerned with their losses in both men and ships. They could not see any end to the destruction of their fleet.

It was announced to the troops that President Roosevelt had died. This news brought a pall of depression over the men that added to the gloom of the battlefields. He was loved and respected as a leader by most of the military's lower ranks and almost no one knew anything about Harry Truman. How would he handle the war?

"We didn't know much about Truman and we didn't think he was very good. It looked like he was too weak to lead us in a war. We didn't have much confidence in him."

April 13, 1945. Last night had been a quiet night and the Marines of 2nd Battalion received some rest, and readied themselves to move into their zones of action again. An air strike was scheduled for George Company's front and the battalion tanks were registered for support in the rear. This time tanks could not go forward with the infantry because the steep and hilly terrain prevented it. The air strike was canceled because the planes were diverted to a hotter spot, so the pre-assault bombardment left a lot to be desired. Fox and Easy moved off with George and all three companies received fire. George received an additional task in the midmorning when they were ordered to pick-up and return Easy Companies' packs that had been dumped and abandoned the previous day.

Enemy firing increased as the day wore on. The area had a number of caves many of which were woven into the pockets of the Japanese defenses. There were pillboxes, bunkers and machine gun emplacements to be destroyed by the Marines of the 2nd Battalion. There were many of the famous Okinawan burial vaults in the area which the Japanese loved to fortify as well as they did the caves. The vaults had to be cleared of Japanese soldiers and then sealed to prevent machine gunners and snipers from re-occupying them. For reasons that were unclear, there were a lot of civilians living in this area and they had chosen not to leave when the fighting started. There were so many that the Marines decided to intern only men of military age and let all of the other people stay where they were.

The 6th Marine Division prepared for their attack on Yae Take which was scheduled for the next morning. Two battalions from the 4th Marine Regiment and the 3rd Battalion from the 29th Marines were moved into place on the west side of the hill mass. For the advance on the eastern side, the Marines would use the other two battalions of the 29th Marines.

Navy command's irritation grew at the Army's lack of movement. The fleet was taking losses from air attacks and wanted the Army to speed up and complete the ground battle. Both the Navy and the Marines thought the Army's method of combat was too slow when fighting the Japanese in their heavily fortified and protected positions. The army, when they ran into opposition would stop and wait for artillery and other fire support to reduce the enemy positions. This kind of fighting didn't work well on Okinawa because artillery failed to kill when the enemy was deep in his cave and bunker defense system. The Army believed their way of fighting saved casualties and it probably did, except in this case, the Navy believed it was costing great damage to both sailors and ships. The Navy wanted the Army prodded into faster movement and talk surfaced about replacing General Buckner. The debate over Buckner in the days ahead grew ugly until Admiral Nimitz, the overall commander of the Pacific forces, put an end to it. Nimitz knew that to relieve the Army general would cause an inter-service problem that could jeopardize current and future joint operations. He knew General MacArthur would be enraged and, to the Admiral's credit, he was not willing to let that happen.

The 96th Division continued to fight on Kakuza Ridge. Late that night the Japanese launched another small counterattack which was turned back with little effort. This attack was made as a part of the larger offensive of the night before.

Japanese air attacks on the fleet were few this day. Only one plane made it through the fleet anti-aircraft fire and patrolling planes and slightly damaged a medium landing ship but there no casualties.

April 14, 1945. 2nd Battalion was patrolling its assigned sector when they encountered approximately one hundred fifty Japanese occupying defensive positions scattered throughout an area of high, wooded, ground in rugged terrain.

"We got a guy killed. He was eight to ten feet away. It was terrible. He was a veteran and he had growths on his feet. They took him to the hospital on Pavava and we carried him around on a stretcher. We carried him back and forth to the chow hall and we carried him to the bathroom until they operated on him and he was back on his feet. He could of went home, but he wouldn't do it. He had one Purple Heart but he was bound and determined to stay. We went up in the morning with him, and we was getting opposition from the top of a hill. The Air Corps said there was a heavy pillbox. We went up to take it. My platoon leader, Slitz, got wounded and the squad leader, Reese, got wounded. He got shot in the hip. We got up there and there wasn't anybody there. They had abandoned it. We got behind it for protection to try to decide where to find the Japanese and this boy, I can't think of his name, he leaned out around the pillbox to look down the path. We heard a smack and he turned around with his hand over his collar bone and said, 'Boy this is my second Purple Heart. I can go home now.' He fell dead in his tracks. Later on I seen the doctor and he said he was shot with a wooden bullet. That was our first experience with them. He said that bullet had hit his collarbone and they was splinters all through his heart. And the wooden bullet, believe it or not, wouldn't hardly scratch a rock but it had this wicked little snap. You see, they was made out of hard maple, with a gas check on the back to keep them from burning up when they went down the barrel. They was wicked. Up close they made a tremendous wound. I got hit with one at Dakeshi."

"The first time you see somebody you know is shot, it is a shock. You know, about all of us was closer than brothers, really. You had to learn the guy, you had to learn what he was like, you had to learn to depend on him. By gosh, your life depended on it."

"We got the guys who shot Melcher, I think that was his name. We got 'em. We almost never left our dead, but that time we got so much fire that we pulled out and left Melcher because there was only two of us left that could still walk. We took Slitz and Reese with us but we had to carry them and drag them and we left Melcher but we went back and got him the next morning. We took a burial detail and brought him back."

The 6th Marines attacked Yae Take from opposing directions, as planned. The Marines on the east side immediately ran into overwhelming fire from well dug in positions, and were pinned down for the rest of the day. Marines coming from the west advanced several hundred yards and then encountered a new Japanese tactic. They had put together small teams built around a heavy machine gun and a few light machine guns. These teams would hide on the rugged slopes and in the ravines with enough concealment that made them almost impossible to spot. They would hold their fire until several Marines had passed their position and then fire a few rounds and run away in order to do it again. This tactic caused a lot of dead and wounded, but it did not stop the Marine units from pushing to their first day target.

The Marines dug in for the night in front of two fortified hills that protected Yae Take. Hill Green and Hill 200 would have to fall before the Yae Take itself could be assaulted. The Marines also needed these hills for their own artillery to be able to support further advances.

96th Division continued to attack the main Japanese defenses in the Kakuza Ridge area. The division was so depleted by casualties and overcome with exhaustion that General Buckner sent his reserve 27th Division into the line. This new division took over the western side of the 96th Division's area of responsibility. Army Command also brought up twelve hundred replacements for both the 96th and the 7th Divisions although this number did not even come close to filling out the divisions ranks.

The Japanese sent their last, small, offensive attack against the American lines. This was the last part of the offensive that had been planned and had actually commenced with a large attack back on April 2. The Japanese offensive was a disaster. It killed and wounded hundreds of soldiers that would have been better used if they had stayed in their defensive positions. The soldiers fought well from concealment and inflicted heavy casualties on the Americans, which was their goal. In the open, on the offensive, they ran into the vastly superior firepower which killed them in great numbers and left their defenses weakened by their losses. There were simply no more Japanese or Okinawan men to replace their casualties.

Only a small number of planes attacked the fleet with the battleship *New York* taking a minor blow. *Sigsbee*, a destroyer, was hit and severely damaged and had to be towed to Guam for repairs. She reported only four killed and seventy-four wounded and was not put back into service until after the war. The destroyer *Dashiell*, on picket station was attacked by no less than twenty planes. All were beaten off except one pilot who dropped a bomb that barely missed but caused some damage to her. The *Hunt*, another destroyer was hit by a plane but stayed on station until being relieved a few days later.

April 15, 1945. The land battle began to change on this date. Most of the American Army units had now made contact and were engaged with defenses that were more than just outposts or scattered pockets. The enemy had now been found and the Army was beginning to understand how the island would be defended. The fight would be in the south.

The 7th Marines kept their battalions patrolling their assigned sectors on the east coast. They killed or wounded a lot of individual soldiers and wiped out small pockets of resistance. Japanese snipers fired on supply trucks on the roads at night and hid from the American scout/snipers during the day.

Small groups of enemy soldiers had been bypassed because of the speed of the Marine's offensive and had to be dealt with by rear area support Marines. Because of the unique nature of the Marine Corps, all Marines were considered riflemen first regardless of whatever other job they filled, so it was not necessary to pull any combat Marines back to deal with the enemy left in the rear. The support Marines were well up to the task.

"A day never went by that you didn't have snipers after you. You just got used to them just like everything else. Back in the rest areas we didn't even go after them unless they got to shooting too much and hitting guys. You knew about where he was and where he could shoot so you just avoided those areas. If you had to get him, you have a bunch of guys shooting about where you thought he was. That would pin him down till somebody could sneak up there and get him."

The 6th Marine Division had finished sealing off all of the Motobu Peninsula and could now send more forces to continue the attack on Yae Take since the 1st Marine Division had reached the northern tip of Okinawa and could protect their sister division's rear. The Marines on the east side of the defenses were still pinned down and would remain in their positions for another day. This left the burden of the advance to the men on the western slopes and they commenced their attack on the two hills (Green Hill and Hill 200) guarding Yae Take. During the morning the Japanese "hit" teams operated as they had the previous day, but by noon the Marines encountered dug in positions and the fighting became fierce and casualties mounted. By the end of the day the Marines were on the crest of Hill 200 and the battalion attacking Green Hill was digging in just below their crest. In addition to losing a lot of men, the survivors were too exhausted to fight any more. General Shepherd decided that his tired men would continue the fight the next day but that he could relieve some of the pressure by attacking with strong elements from a fresh regiment. He would send these units from the south which would put them up against the Japanese flank. Shepherd was certain the Japanese did not have enough men to protect this south flank.

The Army's advances had been brought to a complete halt all across southern Okinawa. There was no known way into the Japanese outer defenses except head on assaults that continued to fail, each attack bringing heavy casualties. So, the Army held their positions and began recon missions in force to try to find a weakness in the defense system.

A few planes were sent out to keep up pressure on the fleet. They hit two destroyers and a fleet oiler. The only other damage was to the emotions of the already nerve jangled ship's exhausted crews who kept working at alert status. The Navy sent a sizable force of planes to attack the airfields on southern Japan in hopes of destroying a large number of enemy planes on the ground. The fleet oiler damaged, the *Taluga,* was hit by a Kamikaze while in route to Okinawa with three hundred gallons of aviation fuel. The plane pierced her deck and came to rest in a compartment next to the fuel tanks. Firefighting efforts by her crew kept the ship from exploding and she continued on with her cargo.

April 16, 1945. Men of the 7th Marines were becoming overwhelmed by civilians who increased in number every day, now. They clogged the roads and had to be cared for in a number of ways that distracted the Marines from their mission. Patrols would find evidence of human activity in cave complexes. They hoped they had found enemy positions, but too often the caves were filled with civilians in dire need of food and medical care. Each group had to be searched for disguised Japanese soldiers or Home Guardsmen before being transported to the west side of Okinawa to the detainee camps. There were now huge numbers in the detainee camps and most of the people were suffering from malnutrition and a variety of medical problems that diverted support from the American fighting men.

Marine Battalions of 6th Division began the main assault on Green Hill in front of the heights of Yae Take. By late afternoon, they had men on the crest of Green Hill and had slaughtered the defenders, but the Japanese still held many of the lower ridges around the crests and launched several counterattacks. The Marine advance against the south flank had brought success in turning back the counterattacks and helped to shatter the defense of Green Hill. The Battalion that had taken Hill 200 the previous day pushed to the crest of Yae Take itself and defeated the Japanese there with close-in fighting. After nightfall, the Japanese counterattacked with every soldier who could move but the Marines drove them off and by morning it was discovered that the defenders who lived had left. There were three hundred fifty Japanese dead, as counted by the Marines, from the counterattack. The division's problem, now, was to stop the fleeing Japanese from escaping and setting up new defenses.

The two battalions that were assigned to advance from the east had made no headway at all toward Yae Take, so they gave up the effort and began to proceed down the Itomi-Toguchi road. This movement managed to cut off and then destroy hundreds of fleeing Japanese who were trying to go deeper into the Motobu Peninsula. Several hundred men, along with the commander of the Japanese forces in northern Okinawa, Colonel Udo, escaped from the Peninsula into the vast northern area. His intent was to carry out guerrilla warfare, but the Marines were already in the area and he spent the rest of the campaign trying to avoid the Marines hunting for him and his men. His presence did, however, force the Americans to keep an entire division in the north in order to deal with his small force.

There is an eleven square mile island located west and slightly north of the Motobu Peninsula in northern Okinawa. This small island, named Le Shima, held the largest airfield in all of Asia and was valuable for the setting-up of radar for an early warning system for the American fleet. The Japanese knew the value of the island and had two thousand soldiers well dug in to counter the American attack they knew was coming. There were five thousand civilians scattered among the Japanese on the island when the pre-invasion bombardments had started in mid-March. Many of these civilians would startle the invaders when they took part in the fighting. Women attacking with wooden spears were a deadly surprise!

The Army's 77th Division was handed the task of securing Le Shima and landed on the island in the early morning of this date. By the end of the day the airfields had been taken. Luckily for the division, the Marines on the Mobuto Peninsula had captured two enemy 150 mm guns that had been trained on the Le Shima airfields. The gun crews were waiting for the Americans to take the airfields, then they would have opened fire and likely killed and injured many American soldiers. That night the Japanese counterattacked in a fury. The division commander was stunned by their attack, and after surveying the always incredible defensive positions, asked for and received reinforcements.

The American Fleet had been attacked every day in April by small groups of planes but this day the Japanese attacked in force with one hundred sixty Kamikazes and two hundred forty-six fighters and bombers. One ship, the destroyer *Pringle,* was lost and several others suffered heavy damages. The *Pringle* had been hit by a Kamikaze near the Philippines in December of 1944. She was badly damaged but repaired and returned to action. The crew was highly experienced, but this time a plane crashed into her and the bombs from the plane penetrated her decks and exploded. She was broken apart and sank in six minutes. Fortunately two hundred fifty-eight men survived. The good news in this third massed attack, was that only one plane made it through to the carriers or the other major ships supporting the shore battle. The carrier *Intrepid* was damaged so badly that she had to withdraw to a shipyard for repairs as did three other destroyers and two minesweepers. Some sailors in this battle suffered beyond human endurance because burns were the most common form of death and injury aboard warships.

The destroyer *Laffey*, while on radar picket duty had twenty-two separate plane attacks in less than an hour and a half. She destroyed seventeen of them but was hit by four bombs and six Kamikazes, causing a hundred casualties. Through heroic effort, *Laffey* stayed afloat and battled until the attack ended. The Japanese seemed obsessed with attacking the radar picket ships instead of saving their pilots and planes for the carriers and other major ships. Efforts of the *Laffey* crew and the other sister ships' crews on picket duty saved the Navy untold numbers of the major war vessels and transport and vital supply ships. Six hundred thirty-six officers and men of the American fleet were killed or wounded before the day ended.

The Japanese had scheduled two thousand aircraft to be used for the battle for Okinawa. Of that number, six hundred had already been destroyed. Only four hundred six of the balance were available for attacks on the American ships. The rest had other duties. The Japanese had to wait for further mass attacks until more planes and pilots could be drawn from the Home Island training commands.

April 17, 1945. Patrols continued for the Battalions of the 7th Marines. They were becoming very adept at sorting out the cave complexes that were everywhere in their sector. Some were empty, some were used as storage by the Okinawans, some had contained Japanese soldiers but were abandoned as many Japanese began to infiltrate south to the Japanese defense concentration. Some of the caves were filled with civilians hiding in fear of the Marines. By now the Marines were simply searching the civilians for men of military age for detainment and turning the rest loose where they were. They had used caves close to their homes so now they just went home again. If they required food and medical treatment, it was provided by the Marines and Navy medical personnel.

"When we came up to something, I didn't have to do anything because up there I was just sniping' for the first 30 days. If the SeaBees had trouble building a bridge or something, I would get rid of the snipers for them. If there was a big gun they couldn't find I would go locate it, if I could. Then the Air Corps would get rid of it."

The 6th Marine Division began mop-up operations at Yae Take and the surrounding area and began the chase for the Japanese who had managed to escape. The few holdouts were cleared away and the division would have little to do until they were called south at the end of the month and thrown into the "Shuri Line." They had fought a difficult battle and had nine hundred seventy casualties to show for it, along with a body count of two thousand Japanese. All organized resistance in the northern part of Okinawa was over. The Marines would spend the next several days patrolling, resting and listening to the ever increasing rumors about major fighting in the south. They tried not to even think of the possibility of them being sent south, but they knew that it was only a matter of time. No one believed that if there were battles in the south they would be left out. That wasn't how things worked with the military and they didn't trust that the Army could ever get along without Marines, if there were any around. And there were plenty of battle hardened Marines around!

The 77th Division fighting to capture Le Shima was having a lot of difficulty in penetrating the defensive positions. The Japanese, as a part of their defense, were throwing constant counterattacks against the Americans. The attacks were composed of a mixture of Japanese soldiers and civilians, the later included women on an ever increasing scale. The American soldiers were demoralized by having to shoot civilians, especially the woman. The division kept switching units around into different directions, trying to out maneuver strongholds and take the mountain called the Pinnacle that commanded the whole island.

Japanese air attacks on the fleet were light but some minor damage occurred to a radar picket duty ship, the destroyer *Benham*. Large Kamikaze attacks were being scheduled but the planners still did not have enough aircraft and pilots ready to send the massed attacks that were needed to ensure sinking or damaging the major vessels.

CHAPTER FIVE
THE MARINES GO SOUTH INTO BATTLE

April 18, 1945. The 7th Marines' 2nd Battalion's patrols ran into an enemy position on high wooded ground in extremely rugged terrain. It was estimated that there were one hundred fifty Japanese soldiers well dug into the large area. There was no way to get them out without individually killing them. Neither Air strikes nor artillery would have had any affect, so the battalion began assaulting this "pocket" using small unit tactics.

"This was the first time and only time that I ever seen the battalion commander up on the front lines. I was by myself and it was late in the afternoon. I come up on this sunken ox cart track. They wasn't nobody around and I leaned back against a tree stump on top of the bank. I was intending to take a nap. I laid my pack down beside me and I heard a noise down in the ox cart track. I peeked over the edge and there was Colonel Berger sitting right below me. He was a real big, hairy guy. He was leaning against the side of the bank just digging at the fleas on his chest with both hands. I didn't want to have nothing to do with any colonel, so I just eased back out of sight."

"SNAP! A bullet hit my pack. I grabbed my pack on the way down and just dove into the ox cart track. I landed on my head right next to Berger and I must have shook him up. He wanted to know what the hell I thought I was doing. I showed him the bullet hole in my pack and told him there was snipers out there. He said snipers didn't scare him none and the idiot stood up. I started to tell him that he was exposed and they might even have them little machine guns. Before I ever got a word out, a hole in the clay about a foot around just appeared, right beside his head. Some sniper had fired three or four rounds from a Nambu. The last thing I saw of Berger, he was on his hands and knees heading back down that ox track. He was going so fast that his arms and legs was just a blur. I never did know what he was doing there and why he was by himself. Colonels never ever went anyplace without taking a whole bunch of guys with them."

The 6th Marine Division continued patrolling the north and waited for the dreaded call that would send them south.

General Buckner, the overall commander of all of the ground forces, closed his command post in the vessel *Eldorado* and reopened it nearly two miles southwest of Kadena Airfield. He was very satisfied with the Marines' progress in the north. He committed the Army's 27th Division, held in reserve until this day, to the line to reinforce the other two divisions. They found themselves pushing against the Japanese main line of defense called the Machinato Line because it started on the west coast at Machinato Inlet. They now faced the best Japanese troops on the island. A major assault by all three divisions was planned for the next day. Since the Japanese knew that the Americans never advanced at night they were somewhat less vigilant than they should have been and this flaw was utilized by the attackers. An advance over open ground of one thousand yards could be made if kept secret from the defenders. Engineers had to construct bridges across an inlet before an advance would be possible. They began building at dark and were finished by 0300 hours except for their largest bridge needed to ferry large trucks. Construction noise was covered by, the now standard, nightly bombardments provided by artillery and ships. Two battalions crossed the inlet and the open ground and were in attack positions by daylight of April 19. The surprise nighttime maneuver had worked, but Buckner and his soldiers didn't know that the Japanese had reinforced their line and were even stronger than the earlier attack, which failed, by the 7th and 96th Divisions.

Ernie Plye, who had landed on Okinawa on April 1, had gone to Le Shima the day before to visit the 77th Division. Pile was riding in a jeep with division troops over what was thought to be safe ground when he was killed by a Japanese machine gunner. The division kept up constant attacks on the enemy and casualties began to rise on both sides until April 21, when the Japanese made another counterattack. This time, it was a major attack and included civilians and women with spears. The attackers were destroyed but not before the Americans had suffered severe losses.

Single Kamikaze planes were sent against the fleet but there was no damage from the raids. Admiral Nimitz's own strikes against airfields on the Home Islands were destroying large numbers of planes on the ground and the Navy and Marine fighters were having a field day against the Japanese pilots sent up to challenge them. Difficulties increased, many fold, for the Japanese planners trying to mass planes and Kamikaze pilots to launch at the American ships.

April 19, 1944. Two battalions of the 7th Marines continued patrolling but found nothing except caves and hoards of civilians. The 2nd Battalion resumed their attack on the Japanese defensive pocket they found the day before. The terrain was so hostile they were forced to move exceedingly slow and the Japanese, although small in number, fought as hard as they ever had. Casualties in the battalion mounted due mainly to the slow progress being made.

Part of the 6th Marine Division at the tip of northern Okinawa and patrolling southward started to run into men from the 1st Marine Division who had advanced north on the east coast road. This meant the northern section of the island campaign was over except for the few Japanese stragglers who would be hunted until the end of the whole campaign.

The three Army divisions were set to commence their concentrated attack against the defensive line known as the Machinato Line. They faced the elite Japanese 67th Division who would have to be defeated in order to reach the Shuri Heights' outer defenses which lay just to the rear of the ridges making up the Machinato Line. The attack started with a massive shelling from six battleships and several cruisers and destroyers and an air strike of several hundred planes. The Army artillery and some "borrowed" Marine artillery fired the most concentrated mission yet seen in the Pacific Theater. Nearly twenty thousand shells, along with bombs and napalm rained down on the enemy but caused them little damage. Troops of the Japanese 67th Division had hidden in deep caves and shelters until the shelling stopped, then they manned their positions to deal with the American advance. During the advance, the 27th Division had bypassed a critical stronghold known as Kakazu Ridge. This maneuver managed to open a one mile gap in the American lines and gave the Japanese a perfect position from which to counterattack come nightfall. The gap and its danger was recognized and most of the day was spent holding up the other divisions while the 27th

Division corrected its mistake and filled the gap. Kakazue Ridge was now included in the advance, but night was coming and the three American divisions fell back a short distance without making any headway at all except to kill and wound many of the defenders.

96th Division jumped off against the Nishibaru Ridge area and experienced counterattacks throughout the day. Casualties mounted on both sides, but the Americans had gained ground to the gorge just in front of the strongly defended Ridge itself.

A few Japanese planes spent themselves on the picket duty ships without causing any harm.

April 20, 1945. Two battalions of the 7th Marines still patrolled their sectors but could not find an enemy to fight. The 2nd Battalion was winding down their operation by overrunning and killing the Japanese they faced. There was no one to tap for reinforcements so each soldier killed or wounded weakened the enemy sector.

The campaign in the north was over for the 6th Marine Division and they set up headquarters in the town of Nago. This area then became the central supply depot for the entire on shore operation. The Marines were supposed to have been relieved by the 27th Army Division by this time. The original plan was for the 27th Division to go ashore at this time instead of when they did, relieve the Marines and operate as the occupation force for the northern section of Okinawa. When the island campaign was completed, they were to serve as occupiers for all of Okinawa. The Marine division upon being replaced was to be moved to a rear staging area on Guam and begin preparations for the invasion of the Japanese Home Islands. These plans had collapsed when the 27th Division had been thrown into combat, as the reserve division, earlier in the month at the Shuri Line outer defenses. Instead of being saved for occupation duty, the division was being cut to ribbons at Kakazu. The Marines knew, without being told, that instead of going to Guam, they were going south to the Shuri defenses.

The Army carried on their attack along the three division front. The fire they encountered was murderous. The Division was ordered to get over Kakazu Ridge by that night and by late afternoon the division was at the eastern end of the ridge. Then they were stopped in their tracks at the ridge by the rest of the defense complex which included connected ridges and high points. Casualties mounted, platoons and even companies began to melt away. There were only enough replacements to fill a fraction of what was needed and they had bypassed strong points and defensive pockets throughout the day. The division found itself with a serious problem because they could not continue forward and they now had enemy troops to their rear. Division casualties numbered five hundred six on this day alone. For one time, in only a few times during the battle for Okinawa, American units ran from the enemy. Two companies advanced too far and found themselves surrounded. They panicked and instead of trying to fight their way free they ran in total disorder.

Attacks began again by the 96th Division all along their line of responsibility. When the day was done, little ground had been taken, but casualties and exhaustion had escalated to an alarming rate.

The 7th Division, near the Machinato Inlet, was holding in place. They could not move until their sister division cleared the Kakazu complex. Otherwise their flank would be exposed. They spent the day attacking defenses close to their line and experiencing heavy enemy fire from the heights above them. There was a constant and steady increasing casualty rate that depleted whole units.

Again, a few attacks were made on the radar picket ships but none were hit. The destroyer *Ammen* had a bomb dropped next to her. While there wasn't any damage to the vessel, bomb fragments wounded eleven sailors. It had been several days since the larger ships had even seen an enemy war plane.

April 21, 1945. Jack and the 2nd Battalion continued killing the small enemy force that by now had broken up into groups of two or three and sometimes individually and were trying to escape to the south.

Frank Moody. "We had gone into the mountains, back on April 12, to get the wounded from Easy company out. I had taken a platoon up there and then they had sent the whole company up near where we were the first night. We had lost a lieutenant that night. His name was Jenteny. I've always remembered his name. We couldn't find him. He was supposed to be where we had located about thirty of the wounded guys from E Company, but we couldn't find him. We never did find any Japs, and after being up there for nine days, we was coming out. I was coming down a ridge leading about two hundred fifty guys when I ran right up on this dead guy. He was the lost lieutenant and I just kind of walked right up on him. It was kind of lucky, like. He had been laying out there for nine days, of course. The Japs had a long pole twelve or fifteen feet long. They had that pole run through his battle jacket which is just a light jacket, which was just like a shirt, you know. They run that pole through his jacket and on the other end they had tied his boots to that pole by his laces. I never did know what they did that for. He had been there for nine days and the weather had gotten pretty hot by then. We couldn't take him out right then. I found him and the captain came up and looked at him but for some reason we couldn't take him out with us. We had to get out first and come back for him. I couldn't tell if he had been tortured. He might have been, but I couldn't see anything. I don't know what he would be on that pole for. He was quite a ways from where we had looked for him, where he should have been. I don't know why they would of packed him around that way. I couldn't see anything but he was in pretty bad shape, you couldn't really tell if they had done anything to him, only just packed him on that stick over their shoulder. Anyway, we left him and that was my nineteenth birthday. What a hell of a way to spend your birthday!"

The 6th Marine Division carried out routine operations and waited for the dreadful call that would send them south into the heavy combat they knew was going on there.

The Army's 27th Division was now in serious difficulty. The Japanese had pushed reinforcements into their Kakazu defenses the night before. Now, the division faced a stronger enemy than they had faced the day before and now had organized forces to their rear and a widening gap between them and the 7th Division. The flanks of both divisions were open and the situation was frightening to the commanders. This situation required quick, drastic, action. A battalion was "borrowed" from the 7th Division and an engineering battalion was assembled and armed as infantry. Preparations were made for an all out assault on April 24 and another "borrowed" battalion, this time, from the 96th Division was on its way to help out.

On Ie Shima, the major Japanese counterattack was destroyed leaving three hundred sixty-four Japanese and civilian bodies lying within the positions of one American battalion. The 77th division had continued wiping out the Japanese holdouts and declared the island of Ie Shima secured by mid-afternoon, after sustaining eleven hundred casualties. Japanese casualties numbered forty-seven hundred killed, including fifteen civilians.

Back on Okinawa, Nishibaru Ridge was attacked by a regiment from the 96th Division. The Japanese launched three counterattacks during the day and when the day ended the Americans were in the same positions as they were when they started. Except, now, the regiment was reduced to 50% strength because of casualties.

The fleet spent another day carrying out their duties without having to bother with fighting the dreaded Kamikazes. They launched carrier aircraft strikes against the southern Japanese airfields and provided air support to the ground forces and continued pouring supplies and men onto the island.

April 22, 1945. The 7th Marines remained in the vicinity of Kin with patrols mopping up small pockets of the enemy and the ever present snipers. 2nd Battalion had finished clearing the enemy from the pocket of resistance they had discovered a few days ago. They went back to their extensive patrols and numerous small scouting parties, but they couldn't find any of the enemy. Twenty-five mortar rounds fell in the battalion area causing several casualties, but the mortar locations could not be located in the hideous terrain of caves.

Frank Moody. "The day before, on my nineteenth birthday, I had found that dead lieutenant, so they wanted to know if I would go back with a stretcher and some guys and bring him out. They sent four guys to pack him out on the stretcher. They sent me and another guy to guard them. I was the only one who knew where he was at. I, like Dolan, was raised in rough country, so I was good in the mountains. They wanted to know if I would go get him. I said, 'Sure'. I was only nineteen years old that morning. Think about that!"

"We went back, moving pretty fast. I had borrowed my squad leader's tommy gun because it was light and if there was any trouble we was gonna be moving out fast. We couldn't stand and fight with just six guys altogether. We all had guns and would have to pack him out, too. We didn't know how many Japs could be there. We got him. He was not in very good shape. He was so full of maggots he was just about moving. We sprayed him with some kind of a deal to kill the maggots and kill the smell a little bit so we could pack him. We rolled him on the stretcher and took him out. It wasn't all that far, it was a few miles but not that far. Shoot, the whole island wasn't but sixty miles long and we wasn't very far north. It was a few hours though, but we got him out. That was the last time I ever heard of him, but I remember him on every birthday I've ever had." It always seems like it just happened and it was fifty some years ago."

The 6th Marine Division carried on with camp duties and supply working parties without knowing what the future held for them.

Again, the 96th Division attacked all along their line. They gained the front edge of Nishibaru Ridge and just like the previous days, suffered heavy casualties before the day ended.

Kamikaze and bomber attacks on the fleet had dropped to practically nothing, but on this day they came back. The minesweeper *Swallow* was engaged in antisubmarine patrolling when an undetected enemy plane came out of very low clouds and plowed into the side of the ship. The crew was forced to abandon the ship and she sank in less than an hour. A very determined Kamikaze pilot crashed his plane into the stern of the destroyer *Isherwood* causing some of her depth charges to explode. The destroyer had to be towed from the battle area for repairs but later returned to duty. These attacks brought the Navy another one hundred twenty killed and wounded.

April 23, 1945. All of the companies of 2nd Battalion continued to patrol their assigned areas. One Japanese soldier was taken prisoner and a large number of civilians were taken and turned over to the division military police for processing. Bodies of an officer and two enlisted men were recovered by a patrol sent to find them.

"When they found Lt. Spindler and the other two guys, they had been bayoneted to death. They was cut to pieces like they had all practiced on them. We decided right quick that we wasn't gonna take any Japanese prisoners if we could help it."

The 6th Marine Division patrolled, guarded supplies and waited.

A bulldozer was sent to help the 96th Division cross its medium tanks over the gorge to its front. Flame throwing tanks then joined the other tanks and burned out the defenders except for two strongholds which were to be attacked the next day.

The fleet spent another day without being bothered by Japanese planes, with a few exceptions. If the Japanese sent twenty or fewer planes, which they did every day when a mass attack didn't occur, the Navy considered it a quiet day. Gun crews and other overworked sailors were rested on these "light" days. At least as much as they could, since every sailor on every ship had a difficult job to carry out in addition to his battle duties.

April 24, 1945. The 7th Marines searched in vain throughout the day for some sign of the enemy. The longer they went without finding anything, the tighter the tension became. The rumbling of artillery to the south and the rumors of the army's difficulties brought apprehension that they would soon be sent south unless they could find an enemy of their own to engage.

"We was at a town on the coast that had the ocean on one side and a moat around the other three sides, with draw bridges. They had put over a thousand civilians in there and a few prisoners. The Japanese or Home Guard was prisoners while they called the civilians detainees. They had all been turned over to the Army MPs they had sent there as guards. First they was turned over to the Navy for interrogation, then turned over to the MPs. The Army guys was wearing state side uniforms and white helmets and arm bands, and we wasn't all that far from the front lines. They had a field kitchen for hot chow and everything. We ate C Rations."

"My squad was full, thirteen men. I didn't want to lay out there in the mud anymore so I took over a little house. It was bamboo inside. The walls was real thick and lacquered, beautifully. It had sliding doors in it. All of the storage was in the middle supporting walls. I would go in there, crawl up on a storage shelf and pull the door shut. Nobody could find me except everybody in the squad knowed where I was, including all of the squad leaders. If you was out in the open somebody would always grab you and put you on a working party. Day or night. I figured it was my job to fight not unload ammunition or supplies. They had more than enough rear echelon troops to do that. But they avoided the front lines like they wasn't really Marines."

"The Army was in charge of all the civilians. There was over a thousand of them. They would put them in the town at night and take off all the draw bridges. In the morning they would put the bridges back and let them out to work in the fields. We didn't have enough food for ourselves, so they had to let them work."

"We was just standing there watching them go out. We seen one guy and he was questionable age. He looked like he was over sixteen. Somebody said, when he was going over the bridge that he would bet the guy was a Japanese soldier. He said he didn't walk like them Okinawans but they was letting him go out to the fields. The fields started about a mile from were we was. Norton came out and started watching him through his field glasses. They went out about a quarter of a mile. There was a guard but the old men and women would get way off from guard. This old boy sauntered off from the rest and started digging for something. He dug up something, you couldn't see what, and took off running with it. He got away. We was always feuding with the Army and it wasn't our job, but Norton told me to go get that guy. I asked him what he meant by 'go get that guy'. He was already heading back toward the hills. I thought Norton meant for me to go shoot him, but I wasn't sure. Norton said to go get him and bring him back. I sure didn't want to do that, so I asked him how much time he wanted me to spend chasing that guy. Norton said he didn't care how long it took, just to do it."

"So I started out and tracked him till dark. He had hobnailed boots on. Nobody else ever had any hobnailed boots. I had tracked him for about five miles. He had to stick to the trail. That was about as rough a country as you've ever seen. It was muddy so he was easy to track. Well, I run him into a little village just about dark. I crawled up the slope into the brush and went around the village. It wasn't more than three hundred yards long with just two little rows of shacks along the trail. I got to the other end and went to sleep. I was gonna wake up real early and catch him when he went by. I over slept so I run down to the trail and there was his hobnailed boot tracks going on by. He had beat me out and I missed him. I tracked him up north away and then back down the island almost on the west side."

"I came around a corner and I had come up on a Japanese Army barracks. It was down in a valley and I was up on the trail on a slope. When I seen that barracks, I thought that's where that guy is going. I could, also, see a destroyer just off the coast out there. I was still tracking him on the footpath when I heard a whistle and I knew what it was. They hollowed out pieces of bamboo and made whistles out of them. They used them to warn one another. It was morning and I had walked into a whole mess of them. Their whistles just blew and blew. When I heard the first one I had just flattened out, right now. I must have laid there for about an hour or a hour and a half. Nothing happened. I didn't see or hear anything, so I eased up. The old boy that I was tracking had walked right through the middle of about fifteen or twenty of them. They was Home Guard and they had been sleeping in a circle of little slit trenches. Somebody fired at me from someplace. I knew I was over in the 6th Division's area. I tried calling them on my Walkie Talkie. I raised somebody and I told them who I was and where I was and I needed some support. They must have contacted that destroyer out there because she started firing out ahead of me. She fired for about an hour. Then somebody called me and said they was southwest of me, three or four miles and was coming right at where I was at."

"I had backed up a good ways when that ship started firing and that big barracks complex was right to my left. I had lost the old boy, but I figured that he had probably went to that barracks. I couldn't keep going down the trail anymore because there was too many Japanese on it. I went way back around and come into that barracks complex from the other side. They was nice pine buildings built up on stilts. It was neat and clean, even the beds was made. I supposed they had taken out and gone to the south end of the island. I went down the valley away to where I thought I was past where those Home Guard was dug in and went back up on the trail. I saw those hobnailed boot tracks again. Pretty soon I saw what that fellow had dug up. He had throwed it away. It was a machine gun barrel in a shinny bamboo case. I guess he thought I had got too close and he didn't want to get caught with that thing on him. The guys that said they was coming toward me was coming up a road that intersected the trail I was on. They didn't see me because I was sneaking down that trail, looking right and left now, because I knowed I was real close to him. I come to that intersection and somebody yelled at me from up the road. They asked me if I was looking for the follow that they had there. I said that I was looking for a Nip that I had been tracking. They told me that I didn't have to track him anymore, they had him. That guy had slipped up that road and was sitting there watching for me when they had come up behind him. They captured him. They give him to me and I started back with him."

The 6th Marine Division continued their now rear area duties. Logistics personnel were stockpiling massive quantities of all types of equipment, fuel, ammunition and other vital supplies. The dumps were not only for the current battle but were for the troop build-up afterward to turn the island into a base for the next invasion, Japan. Since they had a whole Marine division for guard duty, the Japan invasion planners had stepped up their logistics schedules.

In order to correct the Kakazu Ridge disaster, battalions from all the Army divisions were reinforced with tanks and sent against the ridge area in a do or die operation. They only found that the Japanese had withdrawn to new defenses behind their former defense line, much closer to the Shuri Heights.

With the enemy withdrawn, the 27th Division had cleared the Kakazu area but the entire division had been badly mauled and was exhausted as a fighting unit. They were ordered to hold in place until decisions could be made about their future and what to do about their position on the attack line.

96th Division was now massed on the Nishibaru to Tanabura defense line and ready to take the final strong points when it was discovered that the Japanese had pulled back and abandoned their positions to the American Army. The Army's divisions were now spent, but they held good positions since the Japanese had withdrawn their survivors to their secondary line of defense. Planners and commanders realized the 96th and the 27th Divisions would have to be replaced before any more major assaults could begin and a shuffling of units began. It was decided to bring the two Marine divisions down from the north and to bring the 77th Division from Le Shima to replace the two Army divisions, leaving the Army's 7th Division in place because they had not engaged in the heavy battles that the other two divisions had. The Japanese were now facing more and fresher attackers than in the preceding weeks.

Before bringing the Marines and 77th Division into the battle, the Army wanted to consolidate their holdings, so they sent what was left of their battered divisions forward to complete the destruction of the Shuri outer defenses they had been fighting for the last five days. All three divisions moved forward with only the 24th Division being stopped. They had been attacking a place called Item Pocket for several days and the defenders were just as difficult as before. This pocket was tied to the inter-defense line and had even been reinforced in the night. The depleted outer defenses encountered by the other two divisions provided a welcome surprise for the American soldiers. The Japanese had used the night to withdraw completely from the area and take up new positions within the inter-defenses. The Army, except the 24th Division, moved forward one thousand yards and began preparations to attack their new targets which were the next set of hills, ridges and ravines in front of the Shuri Heights themselves.

The fleet, again, had a damage free day, as far as enemy attacks were concerned. There were the always present accidents that made duty on warships a lot less than safe places to live and work.

April 25, 1945. All of the battalions in the 7th Marines sent out long range patrols, but they could not make any contact with the enemy. Command Post personnel and support companies were making preparations in expectation of a move south. Rumors grew of the hard fighting the Army was engaged in. The Marines also heard of the lack of advance of the Army and of the high casualty numbers.

The 6th Marines Division carried out their routine functions and worried about their upcoming trip south. Occupation services personnel had landed and taken over responsibility for the civilians. They relieved the division of many other duties so the Marines could be released for combat at the Shuri Line.

Back on April 20, while the Army's 27th Division worked to consolidate their positions and expand them where possible, they had sent their reserve, the 165th Regiment, straight down the west coast on Highway 1 to capture the Machinato Airstrip. The 165th had been bogged down in an ingeniously designed defense known as Item Pocket. This day the soldiers attained and held a critical Japanese defense ridge crest. This ridge conquest made Item Pocket indefensible and turned the battle into a mop up action. It would take several more days before the highway could be traveled and the pocket could be completely cleared.

The Japanese sent only a few single planes against the fleet and caused no damage. However, the carrier *Steamer Bay* and the destroyer *Hale* managed to collide with each other during the night.

April 26, 1945. Another uneventful day passed for the battalions of the 7th Marines and preparations continued for the trip south.

"I got back with the prisoner Norton sent me out after and turned him over to the Navy for interrogation. I never told anybody that I wasn't the one that caught him. I still don't even know why Norton had done that. There just wasn't no reason to send me out there to track one guy. I guess it was just his pride. The Army let him get away and the Marines brought him back. I had tracked him for two and a half days, up to the north and back to the south. There wasn't hardly anybody left in that part of the island, not even civilians. There wasn't hardly any fighting going on at all. I still wonder why Norton made me do that. We was supposed to be in a rest area. Maybe Norton knowed that I had been hiding from work parties and wanted to get even with me."

The 6th Marine Division continued turning over rear area duties to service personnel and packing material for their trip South.

At the Shuri Line, the Army divisions found that they had advanced far enough to run into a line of new defensive positions. These ran east from Item Pocket across escarpments to a position called Kochi Ridge. When the Army made contact with this area, they were brought to a complete stop. These defenses were as well prepared as those already encountered, but there was one new factor posed for the Army. The new defenses contained many more defenders than the Army had ever encountered. The Japanese had switched their battered troops with a fresh division. The commanding officer, General Ushijima, had kept a Brigade south of Shuri to combat any landing the Americans might make on the east coast behind Shuri. He, now, brought these well-rested soldiers up to the Shuri Line and placed them directly behind his new division now facing the American Army. This left the Japanese rear unguarded but it was more important to prevent a breakthrough of the Shuri Line than to keep troops waiting for another American landing that might not take place. Ushijima's decision was correct. General Buckner would not permit another landing no matter how many senior officers tried to convince him otherwise.

The Navy had another day relatively free from air attacks. The destroyer *Hutchins* was working close in to the island providing gunfire support for the ground troops. In the night, a Japanese suicide boat slipped up on the ship and dropped a depth charge near her side. The explosion didn't injure anyone but it did buckle the underwater plating enough that the ship had to withdraw for repairs.

April 27, 1945. Jack's battalion had to send its Fox Company back into the rugged terrain they had fought over days before to rescue three rear area service Marines who went into the old battlefield to hunt and recover souvenirs. The three Marines had been pinned down by sniper fire and could not get out on their own. Fox Company killed four of the snipers and brought the frightened and embarrassed men back into the battalion lines.

"While we was in that area there was quite a bit of Army around there. All of the civilians and prisoners had been turned over to the Army. The engineers and the Seabees was bulldozing on the roads trying to get supplies through the mud. They would hook a train of amphibious vehicles together and pull them through the mud. After a while the mud would get so bad that nothing could get through it, so they would move over and start a new road and the same thing would happen. There was one spot where they had run out of a place to make a new road. They couldn't get through it or around it. A Seabee had brought a tracked crane down there. He would pick up stuff on one side and set it down on the other side. Well, some Army brass come up there in a jeep. They wanted that Seabee to stop what he was doing and swing them across on his hook. He didn't want to stop working supplies so he told them he would take them across for a dollar a person. They fussed and fumed but there wasn't anything they could do to that Seabee. They wouldn't pay, so they got out and waded through the mud. They was wearing uniforms just like they was back home. (There was a special Army unit sent to Okinawa to administrate and govern. These officers were probably from that unit.) After they was out of sight, the Seabee hooked on to their jeep and put it over on the other side. When those officers come back they had to wade back through the mud and of course, their jeep was gone. They had a fit and stomped off down the road. Willie, the old supply sergeant took the jeep back away and painted it camouflage, like our jeeps was painted. He drove that thing all over the rest of the island. Him and a little private of his had stole everything they could get their hands on from the Army. Willie handled ordinance, too. That was how I got that Tommy gun. Somebody had lost it and it was turned in to Willie and he gave it to me. He was the one who shipped my Japanese rifle home to me."

The 6th Marine Division now knew for sure that they were going south into heavy combat and began completing their final preparations. They were well rested, even the regiments who had cleared Motobu, over strength and properly supplied for what they thought was in store for them.

The Army stood before the new and heavily reinforced defenses at the Shuri Line. They were so beaten up that they could not advance. General Buckner was receiving replacements, but so slowly that it would be a long time before any attack could be made. In addition to his divisions already in the line, Buckner now had three fresh divisions available to him to use as he saw fit. The 77th Army Division had returned from their successful invasion of Ie Shima and the two Marine divisions in the north were ready for new assignments.

The commanding officer, Major General Bruce of the 77th Division, tried to convince Buckner to land his division on the east coast south of Shuri and then either outflank the Shuri Line or secure the southern tip of Okinawa.

Either way the enemy would be surrounded with no escape possible. Buckner vetoed the landing to the rear recommendation as too slow and too difficult to supply, especially with ammunition. He felt it would have been a logistical nightmare. Buckner had decided that the best way to victory was to punch through the Shuri Line as fast as possible, so he decided to put the 77th Division in an assault position by sending them to relieve the casualty weakened 6th Division. These soldiers had been in continuous combat from the very beginning. They had suffered, by far, more killed and wounded than any other division thus far in the invasion of the island. The 6th Division was to be pulled back into reserve for rest and rebuilding with replacements.

Buckner decided to send the 1st Marine Division to relieve the 27th Army Division. This latter division had fought with great distinction since being thrown into battle from their reserve position shortly after the battle for Okinawa had begun. They were actually a New York National Guard Division trained and brought to Okinawa as garrison troops. There had been no intent to put them into combat. The extent of their casualties had finished them as combat effective until they could be rested and train their replacements. Buckner, instead of holding this unit in reserve, sent them north where they would not face battle again. He decided to bring the Marine 6th Division down from the north and place them on his right flank so they could push south along the west coast just to the right of the 1st Marine Division. The new American assault line would stretch east across the island beginning on the west coast with the 96th Marine Divisions, on their left flank and in the middle he would place the 1st Marine Division with the Army 7th Division to their left on the east coast protecting the left flank of the line.

An ammunition ship, *Canada Victory*, was sunk by Kamikazes with thirty-nine casualties. These men were not counted on the Navy casualty list because the ship was crewed by the Merchant Marine. The cruiser *Wichita* while operating close-in for gunfire support and counter-battery fire, was hit with several shells from shore batteries. Damage was slight and she kept to her duties. The destroyer *Talbot* had just arrived at Okinawa for duty the day before. Less than twenty-four hours later a Kamikaze sent her to the rear for repairs. *Rathburne*, a WWI destroyer converted to a high speed transport, was hit by a plane and damaged beyond repair. A suicide boat crashed into the destroyer *Hutchins* causing no casualties but damage was so severe the ship had to be scrapped.

April 28, 1945. Patrols of 2nd Battalion of the 1st Marine Division rounded up fifty civilians and killed three enemy soldiers who tried to run from the Marines. Marines of this division had now received official word that they were going south to replace an Army division that was in the thick of combat at the Shuri Line.

"We knew that we was going south in a couple of days so we stayed pretty close to home. We heard that the fighting was pretty bad down there. There was some guys that would do almost anything not to go into that fight. You could shoot yourself and that would get you off the line but you could get a dishonorable discharge, too. One day, I saw these two guys from our outfit climbing up this slope where there was a small cave. I had been in that cave a day or two before and knew there wasn't nothing in it. They would have known that too. Because they was acting kind of funny, I sat down and watched them. They walked over to the cave and looked inside then they got on each side of it and kind of stuck their butts in the entrance. One of them tossed a grenade inside and then I knowed what they was doing. They was trying to get wounded so they could go home! That grenade went off and they fell down and started yelling for a corpsman. I ran up there. I told them that I saw what they was doing and they wasn't gonna get away with it. They just had some scratches and little shrapnel holes. I took them to the corpsman and got them patched up. I told them they wasn't going anywhere except back to their unit. I was so mad that I told them that if they ever tried that again that I would shoot them myself. As far as I know, they never did. Imagine a Marine doing something like that! I was ashamed of them."

The 6th Marine Division was now ready to move south whenever they received orders.

General Buckner's new strategy was now confirmed. The three fresh divisions would be brought down from the north to be sent into battle along the Shuri Line with the 7th Army Division that had been there from the start. The battered 96th Division would be pulled back into reserve and the severely damaged 27th Division would be sent north to fight no more.

Wave one of the fourth massed air attacks was sent against the fleet with wave two to take place the next day. The picket duty destroyers *Wadsworth*, *Daly*, *Twiggs* and *Bennion* were targets this day and all received some damage. They did, along with six Marine fighter planes, destroy twenty-two of the enemy planes attacking them. A minesweeper, the *Butler* was damaged so badly that she was withdrawn from any further combat. Eleven of her crew were killed during the action. The well lighted, well marked hospital ships *Pinkney* and *Comfort* were singled out for attack and damaged. Structural damage was limited, but six nurses and several surgeons were among the one hundred twenty-two killed and wounded aboard the two vessels.

April 29, 1945. Jack's unit along with the entire division was fully engaged in preparations to move south. They kept patrols out but with orders not to travel far and to be ready to return to the division's lines on short notice.

The 6th Marines Division was ready to move and awaited orders to do so.

The Army's 96th Division had killed at least two thousand Japanese during their current movement, but two of their regiments had so many casualties that their combat effectiveness was so reduced that they could not continue. Two regiments of the rested 77th Division relieved them and continued the attack, but they now faced an escarpment with a cliff that seemed to provide no way to its top. Their advance was halted until a way to the top could be determined.

The second wave of the massed air attack that had started yesterday struck the fleet. Two destroyers, the *Haggard* and the *Hazelwood* suffered massive damage with heavy loss of life. Three Kamikazes went after the *Hazelwood* while she was escorting a carrier group. The first two planes missed but the third crashed into the bridge and exploded. Flaming fuel from the plane washed over the decks burning ten officers and sixty-seven sailors to death within seconds. The balance of her crew saved the ship, but she was knocked out of the war. The *Haggard* had been performing carrier screening duty but was detached and sent to a radar picket station. Before she arrived, a Kamikaze crashed into her side. The planes' bomb penetrated the ship's skin and exploded in her engine room killing all the men there and creating sudden flooding. Her crew saved the ship, but she had to be towed from combat and did not return. Fifty-six men were killed and another sixty-six were wounded.

The Japanese commander, General Ushijima, in view of the advances made by the Americans thus far, convened a staff meeting to determine if the Japanese battle strategy should change. The General wondered, if in view of the American penetrations of his defenses, deep in some locations, did not dictate a change from defense to offense. A major counterattack could restore his original lines, kill a lot of his enemies and raise the moral of his army. Japanese soldiers felt it was more honorable to die on the attack than it was to be killed sitting in holes and caves. General Ushijima did not attend the meeting in order to give his staff officers freedom of speech and action without any influence from his presence.

Ushijima's chief staff officer held that to stay on the defensive would bring defeat before the end of May. He saw that the American forces were growing stronger each day with their superior fire power and ability to bring ammunition, supplies and replacements ashore at will. Each Japanese bullet fired, each ration eaten and each soldier killed weakened the effort to hold Okinawa for any appreciative time. No matter what was tried, there could be no resupply nor any reinforcements. Whatever resources were available this day were all there would ever be. A full scale counterattack might not succeed, but the kill rate it might generate among the American forces could shock them so much they might not be willing to attack Japan proper.

Colonel Yahara was an important staff member and a close adviser to General Ushijima. He alone in the meeting opposed a counterattack based of the facts that the Japanese had kept their Army mostly intact and had inflicted heavy losses on the Americans. Resistance could be greatly prolonged by bringing their reserve division and brigade that was stationed behind the Shuri Heights forward into the remaining defensive positions. He felt that no matter what was done, their fate was to die while killing as many of the enemy as possible. The best way to use their forces was to remain where they were.

The entire staff, except Yahara, decided that the whole Army would go on the offensive May 4. The staff decision was taken to General Ushijima late in the night, and he agreed with the decision even after hearing Yahara's counter-argument and ordered detailed plans to be written.

April 30, 1945. Colonel Snedeker, CO of the 7th Marines ordered his patrols to return to their battalion areas, then he traveled to the Shuri Line with the CO of the division to look at where their new positions would be. Final decisions were then made to move the Marines, and the senior officers issued orders as exactly where to insert their men to relieve the Army units and where and how to continue the attack on the Shuri defenses. Out of combat for the moment, but with the threat of combat worse to come, five

Marines still had breakdowns and had to be evacuated.

For the month of April, the regiment counted three hundred sixty-six casualties with a hundred wounded and psychiatric casualties returned to their units. The net loss was two hundred twenty-four. Jack's battalion suffered far more than the other battalions and attached units put together. Their non returned losses were a hundred forty-four. The figures of the 2nd Battalion are striking and when examination reveals that of the net figure of a hundred forty-four, sixty-four were psychiatric losses. Another interesting item to note is that there were only twenty-three killed of the total battalion loss.

The 6th Marine Division was still waiting for orders to move south.

The newly arrived 77th Division (from Ie Shimi) had now relieved the 96th Division but found no way to proceed without getting to the top of the cliff and on the escarpment that faced them. They could not find a way around the cliff and decided that the only way to get to the top would be straight up the cliff. They brought in ladders and Navy cargo nets and prepared to renew the attack the next morning.

Only a few stray Kamikazes pilots, who mostly proved to be harmless, went at the fleet. One plane did make it to the Merchant Marine cargo ship, *S. H. Young*, producing only minor damage but killing forty-eight Merchant Marine sailors.

In Germany, Adolf Hitler committed suicide.

CHAPTER SIX
ADVANCING TOWARD SHURI

The Marines were heading into the close, deadly combat already going on at the Shuri Heights defenses. There would be a similarity at Shuri to World War I trench warfare, the same ground would be fought over for weeks. This combat would prove to be an assailant to all of the men's senses. They saw tracers coming at them, their buddies being shot and blown up, explosions and enemy soldiers coming at them. They heard the screams of wounded Marines and Japanese soldiers, shells screeching as they flew through the air and the following explosions, the whoosh of flamethrowers, the snap of bullets passing by, machine gun and rifle fire. Their touch was of the blood and gore of wounded buddies, the bite of fleas, the cold rain, the feel of sleeping in mud. They tasted cordite, foul water and teeth unbrushed for days. There was a constant smell of body order, blood and rotting bodies. They had no appetite, they ate the C rations and chocolate bars just to keep going so they, in effect, were slowly starving to death. Their emotions were hammered by their life style and constant fear. Most Marines proved that the human body could withstand and survive great torture and misery. The mind was different, though. All of their minds were affected to a lesser or greater extent. Some would bury their experiences within them and try to act as though there was little or nothing wrong. Some would break on the battlefield and become just as much of a casualty as if they had been shot. Some held it together for years and even decades before falling apart. These latter veterans would be casualties that would never be counted or recorded.

Some people, even veterans, think that the World War II Pacific Theater veterans got over their experiences with time. Most did not. They just got used to living with them.

May 1, 1945. The 7th Marines suspended all of their patrol operations and moved forward echelons of the regiment and each battalion to the south near the village of Uchitomari where headquarters would be established.

Jack's battalion commander, Lt. Col. Berger, ordered the final preparations completed for moving the battalion south. He reported to his boss, Colonel Snedeker, that the battalion had suffered greatly from the lack of supplies. He made several recommendations to correct the logistics problem in the future fighting, but all were ignored. The lack of supplies would continue to plague the Marines throughout the battle. There were plenty of supplies on the island by this time and the rear echelon troops lived well. The problem was an inability to move the supplies to the front lines. The Japanese had plenty of artillery and a good line of sight from their high positions. Roads were few, poor and dangerous from snipers and the enemy artillery. Rain stopped all movement as practically every vehicle was forced to a halt in the deep muck that the roads turned into. There was no lack of effort by the support and service people in trying to get supplies to the front. It just didn't work. The regimental commander believed and reported to his superiors that rest areas provided showers and new clothing to his men. That may have happened for some Marine units but not for Jack's.

"I didn't see no showers. Sometimes there would be water but all you got to wash with was a helmet full, so you couldn't get very clean. When I got wounded I was wearing a shirt that the Seebees give me and a pair of Japanese trousers that I had found. My clothes had worn and rotted plumb out. Sometimes you could wash a little when it rained, but you couldn't wash your clothes. Well you could try but it wouldn't do you no good "

The 6th Marine Division had arrived in the south. They were bivouacked a little way north of the Machinato Airfield and north west of where the 1st Marine Division was to be located when their spearhead battalions got there the next day. They were expecting to take over the zone of action that was now held by the Army's 27th Division. This latter division had set itself into a defensive perimeter and was just waiting to be pulled back. They had no fight left in them. Both divisions were ready to complete the relief movement when the overall commander, General Buckner, gave them the order.

The newly arrived, 77th Division had to get on top of the escarpment facing them. They went straight up the cliff on ladders and Navy cargo nets and gained the top. Fierce mortar and machine gun fire met them as small Japanese units counterattacked. They held the positions they had captured until midnight when a counterattack, in force, drove them back down the cliff. It took a great effort to provide enough accurate support fire at the cliff bottom to drive the Japanese back, in order for the soldiers to withdraw from the counterattack. The companies who had gained the top of the cliff barely escaped being wiped out, but they would go back the very next morning.

The first day of the new month found the skies over the fleet clear of any Japanese aircraft. The ships went about their support duties and watched the skies, waiting. No one could have known that the enemy had grounded their planes until the day of the land-based counterattack that the Japanese had planned. They were also searching for and assembling every aircraft the High Command would allow them to use to support their attack.

May 2, 1945. 2nd Battalion, along with rest of the regiment, was loaded into trucks and sent south. Two tank battalions and several other attached combat units from the regiment, even a 105mm gun platoon accompanied them. The Marines were unloaded in a rear area bivouac just behind and to the northwest of their assigned combat location. They were placed closer to the battle lines than the 6th Marine Division and just close enough to receive a few enemy shells that caused no harm except to interrupt the Marines' sleep. They had been ordered to insert themselves into the battle between the 6th Division on the west coast and the Army's 77th Division near the center of the Island. The latter division would slide further east to make room for the Marines. These units weren't really replacing anyone, they were meant to reinforce the attack on the Shuri defenses as would the Army's Division when they were put back in the lines a few days later. With the new arrivals General Buckner would have five divisions to crack the Shuri Line instead of the two divisions he had used throughout April. The 6th Marine Division would take over the Army's 27th Division on the extreme west coast and head for Naha. These Marines had not arrived yet and there was alarm that the 27th Division was no longer combat effective. There was concern that they could neither attack nor withstand an attack so the 1st Marine Division was hustled into their positions on their left flank until the 6th Marine Division could get there. The 1st Marine Division could then move east and take up their original place in the battle plan. This movement was a stroke of luck because the Japanese counterattacked in force two days later. Later, no one could even speculate on what might have happened if the shattered 27th Division had been left in place to await the relief by the Marines 6th Division.

"There was still a bunch of Army guys around there. It had rained some up in the hills and the ditches was running full of water. Some Army guys pulled up along the road there. They all jumped out and filled their canteens. It was running pretty clean but it was running over a bunch of dead Japanese that was upstream. We all knew that and thought this was a pretty funny joke."

The 6th Marine Division was sitting north of Machinato Airfield getting ready to move into the Army's 27th Division's positions. The soldiers of the latter division took on a new worry. Would they be able break off contact and get to the safety of the rear without being killed or wounded? No one wanted to die when they knew their war was basically over, or at least this frenzied hell they had been pushed into was at an end. Some would die and some would be wounded in the division exchange.

Men from the 77th Division went back up the cliff and this time managed to hold their positions on the escarpment the rest of the day and throughout the night.

For the second day in May no Japanese planes went at the fleet. The sailors were glad, but didn't understand why they were not being attacked. Suspicions rose that they were in store for another massed attack. Dread crept into the sailors, especially among the gun crews who were always eye witnesses to the Kamikaze induced terror.

May 3, 1945. The 7th Marines moved the 1st Battalion forward to a position Northwest of the Machinato Airfield where they sent out patrols and set up a perimeter along the beach. 2nd Battalion spent the day walking to their next bivouac that would put them in a position to begin replacing the soldiers they had been sent to relieve. They were just on the right flank of the 1st Battalion and could support each other. The two battalions settled in for a restless night because they were now close to the lines and they knew they would be in combat the next day. They were located west of the center of the island slightly north of Machinato Airfield facing toward the defenses that led directly to the Shuri Castle stronghold. The 6th Marine Division was north of them and just to their right hugging the coast. The plan was still to send the 6th Division down the coast and turn the 1st Division inland near the center of the island to directly attack the Shuri Heights once they got through the outer defenses. Three Army divisions would cover their left flank and also extend to the east coast with the 7th Army Division operating on that coast.

This plan was delayed for a short time by the Japanese counterattack that would begin with quiet troop movements just before midnight this very night. Regiments of the 1st Division had to be rushed into the positions on the shore line to reinforce the 1st Battalion to repel the Japanese landing attempt. These positions were actually reserved for the 6th Division, but as a part of the job of guarding the southern part of the airfield the 1st Division was there when the attack started. The Japanese mission, here, as a part of the full scale counterattack, was to get ashore behind the 1st Division, cut them off and attack them and elements of the 27th Division from the rear. They certainly had not intended to run directly into a large force of Marines. They fell short of the landing site and landed right in the middle of the 7th's Marines' 1st Battalion's units stationed alone the coast. They didn't expect to be spotted and attacked out on the reef by Marine amphibious trackers either but they were. It was fortuitous that most of the 7th Marines had been plunked down right where the Japanese landed. Commanders had never dismissed the fact that the Japanese might attack but when they did it was a complete surprise to General Buckner and his staff.

The 6th Marine Division had assembled too far away to oppose the Japanese landing. They had to stay in place until the 1st Division beat back the amphibious landing and do enough mop up so they could move to their own zone of responsibility and turn the coastal area over to the proper division. They did have some excitement when about sixty Japanese did make it the to actual landing site. They tried to scatter throughout the area but they had landed in the division's zone. By the end of the next day they had all been hunted down and killed.

7th Division units held the front part of the escarpment they had taken the day before. Now they attacked the enemy reverse slope positions. The slope was covered with caves in which the Japanese hid before coming out to pour fire on their attackers. Explosives, grenades and flames were the only weapons that would kill the defenders who were basically inside the escarpment instead of on it. The fighting was so close and terrible that it was reported by witnesses that many American soldiers cried in terror, frustration and rage as they blasted and burned the Japanese in their caves. A soldier would climb to the top of cave openings while riflemen tried to protect him. If he made it, he could throw an explosive charge into the cave. If he was killed or wounded, another soldier would take his place without any orders being needed. At other caves, flamethrowers were used with the operators knowing they had a very short life span. This fight on the escarpment revealed to General Buckner that these tactics, invented by necessity, would be the only way to reduce the Japanese defenses. In the future, where possible, he would add tanks including flamethrower tanks and air dropped napalm and even gasoline to the deadly mix. He also understood that the going would be much slower than anyone thought and would cost dearly in American lives.

It has been speculated that Buckner thought that once the defenses he was now facing were breached, that Shuri itself would fall. If he had known that the fight for Shuri would take several weeks and kill thousands of Americans perhaps he would have made a new amphibious landing behind Shuri that many senior officers had recommended.

A third day began in the fleet without enemy air attacks. They were now certain. Something big was coming and soon. The ships maintained a high degree of alert.

The Japanese were ready for their counterattack. They would begin troop movements when night fell in order to be in attack positions with the dawn on May 4. They sent a number of planes against the fleet in the late afternoon and early evening. Before the destroyer minelayer, *Aaron Ward,* ended her short career, she had been commissioned for only four months, she had shot down eleven Japanese planes. She was hit by six Kamikazes but managed to stay afloat and was towed out of the battle. She did not see any further action and was scraped a short time later. Also put out of further action were the heavy cruiser *Indianapolis* and the minesweeper *Macomb. Bache*, a destroyer was hit but her damage was minor. Some landing craft and a gunboat were put out of action but the biggest ship loss this day was the sinking of the destroyer *Little* after being struck by six Kamikazes. The real loss, of course, was that of the two hundred forty-eight sailors who were killed and wounded. The Navy was stunned that it had only taken twenty Japanese planes to accomplish so much destruction.

During the early evening Japanese planes bombed and strafed Kadena and Yomitan Airfields as a preliminary strike and to destroy and ground as many aircraft as they could. The planes came in force but caused little damage to the runways or the planes. The pilots were able to fly just as if no attack had occurred.

After daylight, the enemy planes went after the 77th Division. Few reached their targets and before any damage could be done, the sky was swept clean by American fighter planes.

May 4, 1945. Instead of being awakened in the morning to move forward into the Army's front positions, the 2nd Battalion was assembled at 0300. The Japanese were making their counterattack and had sent a landing party north. They had been detected near the beach where the regiment's 1st battalion was bivouacked. The regimental commander wanted to reinforce his 1st Battalion and ordered Jack's battalion south and attached them to the 1st Battalion. They moved fast to take up new positions south of the nearby Machinato airfield on the west coast. They didn't know it at the time, but the Japanese were starting a large scale attack all along the lines. The enemy began firing an artillery barrage that caught 2nd Battalion out in the open just about half way to Machinato. Army personnel pulling back suffered several casualties from the bombardment, but the Marines had only one man injured.

Shortly after their arrival, Lt. Col. Berger learned that there were about two hundred Japanese troops in the landing operation and the 1st battalion commander had no plan for him and was not going to be putting his battalion in the line facing the landing party, so they just sat near the airfield and waited for morning. What the Marines didn't know was that the Navy had caught much of the landing party out on the reef and in the open. They were cut down by the dozens by Marine am tracks and Navy gunboats. When it was over, there were about twice as many Japanese soldiers as Berger thought there were. Although the Japanese were totally overwhelmed by Marine and Naval fire power, they still brought about seventy-four Marine casualties in the one-sided fight.

Frank Moody. "One night, I think it was about the 4th of May, there was a bunch of them that tried to land on the west side. We went over there. There was shooting back and forth. I was laying down pretty tight. There was tracers and bullets going over the top of us. We couldn't get out on the bluff to see the Japs that well. You had to be careful. There was shooting both ways and we were up on that little ridge a little higher than everybody who was shooting. The Japs shot them up pretty good all up and down there. That night Dolan looked me up. He ran me down and found me. We was in the same company so he couldn't have been very far away. The weather was dry, it wasn't raining like it usually was. I had moved down the ridge a little and was under the bullets, so they couldn't hit us. We was sitting on something that was off the ground. I told Jack to come on over and sit. He come on over and sat by me. You couldn't see anything, of course. He sat there and we let our feet dangle. Something we was sitting on was pretty good sized. I thought it was a rock or something. It really didn't make any difference, we didn't have to sit or lay on the hard ground. It felt good just to be able to sit up for a while. The bullets was going quite a ways over the top of us, so we just sat there. It finally got light in the morning. Jack had sat there for a long time. His platoon had come up right besides us by then, so he had stayed sitting there. We saw we was sitting on a five hundred pound bomb that had not gone off. We laughed and laughed about it, a lot. I had invited him to sit on a bomb! We have always laughed about that."

Jack Dolan, "When they made that beach landing there was places where they couldn't get over the wall. There was drain pipes that went through the wall so the road would have a place to drain. When it started getting light, the tide went out and they would find the ends of the drain pipes and crawl up them to get ashore. Well, Frank Looke went down there and started shooting them as they crawled up through there and come out. He killed so many that he got decorated for it."

When it got light, Jack's George Company was moved closer to the shore where they relieved a company that had taken the Japanese under fire during the night. The relieved company simply headed south to kill any enemy soldiers who might have made it ashore. At full light, George Company began patrolling their area and found it to be heavily mined. The battalion command post, who they thought was a safe area, came under fire from riflemen and light machine gunners. They were from the landing party and had concealed themselves behind the sea wall less than a hundred yards away. The Marines had sent amphibious tractors along the shore to help eliminate any surviving Japanese and they killed the soldiers who were firing at the Command Post.

The battalion patrols spent the day mopping up the area and, with the amphibious tractors, accounted for the deaths of forty-two Japanese who had made it ashore during the night. During the effort of hunting down the Japanese stragglers, the battalion lost twenty-one men.

The 1st Battalion had borne the brunt of the landing attempt, but the 2nd Battalion still lost seventy-four men in the mop up operations. The military's so called non battle casualties had been only an annoyance until now. The trickle of men lost from the lines because they broke down was picking up. This loss of fighting men without wounds, was noticed but rarely discussed by commanders. The men were well aware of it, though, and knew it could happen to anyone at anytime. Jack's regiment had taken one hundred nine casualties in the four days they had been in the south and fifty of those were the non battle variety. This latter number would increase dramatically as the fighting intensified and time in the line lengthened.

"That happened to lots of guys. That happened to a guy that I knew later on down the island."

The 6th Marine Division was supposed to move into their assigned zone of action, but their orders were momentarily suspended. No one quite understood at this point that the Japanese had commenced a major offensive that traversed the island and included amphibious landings on both coasts. They did know that there was a landing to the south and that elements of the 1st Division were engaged in battle. They also knew that this fight was taking place across their line of march and that alone prevented them from doing anything except holding in place. Some short time after the landing started south of their positions, the 6th was startled to discover that some of the Japanese, about sixty, had landed in their own area. These troops made it ashore and scattered inland. When daylight came, the division sent Marines out to find these now wayward soldiers. All of them were hunted down and killed.

As a part of their offensive that began this day, the Japanese sent another amphibious force up the east coast. Their mission was to land behind the Army's 7th Division whose zone of action started on the east coast and went west, inland, to tie into the 77th Division's left flank. They would land behind the 7th, hide until daylight and then attack the rear of the 7th where senior officers and supply dumps were located. The American division would have to pull infantry out of the lines to deal with them and thus weaken the lines. Because of a lack of equipment, the Japanese had to use row boats and hug the shoreline. When the boats came opposite the 7th Division's position before dawn, they were spotted by Naval craft stationed there to provide gunfire support. The Navy took the boats under fire and sank all of them. The few survivors who managed to escape the navy's big guns where shot by 7th Division soldiers before they could reach the shore. The American line in this area would remain as strong as it was before the ill-fated landing attempt. American commanders counted some and estimated others and came to the conclusion that at least a thousand Japanese had participated in the two landing attempts. It was further noted that they were service troops, not hardened infantry and their loss served only to reduce the Japanese defending forces.

The Japanese artillery pieces were hidden in caves, houses and other natural concealment. It was standard operating procedure to unveil the guns only long enough to fire two or three rounds then, re-conceal them. This made it extremely difficult to spot the Japanese gun emplacements. Even if they were spotted, once they were retracted back into the caves it took luck and a lot of effort to put them out of action. This practice would have to change once their offensive commenced. In order to support their infantry, the Japanese had to pull most of their artillery from concealment. It was to be used to soften up the American positions for the initial advance and would then have to be moved forward to keep up with the infantry. They expected little harm by revealing their guns. The Americans would have to withdraw once their lines were penetrated and fighting began to their rear. The Japanese expected to reach the American artillery positions and destroy them before they could react much to the attack. The Japanese would move their big guns forward and take back all of the defensive positions they had lost. Their plan didn't work and they lost many artillery pieces and gun crews, neither of which could be replaced.

The shelling was mostly massed in the area where the 7th and 77th Divisions tied in with each other. About the only damage suffered by American soldiers was another battlefield horror of heavy artillery fire concentrated in a small area. An estimated twelve thousand shells hit between the divisions where the Japanese intended to penetrate the lines. When the shelling stopped the soldiers heard Japanese tanks coming at them. These sounds added to their already jittery nerves. They could now be certain a major force was coming at them. Despite what they had already experienced, the 7th Division held their ground, and halted the attack all along their lines. The groups that made it to the American lines were in turn attacked and destroyed. Some enemy tanks and artillery pieces were brought up nearly on top of the 7th's lines. The guns, tanks, crews and supporting infantry were destroyed by division tanks and the infantry's heavy machine guns. When Japanese leaders were killed, their soldiers, because of their training, didn't know what to do without orders. They had a tendency to become confused and just, sort of, mill around. When it happened in this attack, they were shot down and blown up in staggering numbers. They were definitely not trained to retreat and didn't even know how without leaders. Two Japanese battalions with artillery and about two thousand men were coming across the east coastal flats to attack the left flank to the 7th Division when daylight caught them in the open. They were spotted and a hail of artillery was directed into their ranks. They turned and ran back to their own lines, but more than a thousand men and many officers were killed before they made it. Most of the survivors had wounds and became ineffective for fighting through the rest of the campaign.

The main thrust of the attack was directed against the 77th Division. In order for their whole attack to succeed they needed to cut through the lines here, turn west and hit the 1st Marine Division before the Marines could deploy into their assigned battle lines. This was so important that they committed more medium and light tanks knowing that all of them could be lost but the risk had to be taken.

Three Japanese infantry battalions and the infantry company from a tank regiment hit the 77th Division's lines manned by the 306th Infantry Regiment. They had not gotten close enough to the American defense lines to be able to avoid artillery before daylight, but they still proceeded with the attack. To do otherwise was unthinkable. Japanese tanks were moved forward into the battle but were spotted and destroyed by American artillery. Other tanks that got too close were knocked out by bazooka carrying infantrymen. Without tank support, the Japanese simply could not penetrate the 77th's Lines.

The Japanese commanders were trying to watch the battle unfold from atop the Shuri Heights. They hoped to be able to see their troops approaching their enemy's rear positions, but by noon they knew it would never happen. General Ushijima had moved his 44th Brigade forward to pour through the Americans once the lines had been penetrated. These were fresh men who had been held behind the main defense line as reserves. Ushijima knew that to commit them now would only be to lose them. He decided, however, that his offensive was not over yet. The survivors of the battalions and regiments that had fought that day would regroup and push through the American line near Maeda, capture and occupy the high ground they had given up back on April 23. This was far enough in the American rear that the going was expected to be easy once they broke through the front line. This tactic would give them the high ground in the rear and also provide the new brigade, ready and poised, with a path straight through the American line. A gap would first appear, then the brigade would begin to roll up the American division's flanks. It was possible the Americans could be pushed back to where the battle had started nearly a month ago. The Americans would be defeated and at the least, they would have to start all over again. The loss would be catastrophic and the invasion of Japan might never take place. It seemed to be worth the effort and the loss of men and guns to Ushijima. Some of his staff officers now had grave doubts by seeing the prodigious loss of soldiers who could not be replaced. They wondered if the only thing that would come out of the offensive would be nothing but a weakening of their own defensive forces.

The Japanese large scale land counterattacks had begun at daylight and a massed air attack of one hundred fifty planes struck the fleet to support the fighting ashore. The light cruiser *Birmingham*, destroyer *Ingraham* , escort carrier *Sangamom* and minelayer *Shea* were hit badly enough that they had to be withdrawn from the war. The British carrier *Formidable* and the U. S. minesweeper *Gayety*, the minelayer *Gwin* and the destroyer *Lowry* received minor damage. The destroyers *Luce* and *Morrison* and a few landing craft were sunk. The loss of life was severe, the *Luce* sank so fast that more than a third of the crew went down with her and over half of the *Morrison's* men were lost. *Morrison* was hit by a Kamikaze that caused grave damage. While her crew fought to save her, three old, slow flying, float biplanes somehow made it through the gunfire and scored hits on the ship sinking her. Four hundred sixty-two sailors died and another five hundred sixty-eight were wounded.

May 5, 1945. 2nd Battalion widened its patrol area south of Machinato Airfield and began blowing and sealing caves. They used the regiment's amphibious tractors like tanks and even captured a 40mm gun after killing the crew. Less than a mile south of the airfield, on the shore line, was a low swampy area known as Asagawa Estuary. The Japanese held all of the land on the south side of this feature and in fact had every inch of the estuary sighted in with their big guns. Lt. Col. Berger sent a platoon from Easy Company to scout the low-lying estuary shores. When they got there, platoon leader Lt. Deland and one man actually crossed the water into Japanese territory and came back a second way. When the Lt. and his patrol returned to the command post, they reported to Berger that amphibious tractors could cross the water and that even tanks could proceed at a low tide. Berger sent a detachment of engineers back to the estuary to build a Bailey Bridge. They were escorted by a platoon reinforced with a machine gun section sent to guard them while they worked on the bridge. The bridge was almost completed when the Japanese opened up with heavy mortars and, obviously, pre-registered artillery. The bridge was destroyed and the fire continued throughout the night to prevent the engineers from trying again.

The Japanese had learned to recognize the Marine scouts by the way they moved. The scouts sometimes traveled alone but often took one or two men with them for various reasons. The Japanese tried to hold their fire when they identified Marine scouts near them, knowing that a scout would soon come back with lots of Marines for them to kill. If lost Marines or souvenir hunters ventured too close, they were promptly shot but not most of the scouts. Apparently the concealed Japanese assumed that Lt. Deland and his companion were scouts and later they did bring lots of Marines to be killed. A trained Marine scout would, surly, have spotted some of the many gun emplacements. Then he would have warned Berger that building a bridge there without a large scale supporting attack, would be suicide for the builders. The trained scouts were highly prized, but there were few of them and patrols couldn't always wait for one of them to make an appearance.

Frank Moody. "Jack and me was always close to each other but not really together. Quite a few Japs had got ashore and was scattered around us. We had a company runner who carried messages and stuff. He was back at the battalion command post somewhere behind us. I was not out on patrol, so I was right there with the infantry companies. The Captain wanted to know if I couldn't get hold of the old Colonel back there behind us a mile, probably. Captain Norton couldn't get in touch with them on the radio. So, he wanted to know if I could take a message to him. I said sure, I was always crazy about doing things like that. It didn't bother me. I didn't try to get out of anything like that. He told me about where the old Colonel was. We was down on the coast on the bluffs where the Japs had tried to land. We were there and the Japs were kind of strung out a little bit all down along there. I took off running. I just had a rifle so I was kind of light. I wanted to keep moving because I didn't know who was around there. Pretty soon I did run into a couple of Jap soldiers. *God,* I thought, *where did they come from?* Blood was still running out of them, hell, they had just got killed. I was sure there were some who had got ashore. There was some of them there and I didn't see nobody. So, I thought if I keep moving and they saw me, they would have a harder target. Anyway I run into this guy, the company runner. His name was Haynes. He was from Ohio. He was one of the guys in our outfit. Somehow, he was back there with the Colonel. Somebody had probably sent him back there to guard the Colonel. He might of been guarding the Colonel or it might of been some other higher up. Anyway, the message the Captain give me to give to the Colonel was for this Haynes. I run right into him. He was in a big shell hole. He was the only guy in the shell hole when

I found him. I don't even know how you would find the right guy in all that was going on. I was just good at it, I guess. I gave him his note. I said, 'I'll be getting out of here and getting back', so I took off running again. I had only seen the two dead Japs, no noise, none of our guys, no Japs, nobody. You could see down through this sage brush for about a mile or so. I headed out running pretty good and when I got back to the Captain, where he was, I told him that I had delivered the message. He said they had just gotten through on the radio and Haynes had been killed already. (The Marines, in combat, stripped off all signs of rank. There was no saluting and only last names were used, every other measure to prevent the Japanese from identifying and targeting officers and NCO's, was taken.) They could of seen me give him the message and thought he was a big shot. But when I got back to the company he was dead. I had just seen him a few minutes before. You don't know why it happens like that, or the reason. I had just been there and didn't see a sign of anybody. Never heard anybody either and I was good at that. It was my job to know what was going on. They must of seen me give him that note and shot him, figuring he was an officer or something. Little things like that just keep coming to you every day. You can visit buddies and talk about these things, but you don't talk to other people about them. I never even talked to my dad for several years. I never told anybody a thing. That is just the way things are. Oh, I talked about things like Jack sitting on the bomb but never things like Haynes getting killed because I handed him a note out in the open."

The 6th Marine Division had to stand in place for another day since the 1st Division was still fighting in the 6th Division's zone of action.

One Japanese battalion scattered in yesterday's fighting, regrouped and just after midnight, simply walked through the American lines, unopposed. When they made some noise, the men on watch thought they were Americans and held their fire. The enemy battalion remnant made it to the American rear and set up positions around a supply dump belonging to the American 7th Division. The other depleted Japanese units reassembled as much as they could and proceeded to attack American positions wherever they could find them. By daylight, the Japanese attackers had been repulsed all along their area of offensive operations, except for the battalion at the supply dump. Soldiers of the American divisions spent the rest of the day hunting down and eliminating small groups and even individual enemy troops, except for the Japanese battalion of six hundred men at the supply dump. They were well entrenched at their captured dump and in easily defendable terrain on top of an escarpment. American units had to try to climb the cliffs of the escarpment in the face of heavy fire and were thrown back each time. Daylight faded and the Americans delayed any further attacks until the next day. The Japanese problem was that they were surrounded and so far at the rear of the enemy that there was no escape for them. This problem was confounded that evening when General Ushijima realized the futility of his offensive and ordered it to stop. Survivors were sent back to their defensive positions and the battalion at the supply dump was written off.

The massed air attack of the day before had been badly beaten, but not before sinking and damaging several ships with considerable loss of American life. A Kamikaze crushed into the seaplane tender, *St. George*. She was damaged, but the crew managed to affect repairs on their own and she kept operating until routinely relieved. A Kamikaze also found and hit a Navy operated surveying vessel, the *Pathfinder*, but did only minor damage.

May 6, 1945. 2nd Battalion moved forward to relieve the 1st Battalion which now turned to the task of mopping up around the area. After the relief was completed, they waited while heavy Naval gunfire and Marine artillery pounded the Japanese positions just to their front. When the friendly fire was lifted, the battalion moved forward to take the high ground at the north edge of Asagawa Estuary. At the first step of moving forward, they immediately came under enemy fire. The Japanese had withdrawn into their caves and tunnels to wait out the bombardment thrown at them. When the American fire lifted, the Japanese took up their defensive positions, pulled their big guns into firing positions and brought their mortars out into the firing pits dug into the reverse slopes. All of the weapons commenced firing on the battalion including rifles and machine guns. However, the battalion advance was well coordinated with Naval guns, artillery, large mortars and aircraft. This support fire destroyed Japanese positions and counter battery fire eliminated a lot of the enemy guns. The battalion made good progress and advanced four hundred yards before being ordered to halt because they were getting ahead of the rest of the regiment and were coming close to exposing their flanks. The battalion headquarters people were shaken when an air strike dropped napalm near them. They knew they were too close to the battle and some of them wanted to withdraw further from the front. Lt.

Col. Berger would not permit the command post to be moved since it would send a bad signal to the fighting Marines. The Marines were shelled the rest of the day and all through the night, but the high ground, north of the estuary, was in their hands. An 8-inch gun, from a never to be discovered position, began firing during the night. The scream of these large shells passing through the air and the huge explosions gave the Marines a new terror of the night to deal with.

The 1st Marine Division had found the kind of fighting that had nearly destroyed the Army's 27th Division and decimated the 96th Division. They had to fight through a hill complex made up of interconnecting ridges, hills and draws. The entire area was honeycombed with caves and defensive tunnels. Each post or strong point covered each other one. The reverse slopes had been prepared for protected mortar firing. As the Marines moved forward, they found themselves constantly exposed to crossfire. When a Marine unit would fight its way to the top of a slope, they found themselves registered targets of the mortars on the reverse side. Because of the tunnel and cave maze, the Marines would take a position only to find that the Japanese were inside, firing out from carefully concealed and protected openings. The division sent tanks to help, but the terrain was not favorable for their use and the Japanese antitank gunfire sent the tanks back out of range.

By dark the regiment had lost only twenty-five men, but the division had losses of six hundred forty-nine over the past three days. They had not participated, except for the botched landing in the Japanese counterattack, but still had almost as many casualties as the two involved Army divisions combined. The attack would continue the next day, but the tactics would be adjusted to better deal with the situation.

The 6th Division could do nothing more than scout their new area and wait for the 1st Division to reach a point in their fighting that would allow them to be replaced. Then the battle lines could be adjusted and the 6th Division could enter the fight. The 7th Marines would be pulled east and back into their original zone to ready themselves for the all out assault that was planned.

American soldiers continued mopping up stragglers from the failed Japanese counterattack and began preparing themselves to continue their own offensive. The Japanese battalion at the supply dump was becoming seriously depleted from repeated American attacks. After dark, the young

Japanese commander marched what was left of his battalion back the same way they had come and once again they drew no fire. He left three hundred fifty-five dead soldiers at the supply dump.

During the short offensive, the Japanese lost more than 5,000 men and most of their tanks. A good many of the artillery pieces that the Japanese had to expose in support of their infantry, were destroyed. After the failed attempt, American officers could easily tell that the volume of artillery fire they faced had been reduced. The defense of Okinawa had been severely weakened at a cost of six hundred eighty-seven American casualties.

The American Navy was spared from any air attacks. It was now quite clear that the Navy's resources would be tied up in this one location until Okinawa was secured. Planners had wanted to make another landing on the China coast to keep pressing the Japanese and to ensure troops in China would not be rotated back to Japan. The Navy could not spare nearly enough ships to support any landing anywhere. This realization brought even more concern about the importance of ending the battle as soon as possible. It also raised a question. If the Japanese would fight this hard and grind up so many American lives and destroy so many ships at Okinawa, what would happen when the invasion of Japan commenced?

May 7, 1945. Contact with the enemy was maintained during the night. When morning came, the battalion started fanning patrols out through the area's enemy defenses, the goal being to kill the Japanese within their assigned zone of action. Riflemen would move forward until fire was received, then long range machine guns would fire over their heads into the concealed defensive positions with outstanding results. Official records refer to this action as, "Spirited fire fights ensued." The "spirited" enemy poured artillery fire on the battalion, but the patrols were so thinly spread out that casualties were few this day. American artillery, air, and Naval gun fire were freed to fire missions of opportunity. Any enemy position that opened fire would bring accurate counter battery fire or call fire missions from troops spotting the Japanese weapons as they were brought into firing positions. Marine fighter planes roamed the area and unloaded on any Japanese movement. It was a killing field for the Marines, but the majority of the killing was done at ranges of three to four hundred yards by the support fire. This was a rare and welcome sight for the infantrymen who were used to having to do the killing up close. One source of artillery fire, zeroed in on the battalion, was coming from a partially sunken Japanese ship in the harbor just off of Naha. Somehow and sometime the Japanese had managed to place some artillery pieces on the wreck and began firing rounds into the battalion rear. Once it was discovered where this fire was coming from, Navy guns put an end to it.

The Marines' new tactic was to use small units and attack each cave or tunnel opening as they found them. As they burned or blew each position they could safely bring their tanks forward to help. They learned to throw phosphorus grenades in openings and watch for smoke to come out of the ground. The smoke revealed vents for the underground system and had been so well concealed that they were next too impossible to find, without the smoke. Once found, Marines poured gasoline or napalm down the vents and ignited the fluid with a grenade. Massive numbers of soldiers died in the underground facilities. Some would run out of openings trying to escape only to be shot down by the waiting Marines. When the area was secured and mopping up operations began, the Marines searched the cave/tunnel complex as much as they could, depending on the damage to the tunnels themselves. They found dead soldiers and civilians, field hospital facilities, with large quantities of supplies and ammunition where the patients had mostly died of suicide. The Marines had also learned to bring engineers forward to seal the caves and tunnels so the enemy could not re-occupy them. Too many times enemy soldiers had popped up in the rear from caves that were thought to be empty. Sealing all the openings was the only way to be sure this practice would end.

The 6th Marines had to remain in position for another day or risk exposing their flank. This would not be permitted to happen. The 1st Division had to start making a headway down the island before these Marines could move.

On the east coast, the 7th Division moved southwest toward their next objective a small feature called Gaja Ridge. It protected a stronghold about a mile to the west, Kochi Ridge, that would have to be taken before the Division could proceed south. Not to take Kochi Ridge would leave a strong Japanese force on the division's right rear flank. Bypassing Kochi Ridge would also halt the advance of the 77th Division since it would leave a Japanese force to their rear as well. General Ushijima had pulled a regiment from the Gaja area for his counterattack. They had been all but destroyed and no serious resistance could be mounted against the 7th Division's advance to Gaja Ridge.

The Army's 77th Division was set to continue the attack on the Shuri defenses, but the soldiers were stopped in their tracks. The halt was not brought about by the Japanese but by the 7th Army Division to their left and the 1st Marine Division to their right. If they tried to move, the Japanese on Kochi Ridge poured fire into their left flank. On their right, the Marines were bogged down in the Awacha area. If the 77th Division advanced without the Marines being able to advance also, the Japanese could attack their right flank and even move in behind them. To move in this situation would be to move right into a trap so they had to wait.

The Navy was exhausted, but did not have to fight many enemy aircraft on this day. Not a single ship was hit.

Admiral Turner, the overall commander, noted the success of the Army's 77th Division and also noted that the Division CO was using tactics that worked but were crawling forward so slow that the battle seemed to go on forever. Turner wanted to get his carriers and major fighting ships out of Okinawa waters as quickly as possible. The ships needed overhauls and routine maintenance and the crews were desperate for rest. The admiral knew these same ships would be involved in the invasion of Japan. The Navy's battle efficiency was eroding every day and the invasion of the Home Islands might have to be delayed several months. General Buckner's slowness was intended to save the lives of as many men as he could, but it appeared that his tactics were lengthening the war. In addition to the military, the American civilians were weary and tired of the war. This was exactly what the Japanese wanted when they set up their defenses of Okinawa. General Buckner clearly saw Admiral Turner's point and ordered that all four of his divisions attack on May 11 to clear the Japanese from the Shuri Heights.

Germany surrendered. When it was announced to the troops the next day, no one in the front lines cared. It was news that meant absolutely nothing to men still fighting for their very lives against the Japanese. These men were unable to even conceive of an end to their own fighting. All of the ships in the area and all artillery pieces fired at least one salvo to celebrate Germany's end. All of the shells fired were aimed at the Japanese positions and those soldiers were startled, but unknowing as to why they suddenly received so much more attention than usual. They expected a major attack but none came.

May 8, 1945. Preparations for the all out offensive, scheduled for May 11, began all along the American lines. Elements of the 6th Marine Division began arriving so the 7th regiment of the 1st Division could slide to the east and take up positions in order to commence attacking the defenses nearest to the Shuri Castle stronghold. Jack's battalion spent most of the day turning over their positions to the newly arrived Marine regiment and withdrawing and bivouacking just to the rear of the lines. All of this movement was observed by the Japanese and they pumped artillery shells into the area. The new Marines were moving forward and were often exposed to the fire so they had quite a few casualties. The exchange went well for the 2nd Battalion because not many of them were hit. Only thirty-two Marines were lost and the Marine's commander considered this to be "light." The casualties' buddies, of course, had a different view. To them, there was no such thing as "light" casualties.

"About five days before taking Dakeshi, the captain sent a tank commander and his runner to me. He wanted to know if I would take him so he could look the village over. And we did. I had told him that they would probably let us in, but they might not let us back out."

"It was a three stepped hill, a long slope up to an almost straight up and down cliff. On the first shelf there was a road that ran exactly right on the cliff. It made a half moon circle. We was coming in from the east and turned south right into the main street of the village. On the left, when you entered there was a huge cave dug in under a big rock the size of a house. There was a gaping hole up on one level next to the road and down about twenty to thirty feet below was another hole. This one was the entrance from the back side, we seen that. We started in on the road and it was lined with burial tombs and the side hill was lined with burial tombs. They had pulled all the entrance stones out of them and now they was all pillboxes. The first thing I noticed, just a few yards into town was a machine gun slit about four inches above the roadway so we knew the place was completely undermined with caves. The man that was in there was below ground level. I could see a machine gun barrel sticking out. It wasn't five to six feet from us as we walked by. We seen all kinds of emplacements as we went through to the end of the street. At the end it was walled off, a dead end street. The only way to go on was a ladder that went down to the next level. That was the three levels, a sloping hill which was what the guy had to go up when they attacked the ridge. Then the ridge went down and that was the reverse slope where they had mortars. You couldn't get to those mortars except from the town. Then there was the cliff. The emplacements in the cliff covered the slope, too. You could see openings in the cliffs and you knowed there was guns in every one of them. Then there was the ladder that went down into the rice paddies. You could tell that you couldn't take Dakeshi Ridge without taking Dakeshi Town. The town was the only place where you could knock out the mortars on the reverse slope. They was no other way to get at them. You were not gonna be able to take the ridge without getting tanks into the town to knock out those mortars."

"The rice paddies that you could go down to was at the edge of a long valley that went right up to Shuri Castle. They called that valley the Wana Draw. At the end of the street we could see a man-made hill on the edge of Wana Ridge. We had caught them, that day, without the camouflage nets up. I could see at least six or eight big square holes and they was nine inch mortar emplacements. They was really big. None of us had ever seen them before. We got to the end of the street and the old tank commander said, 'Well, what about it, I don't see too much?' I told him that I had seen plenty. I told him that I didn't think we would get out of there but to just turn around and casually walk back down the road. I said not to look to the right or left. They let us walk out but they didn't let us back in that easy."

The 6th Marine Division sent its 22nd Regiment as a spearhead to take up positions on the front and relieve the elements of the 7th Marines who were still in contact with the enemy. The commander of the new division, Major General Shepard, accompanied his Regiment. He exposed himself to enemy fire to meet with Lt. Col. Berger at Berger's command post, where he received a personal briefing and an up close view of the defenses they were preparing to attack.

After the 7th Division took Gaja Ridge they started for Kochi Ridge less than a mile to their west. Dug into the ridge was a Japanese regiment still intact and in a lot better shape than the Americans coming toward them. The soldiers were stopped by the fire from the ridge and from the approaches. They were halted for the day but would advance again the next morning. The 77th Division had to hold in place for another day.

It was another normal battle day for the fleet, if any kind of battle is ever normal. They carried out their assignments of gunfire support, bombing attacks, close air support, resupply, casualty handling and much more. But, they worked without any Kamikazes coming at them.

May 9, 1945. Jack and the 2nd Battalion spent most of the day moving east and taking up a new bivouac close to their assigned zone of action. They spent the balance of day resting as well as they could and waited for further orders. The whole 7th Regiment was now assembled at this spot and ready to jump off with the other two 1st Division infantry regiments. The plan called for the insertion of the 7th Marines into the lines just to the right of the Army's 77th Division. The 7th's mission was to attack and eliminate the Japanese on a ridge named Dakeshi and the town with the same name located to the right rear of the ridge. The 5th Marine regiment, the sister of the 7th Marines, was fighting a hard battle in the Awacha area northwest of Dakeshi Ridge. When they completed capturing the Awacha area, they would move in on the right of the 7th and advance up the right side of Wana Draw after Dakeshi fell. This would tie the 1st Marine Division into the left flank of 6th Marine Division. All of the moving around within Japanese artillery range and the help given to the 5th Marines made this day the worse so far for the Regiment. There was a total of one hundred six Marine casualties. They were now operating in a very dangerous area. The regiment had already exceeded the number of casualties they had during the entire month of April and they had not yet attacked any enemy strongholds.

Marine planners had noted that getting pass Dakeshi Town would put them into a wide, flat, terrain feature known as Wanna Draw which led directly to the Shuri Heights and the castle stronghold. Dakeshi, therefore, was the key to Wana Draw which was the key to Shuri. Only with the capture of Dakeshi could tanks be brought deeper into the battle. Once in Wana Draw without the tried and tested infantry tank teams being able to operate, casualties would decimate the rifle regiments out of existence. Most planners still thought that the capture of Shuri and Naha would bring defeat to the Japanese and the battle for Okinawa would be over. This idea put great pressure on the assault regiments to keep moving at any cost and close down this island slaughterhouse. They were anxious to get on with the invasion plans of Japan itself but they were wrong. The Japanese were not defeated when Shuri fell. The battle would continue on into the latter part of June!

The 6th Marine Division's original mission had been to relieve the Army on the west coast push south and capture Naha, the capitol city. Planners now recognized that there was no value in taking Naha. The city didn't cover any high ground and had been bombed and shelled flat. It was nothing but rubble that concealed a few enemy snipers. Eventually small units of Marines did go into Naha to clean out the small numbers of Japanese hidden there. The worst thing about the city was that bombs had started falling on it back in October of 1944 and it was believed there were at least thirty-five thousand bodies buried in the rubble. Therefore, disease was another issue to consider. The 6th Division was ordered to take the defenses north of Naha, then slant inland toward Shuri. This could flank the Shuri Line on the west side. Patrols were sent to scout the zone and find a way across the river Asakawa which lay in the division's path.

The 7th Division took up their renewed attack on Kochi Ridge and by the end of the day they had captured the crest. They dug in for the night but the Division level officers doubted they could continue with any kind of advance the next day. It was recognized that the soldiers were so exhausted that the combat efficiency of the Division rifle companies was all but gone. Any further fighting was sure to bring significant numbers of non battle casualties and deplete the units to where they might be useless for the rest of the battle. The decision was made to withdraw the Division in the morning and replace it with the 96th Division. This Division had been resting for about 10 days, was resupplied and replacements had swollen the ranks to nearly full. They were deemed ready for sustained combat. The commander of the 77th Division, Major General Bruce, used his down time to relieve his assault regiment with a regiment that had been held in reserve. So when the attack commenced the Japanese would face a rested, rearmed, regiment whose ranks had been filled out with replacement troops.

The Japanese had not been sitting on their hands either, during the lull in the battle in the center of the defense line. They brought men forward from their service units and mixed them in with the survivors of the infantry units depleted during the counterattack. These men were not trained for their new status as infantrymen, but they were just as fanatical and would fight just as hard. General Ushijima's front lines could never be brought back to pre-counterattack strength but they were close enough to hold out for another six weeks.

The destroyer escort *England* had been hit by a Kamikaze on April 27, but the damage was minor and she stayed at her station on the radar picket line. This day she was hit again and with enough damage caused this time to knock her out of the war. Thirty-five of her crew were killed and another twenty-seven injured. The *Oberrender*, another destroyer escort, was also severely damaged and sent out of the battle. Her crew was more fortunate, but they still had eight men killed and fifty-three wounded.

May 10, 1945. The 5th Marines became bogged down in their fight at Awacha, a defensive complex a short distance north of Dakeshi, so the Division ordered George Company detached from 2nd Battalion and sent into the Awacha battle. While the rest of battalion rested, and prepared for the next day's assault on the approaches to Dakeshi Ridge, the Marines of George Company found themselves pinned down by heavy machine gun fire in a ravine at Awacha. They requested that heavy weapons respond to their situation, but the 5th Marines denied them any support. Without any artillery or mortar support, they had to fight their way up the ravine and dig in on a slope for the night. In order to keep the Japanese from infiltrating their positions, they threw grenades into the ravine all night.

Frank Moody. "Around the 10th of May or thereabouts, we was getting to some pretty hairy fighting. It started getting bad. It was so rainy at the time. We were so tired of being so soaked and wet. We were kinda on a long ridge. There was a guy, Jack knew him, from Chicago named Channick. He said, before we even got to Okinawa, that he was gonna get killed. He said, 'I just know it.' Something just told him. He wasn't afraid or anything. It didn't bother him a bit. I had heard that from three other guys and they all did get killed.

Channick was in a hole out on a little point on the ridge where you could see the Japs if they came up the ridge. We were behind them about a hundred yards or so. They were out on the point, Channick and some other guy, I can't remember his name. There was a little rock bluff behind them. They had dug a hole underneath the rock on the front side of that little bluff. It was only about as high as a table. We was sitting there and saw an artillery shell hit in that hole. Some guys went down there and packed them back. Channick was still alive and I recognized him. He died later on that day. The other guy died, too.

Guess who got to go up there? They sent me and my partner up there to get back in that hole out on the point to see if Japs were coming up the ridge or anything. It was raining and miserable. We had to get in that same hole, there wasn't anyplace else to get. It was full of mud and blood about a foot deep. We had a little shelter in back of us from that little bluff, but it was raining in the front of the hole. You laid in that hole so miserable and so cold.

It was dark now. They had got killed just before dark. We tried to look around to see where everybody else was but it was too dark. It was raining hard and you would try to sleep for an hour while the other guy kept watch. You would take turns with one guy trying to guard the other guy. We was so danged tired."

"It was raining so hard that I took my gun, I had an M1 then, and stuck it up in a little niche in the rock. The barrel was up and it rained in it, of course, but it kept the mud out of the barrel, at least. Then I would try to lay on my back right beside the gun. I tried to get my face under the little overhang to try to sleep without it raining on my face. I would sleep a little bit then Martin, my partner, would take over and try to sleep. He got killed on the 13th of May. Martin did. He was from Nebraska and he was a big kid. I had been born in mountain country and I had a good head on me. I had good eyesight and good ears. I had a good way of getting around through the brush and woods and traveling, staying out of sight. He had just never done it. Not like me or Jack. Jack had been hunting around in the woods for years, chasing and hunting deer, rabbits or whatever. He was an outdoors man and I had lived in rougher country than he did."

"We laid our hand grenades around the edge of that hole we were in. There was a little draw on each side of us going down the ridge. It wasn't even real steep though it was pretty steep. We couldn't see and we were always whispering to each other like, 'What the heck is that?' It kept looking like somebody out there. It would never move so we didn't think it could be a Jap. We kept looking at things about ten or fifteen feet out from us, kinda on both sides. We couldn't figure out what it was. Later, when they shot a flare, we saw it was two Japs that had been cut in two. There was two pieces on both sides and we kept looking at those and trying to figure it out. There was a flare sent up every once in a while, but you still couldn't see what could be coming because of the rain. It was kind of a long night. Long, miserable and so wet and cold."

"It got morning and we could see the two dead Japs were cut right in the middle, more or less, real well. Each piece was about two feet apart. They must have been sneaking up on Channick when that shell hit. It was still miserable and raining. I hadn't seen Jack for several days. I didn't even know where he was. I looked down that draw that turned into a canyon and I could see three Jap snipers that had grass suits on. I didn't have my sniper rifle with me because you couldn't see through the scope anyway, in that rain. I had my M1 and this guy beside me, this Martin, had a BAR. I looked again and could still see these three Japs about three hundred yards away. One was crawling on his hands and knees. They were all camouflaged pretty good with those grass suits on. We didn't know how many more was around us. A little while later it got to be the middle of the day and there wasn't anybody around us. So we got to talking a little bit back and forth. You could hear about a mile away so we was whispering. We had been trained for it. Martin had twenty shots in that BAR magazine. I said, 'I'm going to shoot at that guy down there.' I could kill you at any time but it was raining so hard you couldn't hardly see your sights. I thought, 'I'm going to shoot at him.' I put a tracer round in my rifle. You could see him pretty well, but I knew I couldn't hit him because I couldn't see my sights. If I focused on my sights then I couldn't see him, but I knew that I could come pretty close. I told Martin to watch this tracer and when he saw it hit, to empty that twenty rounds. He might just get him if he fired at where the tracer hit. I shot. The guy was on his hands and knees, crawling to his left where there was a little old railroad track down there. I could see the tracer and it went right under him. Right under his belly. It must have made a pretty good noise or the bullet was red hot and it might have sizzled his tummy a little. He just jumped up and took off running. We thought that was funny. That shows that you can get a little bit crazy when you have been out there in the rain and mud for a week or two. Martin didn't even fire."

"That Jap took off running for some timber down there. Everybody that was behind us could see him now. Martin started shooting at him about that time. I hadn't seen where any of the guys around us were, but when he started running about fifty guys around us started shooting. He had to run for about a block to that timber. He made it in there. No one even hit him. It was kinda crazy with all those guys shooting at him. There was fire all around him and he was really moving out. All that shooting made a lot of noise and I started looking for the other two Japs but I couldn't see them."

"I put my rifle back in that little niche and was kind of squatting in the hole trying to stay out of the mud the best I could. I was looking over the edge of the hole where we had put our hand grenades. We were just sitting there like a couple of dummies. We could hear our guys on our left up about fifty yards across a little draw up higher than we were. There was a little trail that kind of went through there. I could hear those guys talking a little bit. There wasn't much happening right then. All along our lines there wasn't that much activity. It was just that we had to be there. This trail came up the draw toward us then it crossed over and went through a big shell hole. Those guys talking didn't tell us where they were, but they had to be in that big shell hole. We didn't know who it was in there. They had to have come there the night before just like we did. I was watching because Martin couldn't see like I could. All night long we would hear a noise and Martin would ask me what it could be. In the dark I couldn't tell either so I would make up something. I would say that it was a horse or a squirrel or maybe even a person. Now that it was light and I could see but Martin still had trouble. All at once, about fifty feet in front of us this Jap came walking up the trail right toward us. We had been shooting right before this, all of those shots. He was coming up the trail right toward us. The trail came right up past us to the top of the ridge but it forked off to the right below us and went right up to where those guys was talking. He was right at us, more or less, but he didn't see us. I reached over for my gun. I couldn't quite reach it and I didn't want to make any noise and I didn't want to move. He would see me if I moved. He had his rifle in his hand and I had to be careful and not get shot. I took a hand grenade out. I thought if something happens I will at least have a hand grenade and I had pulled the pin out. I knew that if I threw it, it would go off. A lot of guys would get excited and forget to pull the pin when they threw a hand grenade. I poked Martin and he saw him. The Jap just kept walking up there. Only two or three seconds, probably, had passed since I first saw him. He was looking right at us and he never saw us. He got about thirty feet from us and still didn't see us. He got to where that trail forked and started to turn and go up where those guys were. I finally got a hold of my rifle but I couldn't move it. The bottom was stuck in the mud. I didn't really want to move it because I was hiding so still so he couldn't see us. He was liable to hit one of us before we could shoot him. The Japs was real speedy. When he turned, I told Martin to shoot him. He was holding his BAR but couldn't raise up enough to shoot without being seen until he turned. Martin raised up and pulled the trigger and it jammed. This BAR was one of those son-of-a-guns that jammed every time you turned around. Two or three shots and then it jammed. It had happened one time before that night and that just about drove me nuts. That other time we had waited all night for a Jap and when one showed up it didn't even shoot one shot. Just the bolt jumped forward making a noise you could hear for five miles. This time it fired two or three times and hit him before it jammed. The Jap went part way down and started to fall over. He crawled behind a big rock and I threw that hand grenade in on him and then started shooting at him, but he was behind that rock and you couldn't see him. We knew he was shot up good, but we didn't know if he was dead or not."

"Those guys up above that hole started laughing and yelling at us, 'Quit making all that danged noise.' It was raining so hard that they just knew there wasn't no Japs around so they were laughing and kidding us. One of them was Dolan. I didn't even know that he was there. He knew it was me though and yelled at me. I told him we had just shot a Jap. He laughed and said, 'What are you doing, there ain't no Japs out there.' He just laughed and laughed and kept saying there wasn't no Japs out there. So I said, 'Come over here and look,' and Jack did. He came down to us and I said, 'He is over behind that rock.' When I told him, he believed it then. He knew it had happened, but the other guys just thought we was playing a joke. Ordinarily, you would never talk above a whisper but we were yelling and laughing. It was just one of those strange days. We never even seen another Jap in that whole area, but we was always watching so one wouldn't crawl up on us."

"Jack sat down with me. I had climbed out of that hole to get out of the mud and everything. I didn't see any more Japs or anything. Jack said, 'I believe I'll run down there and see if he has a flag on him.' He was a crazy guy anyway. I said that I would stay there and cover him. I kept my rifle out so I could shoot the Jap if he wasn't dead. So Jack run down there and run around the rock. The Jap was dead and Jack said, 'I'm gonna get his rifle.' He had always wanted a Jap rifle. He had said he wanted a Jap rifle to shoot a Jap with. He thought that would be fun. So he grabbed the rifle and took off. That Jap was dead but he had a hold of the rifle and Jack jerked him about three or four yards before he let go. I yelled to Jack to go back and see if he had a flag. We all wanted a flag to send home. They carried them in their helmets, sometimes. Jack jumped back and grabbed the guy's helmet and threw it to me. There was a nice big battle flag in the helmet. I laid it down beside me and Jack came running with the rifle. I was watching so no Jap would jump up and shoot him. We looked at the rifle, it had a few dings in it from the grenade but he might have been dead before I even threw it, I don't really know. We was looking at the rifle and the craziest thing, that rifle had a cotton plug in the end of the barrel like he wanted to keep the water out. We opened the bolt and there wasn't a shell in the gun. He had a cartridge belt on like any Jap soldier. If I had known this, I would have just let him walk up on those guys that was up there talking. It just didn't make any sense that he would have just walked up there after we had made all that noise shooting, with his rifle unloaded."

"Jack knew how he could get that rifle sent home, but first he wanted to shoot a Jap with it. He carried his sniper rifle all of the time. Most of us didn't because you couldn't use them at night or in the rain. They was bolt action and you wanted something that shot automatic but Jack always carried his. He carried a Tommy gun, too, that he had cut the stock off of to make it lighter. Now he had this Jap rifle to carry. He went back up to where those guys was, and I didn't see him again for a long time."

The regiment sent it's other two battalions forward to take the approaching ground in front of Dakeshi Ridge so they would be in proper position when all the divisions were ordered to advance the next day. The 3rd Battalion started forward and moved only a few yards before small arms fire from pillboxes and caves on the ridge approaches stopped them. They were pinned down for the entire day, when they received artillery fire from the front of the ridge and mortar fire from the ridge's reverse slope. The 1st Battalion fared better for a while, one of their companies advanced eight hundred yards to the base of the ridge but was so exposed it and the rest of the battalion were withdrawn to their original positions. Two hundred three dead and wounded Marines from the two battalions were removed from the field to the rear. The survivors dealt with infiltrators throughout the night and prepared, as best they could, for the general offensive jumping off the next morning. The Japanese positions on the ridge were shelled all night by Navy ships and ground artillery.

The 6th Marine Division had to cross the Asakawa river and some open ground before they would be in position to join the other three divisions in the full assault scheduled for the next morning. Their scouts had waded across the river and examined the open land they would have to cross to reach their attack positions to go at the high ground Japanese defense positions. The scouts did not find any enemy emplacements, so they thought they would only be exposed to snipers. A lead company was sent across the river without attracting any enemy fire. They reassembled on the enemy side of the river and struck out across the open area. Just as they began to move, Japanese machine guns opened up on them. The Japanese had built a trap for the Marines by digging in and concealing machine gunners and riflemen all through the area. Most of the time the emplacements could not be located until they opened fire, close-up, or even sometimes, behind the Marines. What the Marines viewed as open land was really made up of low inclines and shallow depressions. The Japanese expertise in concealment and cover wasn't even taxed in creating a deathtrap for whoever tried to cross this area.

The Marines pulled back to the river bank to await for reinforcements and tanks to cross the river.

The 96th Division relieved the exhausted and depleted 7th Division where they had bogged down on the crest of Kochi Ridge. Their mission in the upcoming general attack was to protect the flank of the 77th Division and advance down the east coast until they could turn west and flank the Shuri Line.

The 77th Division was ready to commence the attack scheduled by General Buckner for the next morning. They were located in the center of the island. They were facing a long wide valley that led straight to the Shuri Heights just east of Shuri Castle. The valley was cut up with ridges, ravines, slopes and depressions. Its sides contained the, by now, standard Japanese defense complexes of interlocking caves, tunnels and pillboxes overlapping and supporting each other. Artillery and the deadly 47MM antitank guns were placed to support the defenders and the reverse slopes were dotted with mortar positions. Orders for the Division were pretty simple. They were to just continue advancing toward Shuri, destroying the enemy as they went. General Buckner expected that the Division would occupy a large number of the Japanese while the Marines in the west and the two Army divisions to the east would roll up both of General Ushijima flanks and end the battle. He thought there was really no need to push the division. He expected to win the battle on the flanks. He let them proceed at their own speed, which was unusually slow even for the army, in an effort to save soldiers lives. Admiral Turner and the Navy fumed as they followed the divisions' progress toward Shuri.

The 7th Division withdrew to a rest area on the coast north of the fighting. It was expected they would be in reserve for about ten days while they rested, rearmed, resupplied and processed in replacements. While waiting to return to combat the Division received one thousand, six hundred ninety-one new and poorly trained men. They also received back from the hospitals, five hundred forty-six partially healed veterans. Strangely, a number of the returning wounded were not healed at all. They had simply left the hospital on their own in order to return to their units. It was an administrative nightmare reforming the rifle companies with a balance of veterans and replacements to make each unit combat efficient.

The destroyer *Brown* and the minelayer *Harry F. Bauer* were slightly damaged by Kamikazes who missed their targets but crashed close aboard.

May 11, 1945. This was the day of the four Division attacks along the entire front. Lt. Col. Berger, before dawn, ordered his beleaguered George Company to break off contact with the Japanese and return to his battalion. The company was tired but had only lost three men. They were resupplied and in their attack position before daylight. Fox Company was fresh and was chosen to spearhead the attack on Dakeshi Ridge for the battalion with George held in reserve. Berger had requested tanks to support his infantry movement on Dakeshi Ridge but Colonel Snedeker refused. All of the tanks were assigned to the 1st Battalion going up the east side. It was considered that they would be in a much heavier fight and would need the tanks more than Berger's men would. This turned out to be a costly mistake. So without any support from the regiment, except a five minute artillery barrage, Fox Company jumped off in the attack on the key defensive stronghold of Dakeshi.

The Japanese, of course, knew that Dakeshi must be held at any and all costs. To lose it would put the Marines into Wana Draw which was a straight shot to Shuri. Battle hardened Japanese veterans with a will to die for their Emperor waited in their concealed caves, pillboxes, tunnels and spider holes. Artillery on Wana Ridge covered the front slope of Dakeshi Ridge as did mortars on the reverse slope. The Japanese were just not going to lose this position.

Long range fire was brought to bear on Fox Company as soon as they started forward. There were small groups of Japanese soldiers with light machines and "knee mortars" concealed all over the ridge approaches. The Marines used the tactics they had learned a few days ago. They split into small, squad sized, units and used the natural terrain to dislodge and kill the Japanese as they went up the ridge. By 1600, elements of the company had worked their way over the crest of the ridge and were in the edge of the town. The Japanese had been waiting for this and commenced firing their artillery pieces from Wana and other supporting ridges. Fox Company was pushed back over the crest and part way back down the ridge. Japanese who had remained concealed while Fox Company went past them began to reveal themselves and their automatic weapons. The battle changed from trying to get over the ridge into focusing on and knocking out each and every cave and pillbox as they found them. The need for tanks and flame throwing tanks became critical. Their request for the machines fell on deaf ears. Fox Company, in mid-afternoon, advised Berger that without tanks they would have to withdraw. The regimental commander finally realized the situation and sent the badly needed tanks.

The Battalion Command Post had only received a few mortar rounds but by afternoon it was spotted by the Japanese and they brought it under intense fire. This irked Berger even more because he didn't have tanks and couldn't even protect his own headquarters. Tanks finally arrived about 1600 and entered the fray which relieved pressure on the command post by providing the Japanese new targets to shoot at, which were more threatening than a CP. The tanks started operating with the infantry as they had been trained earlier. They began "processing" (A word coined by the 1st Division commanding general to describe destroying the Japanese one position at a time with small unit tactics and tanks) each opening by blowing, burning and sealing them. In conjunction with the tank arrival, Naval gunfire stepped up on the Japanese artillery positions and knocked out another of the Japanese eight inch guns. This one had been concealed in a civilian's house. The fighting was so close and intense that Berger called a halt at 1800 so his Marines could withdraw a short distance and dig in for the night. The tanks had only been on location for a little over an hour. When the infantry fell back the tanks went with them and then went on to the Regimental Tank Park for protection during the night. Artillery fire from both sides continued throughout the evening and into the night. The forces were so close that hand-to-hand fighting and grenade throwing battles went on all night. During the few quiet moments even verbal insults were hurled back and forth.

"We was close enough to talk to each other. You could even hear them talking to each other. For some reason the Japanese didn't like Babe Ruth. One of them would always yell, 'Babe Ruth, he son of bitchie,' and someone else would yell back, 'Yeah, and Tojo eats shit.' It was strange that you could see the Japanese come out of their caves and holes. They would come out and watch us when they knew they was out of small arms range."

During the fighting, officers had found that Dakeshi Town itself was as heavily defended as the ridge, if not more so. The position of the town allowed protection of the ridges' reverse slope. It appeared that the ridge could not be captured without the town being taken at the same time. They decided to withhold George Company from the ridge attack, the next day, and use them to attack the town itself. Easy Company would go into line in the morning to the left of Fox and tie in with the 1st Battalion. All of 1st

Battalion's rifle companies would be engaged on the eastern end of the ridge. Fox Company's commander was mortally wounded and two lieutenants were evacuated with serious wounds. The regiment lost two hundred fifty men on Dakeshi Ridge and the battle had just started. All through the night the Japanese guns shelled the regiment and infiltrators in force brought hand-to-hand combat into the American lines.

The 6th Marine Division had bridged the river and sent tanks across. With the tanks and Naval gunfire support they advanced a mile and a half, southeast to the Asato River estuary. The fighting was just as bad as it always was but the tank and infantry teams opened a path. The Marines dug in for the night in a position that lay on the outskirts of Naha's northeastern suburbs. The importance of their position was that they were now west of Shuri instead of north of it. In the morning, they would turn more to the east, pass through some small hills in the estuary and be in the Kokuba River Valley. This valley was a half mile wide and would lead the Marines behind Shuri. This would encircle the Japanese Shuri defenses and likely bring an end to the battle for Okinawa. The 6th Division wouldn't uncover their plan's stumbling block until they ran into it the next day. Its name would become known as Sugar Loaf Hill.

The 96th Division was fresh and they began mopping up the Kochi Ridge and then proceeded to do the same to the Gaja Ridge as they moved to the south to their main objective. This was a land feature called Conical Hill. It was a steep hill that overlooked the coastal plain on the east. It controlled any movement on the plain and especially the only road on that side of the island, Highway 13. Northeast of Conical was a Japanese airfield called Yonabaru and the town of Yonabaru. The hill and attendant ridges had to be taken if any troops could get behind Shuri on the east. It was impossible for anything to move on the coastal plain or the road without being destroyed by the enemy gunners in Conical Hill. So the Division attacked through Yonabaru Airfield and the town.

The 77th Army Division commenced their attack to coincide with all the other divisions orders to advance. The Division sent a regiment up each side of the valley they were moving through. The regiments would advance until they received fire then they would bring up tanks, flame thrower tanks and call for artillery and Naval gunfire support on the position that had fired on them. Only as a last resort would infantry move on the position. Casualties were just as bad as always though. The slow total reduction of each position, one at a time, was actually harder on the men's nerves and sapped their energy more. It was also harder on equipment, especially the tanks. They and their crews faced fire from other positions while concentrating larger numbers in a small area.

The war ended for the aircraft carrier *Bunker Hill*, the destroyers *Hugh W. Hadley*, and *Evans* and a support landing craft. One hundred seventy sailors were killed and wounded aboard the destroyers and the landing craft. The devastation aboard the *Bunker Hill* was astounding, fires raged and three hundred ninety-six men died. Another two hundred sixty-four were injured, as well.

May 12, 1945. A small Japanese counterattack force struck the positions of the 1st Battalion just before dawn. They were easily repulsed and left forty of their dead in the battalion's line. 2nd Battalion was ready to go at daylight but had to delay for eighty minutes while they waited for the tanks to arrive. They already knew that the ridge could not be taken without tanks and they knew they could not hold it unless the reverse slope was cleared of mortar emplacements. That meant tanks had to be able to get into Dakeshi where it was then possible to bring fire on the reverse slope of the ridge and clear the town defenses at the same time. The tanks arrived eighty minutes late and the attack on Dakeshi Ridge and Dakeshi Town began.

As the battalion went up the ridge, broken into tank support groups for mutual support, the Japanese began filling in behind them. The teams would reduce a cave or tunnel and proceed onward. The Japanese would send fresh troops from behind the ridge through the tunnel system and come out behind the Marines. This required the infantry and tanks to withdraw and again clean out the caves that had been in their rear. The regiment had held its 3rd Battalion in reserve but had to commit them to mop up behind the two assault battalions. The attack also had to slow down in order to seal the caves and tunnel openings as they went. They learned that they could not afford to bypass any openings going up this ridge. Taking out a cave or tunnel opening was slow, dangerous and deadly for everyone involved. If possible, a tank would fire a round (the openings were always protected by other emplacements) into the opening followed by flame from the flame thrower tanks. If it was impossible to use tanks, then the infantry would reduce the openings in various ways. One of their favorites was to throw phosphorus grenades into the opening then watch for smoke coming out of the hidden air vents. They would then pour gasoline and/or napalm in the vents and ignite the fuel. This was highly effective but also killed a lot of civilians hiding in the region's caves.

"If we could get tanks in there, it wasn't too hard to take a bunker. If you couldn't, it was a terrible thing to do. Guys had to carry a flamethrower and try to sneak up on the bunker. Those things weighed a lot and they only held twelve gallons of fuel. Lots of them guys got killed. Those bunkers was usually covered by other emplacements and spider holes. We would take them out first. Our favorite trick was to get a rifleman, two BAR men and a guy with a flamethrower. Then we had a team. The rifleman and the BAR men would get on both sides and pin them down with fire while the flamethrower guy would come up to about five or six yards and flame them. If that didn't get them, we would take a forty-pound pack charge and hang it down over the front hole. That would usually do it. Lots of times they was only one or two guys with a machine gun in there. They wasn't no entrance from the front. They would dig in from the back side and build the bunker, so the entrance was down a tunnel on the back side. If they wanted to or if things got too hairy they could grab their stuff, run out the back and go in another bunker down the line somewhere. You had to find and blow those entrances or they would come back after you was gone and be behind you. They did the same thing with a lot of their real big guns, but they built them facing out to sea and couldn't get us with them."

As Fox, the lead company of the 2nd Battalion went up the slope, artillery fire increased as did mortar fire from the reverse slope. By mid-afternoon two platoons had only one officer and eight men left. The higher they went the more Japanese they encountered. The combat was so close that hand grenades became the weapon of choice for the enemy. Easy Company managed to work its way to the forward approaches of Dakeshi Town and attracted ferocious artillery fire.

All of the Marine companies pulled back a short distance to dig in for the night. This was almost always necessary because the tanks had to withdraw back to a tank park for protection, repairs, rearmament and fueling. The tank park had to be located well to the rear because the machine's safety was paramount. Berger was stunned to learn that his Fox Company could muster only ninety-three men. They had started the day with a hundred eighty-three so the casualty rate was 50 percent. Fox had no or little combat efficiency left and would stay where it was through the rest of the battle for the Dakeshi stronghold, until it could receive some replacements. Jack's George Company was ordered to escort two tanks into Dakeshi the next day. A regular tank and a flamethrower-rigged tank.

By the day's end some high ground on the north that overlooked Dakeshi had been taken. The ridge was ready to fall, by the next day, all hoped. It was the most bloody work yet encountered by the Marine division. The two assault battalions lost another one hundred sixty-five Marines.

The 6th Marine Division set off for the Kokuba River Valley that would lead them behind the Shuri defenses. There were three small hills in their path which didn't appear to pose any threat to their advance. The center hill, Sugar Loaf, was only fifty feet high and flanked on each side by similar small hills dubbed Half-moon and Horseshoe. The estuary and the river valley had long been considered a serious flaw in the Shuri Line by the Japanese. To correct this problem, the hills had been worked into a masterful defense complex. They had been deeply tunneled for protection from American guns and bombs. The tunnels were interconnected for troop movement among the three hills. They were packed with 47 mm antitank guns, pillboxes and mortar emplacements guarded by concealed machine gunners and riflemen. The emplacements were located on the reverse slopes as well as the front of the hills. The three hills protected each other and could bring massive fire on any flanking movement. The little hill complex was only several hundred yards from the Shuri Heights so artillery from the main Japanese defense position provided further protection. There were slightly more than two thousand fresh Japanese soldiers waiting in the little hills for their chance to die for their Emperor.

The Marines were not impressed in any manner by the hills and they sent out patrols to find the best path to the other side. The lead battalion patrolled all day and found the Japanese in force wherever they looked. Not a single soft spot could be found.

7th Division remained in their rest area trying to recover from the weeks of combat. Units of the 96th Division moved south toward Conical Hill and cleared the entire enemy from their path. By evening, the division's spearhead companies were at the north base of their objective.

The 77th Division's attack regiments, the 306th and the 307th advanced up the west side of their mile wide valley. The 305th was assigned to the east side and the soldiers quickly found themselves in very rugged terrain that was fiercely defended. Casualties mounted in the regiments, but more so in the 305th because of the easier defended terrain in which they were advancing. The rains brought the motorized supply vehicles to a halt and Division cooks, clerks, mechanics, etc. were pressed into service carrying ammunition, water, gasoline and food to the front lines. They kept barely enough supplies moving forward to keep the combat troops functional. They encountered a lot of difficulty treating and evacuating their wounded.

The cruiser *Wichita* had a few casualties and some damage from a source that was quite common during the battle for Okinawa. She was hit by a five-inch shell from a "friendly" vessel. The fleet was so congregated and there was so much shooting during air raids that these accidents were just a part of combat. There was just no way to avoid it. The battleship *New Mexico*, commissioned in 1918, had been bombarding Okinawa since before the battle began. The day before, her guns had blown apart eight suicide boats. This day she had no assignment and was heading into anchorage in an assigned berth near the original landing beaches. Just at dusk two planes plunged into her with one carrying a bomb that set her ablaze. Before the fire was brought under control, fifty-four of her crewmen were dead and one hundred nineteen were injured. The old warship was out of action until after the war ended.

CHAPTER SEVEN
DAKESHI AND WANNA DRAW

May 13, 1945. Another counterattack was sprung on Easy Company of the 2nd Battalion just before daylight. All the Japanese accomplished, though, was the loss of forty-five of their lives at the cost of two Marines killed and four wounded. 1st Battalion was also hit and the Marines killed another seventy enemy soldiers. This was a long way from the ratio coveted by the Japanese. Also, two maps that proved very helpful to the battalion were recovered from a dead Japanese officer involved in the early morning fighting. At daylight the regiment sent their 2nd Battalion against the Dakeshi enemy emplacement. 1st and 3rd Battalions were held in reserve and later in the day, committed to the task of sealing the caves. They had to kill a lot of snipers left behind by 2nd Battalion, as they went at the ridge. Jack's George Company struck directly at the town itself. They passed through the decimated Fox Company and headed into the town. Jack was the leader of his squad now and his squad had the specific duty of escorting and protecting two tanks. The rest of the company went in after the town's defenders.

According to regimental reports the tanks arrived on time at the regimental CP and were sent up to the companies to begin the attack. Many Marines dispute this as fact. They claim the tanks always arrived late.

"Tanks was never on time, they was always an hour late. They could be setting right beside you and they would still be an hour late. If you wanted a tank to be someplace at six o'clock, you told him to be there at five o'clock."

"The captain had come to me and said we couldn't take the front slope of the ridge without getting tanks into the town. He said he knew that me and the tank commander had been in the town a few days ago. He wanted to know how we got in there. I said that we just walked right in. No opposition, but it was well armed and we knew that the road was mined. The road was right on top of the cliff. I told Norton that when they blow the road it will crumble right off the cliff and the tanks would be trapped. He didn't care. The town was built on three shelves and the road was on the second one. Well, they sent us two tanks and it was decided that my squad would protect the tanks while the rest of the company would spread out through the town."

"The artillery had throwed smoke for us and we started up the road to go into the village. I seen a Japanese run down the slope and run into one of those burial tombs lining the side of the road. I fired into it and it blew. They must have had high octane gas in it. The Japanese was blown out and here come a flag. It must have been in his helmet. Anyway, it flew out of the tomb and draped itself over a mulberry bush. I grabbed it and stuffed it in my pocket. Later I give it to Carson. He didn't have no souvenirs to take home. If he is still alive, he probably still has it. It was some kind of regimental flag with lots of writing on it, but we didn't know what it said."

"We went around that corner rock, my squad was escorting two tanks and as soon as they got in, they blew the road behind us. We knew the tanks was cut off. We got about half way down the street and got bogged down. It was a fight with hand grenades and guy to guy. They was trying to get to them tanks, throwing smoke and running at them with pack charges. Ralston got hit! He came around to my side of the tank and yelled, 'I got killed, I got killed, I'm gonna die.' His arm was hanging and blood was running down from his armpit. We was about out of ammunition so I told Colthrope to help me get him out of there. Colthrope got a hold of him and I got his good arm around my neck. I had left my sniper rifle, it wasn't no good in there anyway, and we went clear out of town, back to that big rock. They had set up the CP behind that rock. We left Ralston there and grabbed up a load of ammunition and went back. They was still fighting over the tanks, they was throwing smoke and attacking with pack charges. We was shooting them down. I heard someone yell at me. Colthrope was hit! He got hit in the knee and it had busted his kneecap all up. He was a big fellow that would have weighed all of two hundred forty pounds. We was running out of ammunition again so Clancy helped me with Colthrope. I never got such a cussing in my life than I did from Colthrope. He was so big that we couldn't carry him without his bad leg dragging on the ground. He cussed us out all the way back. We got him out and dumped him with Ralston and grabbed up all the ammunition we could carry. It must have been two hundred yards from the rock to where we was fighting. When we got back in, there was a lieutenant from the machine gun crew that was hit. So we took him out and brought back more ammunition. We stayed in there the rest of the day protecting those tanks. Doherty and his

BAR man had come up from some place to help because we only had five guys left. We heard that Fox Company had went up the front slope of the ridge and just got shot to pieces. Frank was with them, for some reason, and somebody told me that he got hit and was back in the hospital."

"I was down to three shells. I just had three left. All of us was running out of ammunition again. You just couldn't carry enough of it to last very long. I knew the tank would have some for my Tommy gun because tankers carried .45 caliber pistols for protection. Their ammunition would fit my Tommy gun. The Japanese throwed smoke on us, again, in an effort to get to the tanks. The rear tank was a flamethrower tank and the front tank fired HE. The tanks couldn't maneuver because of the walls on both sides of the street. He couldn't swing his barrel around. He had to blow the tops of the walls down ahead of him. He couldn't see over the walls. All he could see was down the street. He got to an intersection and I crawled up on the tank, the rear one. He was out of fluid and the flamethrower nozzle runs right down his cannon barrel so he couldn't use it. He could fire his light machine gun and his .50 caliber. They throwed smoke on us with glass chemical grenades that made smoke when they broke. That was the first time I had seen that. They had never throwed smoke on us before so we knowed something was up, that they was going for the tanks. I was up on that tank pounding on the turret and yelling at the guy to give me some ammunition. He finally opened the pistol port and give me a box of ammunition. As he passed it out to me, I saw a Japanese running out of the smoke with what looked like a forty-pound pack charge. It had a short fuse, about three inches. I can still see the fire coming out of that fuse. The three shells I had was in a Browning (BAR). When I ran out of ammunition for my Tommy gun, I had picked up that Browning. It just had three shells in it, I shot the three shells at the Japanese and missed. I throwed the Browning at him and he throwed the pack charge. What they usually done was throw themselves and the pack charge into the track but he threw the pack charge and took off. It went under the front of the tank and I took off into a sweet potato patch and throwed myself down. I had laid my Tommy gun down there because it wasn't no good to me, without ammunition. The charge went off and it looked like it just obliterated everything. It was a cement street. Cement on rolled down coral. It blew a hole and the tank just settled down in it. It had blowed the front of the tank up in the air and just about half of it disappeared down in that hole. When it was over, I loaded my Tommy gun and ran back to the tank. I jumped up on it and asked if they was all right. Their intercom and their radio was out but they was safe. We backed the front tank up, hooked on a cable and pulled them out of the hole."

"We was getting heavy knee mortar attacks. Of course, that didn't mean nothing to the tanks, they just rolled off them like rain. They was getting so thick that you couldn't keep track of them. I had a fellow with me named Dodge. They give him to me out of the brig on the way overseas. He had been raised in Alaska. His father and all his sisters was in the Navy. I had lost track of him, someplace, in the mayhem we was having with those tanks. The knee mortars was getting thick so I ran through another little sweet potato patch to get up against a wall and under the roots of a mango tree. Those trees straddled the walls on big massive roots. Those knee mortars, you could see them till they started down then your eyes couldn't follow them. A knee mortar has no guide fins on it. It would just turn end over end. They was a big bomb crater in the patch and I ran right through it and there was Dodge. He had laid his rifle down at his side and he was laying on his back on the side of that big hole. He had his arms up in the air and he was saying over and over, 'I'm an anti-aircraft gun, boom, boom, boom.' He was pretending to shoot those knee mortars down. I yelled at him to get the hell out of there. He said to me and I'll never forget it, 'Boy, this could be a hell of a war, we could really have a good time if they was shooting popcorn instead of bullets.' He was still boom, boom, booming, when about seven or eight of them showed up crossing each other. I had got under the mango roots and was looking at him. He grabbed his rifle and started crawling up over that shell hole when one of them landed behind his butt. It didn't hurt him at all. It just scooted him up over the edge on his face. It did break up his anti-aircraft play for the day. It didn't matter what happened, Dodge could make fun out of it."

"We pulled back out for the night and dug in. They had sent a sergeant, name of Dixon, from another company to take over our squad. He went in Dakeshi and missed us coming out. He had to stay in there all night, by himself. We heard Tommy gun fire in there but we didn't know what was going on. It turned out to be him shooting. We went back in the next morning to see what was going on. There was old Dixon. He had piled up about half a platoon of Japanese in the street. He had got caught at the end of the street where there was a retaining wall. It was a dead-end street and he got caught there, in the dark. There wasn't no place to dig a hole but we'd knocked them walls down with them tanks. The tanks wanted to shoot at the mortars on the back side of Dakeshi Ridge. They couldn't shoot over the wall so they just shot through them, then they had a hole they could see through. Old Dixon built him up a hole out of that broken stuff. He said that he went to sleep and along in the night he woke up and there come a formation right down the street. They was in formation. The first one looked like he was wearing a Marine uniform and Dixon jumped up to welcome them. That wasn't the right thing to do but he had them between two walls on a bare concrete street and he had a Tommy gun. He cut loose and they all started running. He got a lot of them though. He didn't have any choice and he got decorated for it."

As George Company moved on the town, Easy Company, on their left, began to assault the ridge. Easy Company, as they moved up the ridge, received heavy fire from the cliffs just below the high ground. This was the same ground that had been taken the day before, by the 1st Battalion. This area was just to their north in their left rear. The 1st Battalion immediately set to work to clear the tunnels in the cliffs and caves below them. Easy Company also received heavy fire from the Army's zone of action, farther to their north, because the Army had failed to move and silence the guns there. Of course, they were also under fire from the enemy who still held Dakeshi Ridge.

The two tanks and George Company made it into the town. The tanks could now fire on the enemy emplacements, on the reverse slope of Dakeshi Ridge. Tank fire was also brought to bear on the enemy infantry in positions on the ridge's crest. This would take a lot of Japanese fire support away from the ridge defenders, weakening the ridge positions. Easy Company could now capture the whole ridge.

Before the tanks in Dakeshi Town could concentrate on their ridge targets, they had to save themselves from the enemy positioned in the town. It was thought that the Japanese were using the town merely as support for the ridge defense. When George Company entered the town, they found that the Japanese were defending the town itself, as a stronghold. The fighting in the town was much worse than out on the ridge. The town fighting was in a very confined area. The company was met by a barrage of small arms fire, hand grenades, and knee mortars. The tanks came under less attack because they were behind most of the infantry. Easy Company had moved up the ridge with tanks and self-propelled guns and attacked a complex of caves just down the slope from George Company. In other words, the enemy in this complex was actually inside the cliffs that were underneath George Company and the town. Easy Company killed two hundred fifty enemy soldiers in the caves and discovered there was a brigade command post, supply dumps and medical facilities under the town. There was access to the underground structure to and from the town. That was why it was so heavily defended, beyond being support for the ridge. Easy Company, in addition to killing a lot of enemy soldiers, captured several mortars, field pieces, machine guns, rifles and ammunition for all of the weapons.

George Company had killed more than three hundred fifty of the enemy. After the tanks helped George Company get in the town, they turned their attention to the ridge. Easy Company then moved over the ridge. There was still a lot of mopping up to do but the ridge was taken! The Marines had breached the main Shuri defense line! The battalion had been ordered to take the Wana Ridge, located behind Dakeshi. They moved on it but it was so heavily defended that the order was quickly revoked. The Marines then went about the business of clearing out the left-over Japanese and digging in for the night. George Company pulled back to the edge of the town to spend the night and the tanks went to their regimental home. At no time did the Japanese from Wana Ridge and beyond stop shelling the Marines. In addition, infiltrators were thick throughout the night. More than five hundred Japanese had died in the Dakeshi fighting and there were one hundred twenty-nine Marine casualties.

Frank Moody. "I was wounded but Jack made it almost through the whole thing. We went through different things and all. The fighting had got pretty bad and kept getting worse even after I left. It was bad fighting. We was in different platoons, you could be less than a hundred yards apart and it would be a completely different war going on. We didn't see much of each other after the fighting got real bad but we always asked about each other. In one hour of battle things could happen that would normally take a year. The fighting was just real bad, everybody was getting killed on Dakeshi Ridge."

"There was this Robertson, a gunny sergeant, he was an old guy. Of course, everybody who was even twenty-two or twenty-three was old devils. He was Dolan's Platoon leader. He was a nice old guy and had been in the service quite a while. I think he was probably about twenty-eight but who really knows? He had been in for about ten years. You think of him now as seeming like he was fifty but he was only about twenty-eight. He seemed older than heck. We wondered how he could even have walked. Old Robertson got shot through the leg at Dakeshi."

"Dolan had taken over his own squad. There were supposed to be four, three man fire teams in a squad and he still had most of them. We all started out, early. Dolan took two tanks with him. We always tried to take a tank with each squad and stay with it. You protected the tank and it protected you.

It was a great set-up and we was good at it. The Army didn't ever really do that, guarding the tank and the tank guarding you. It really helped everybody. Jack and his squad took off for Dakeshi Town with two tanks to protect, while I went up Dakeshi Ridge."

"I got wounded by a hand grenade on the ridge. They took me back behind the lines a ways and I stayed there for three days. I wanted to get back and help Dolan but my left knee was shot up pretty bad. I had pieces in it from that hand grenade. It was drawed up pretty bad. I couldn't even sit in a chair because it was drawed up so bad. I couldn't even walk for about three days. It was pulled up real bad. When I could walk, I got up and went again. I was gonna help Jack out, that was my idea. I knew that he needed help. I was really worried about him. That was just the way it was. We were like that. That would be hard for people to realize, I guess. You had to help your buddies. Guys would just get up and walk out of the hospital and go back to their outfits. You didn't try to get out of anything. You always wanted to go back, like me. I wanted to go back and help Jack. I knew he needed help, I knew that there wasn't that many guys left. That day about all our guys got killed. Oh golly! My partner, Martin, (All the scout/snipers had a rifleman assigned to them for spotting and protection.) got killed that day. He got shot, kind of high through the shoulder. He was always the easiest one to get knocked out. He was big, at least to me he was. He was a big kid for those days. He was about six feet and about two hundred pounds. I was about one hundred fifty-five pounds and five-foot six inches. He would get knocked out easy, like going up a hill packing his old BAR and everything. In real hot weather, he would just kind of conk out. I usually walked behind him, because he did it a lot, so I could catch him when he fell over backwards. This day he got shot kind of up high through the shoulder. You didn't think that it would kill him. It kind of knocked him out and you couldn't get to him. You just couldn't move without getting shot. Everybody was getting hit. He came to and he didn't even know where he was at. When he did come to, he was just a few feet away and some guy yelled at him to roll up the hill, where we could get a hold of him. It was only about five feet. He did roll up to us but he died from it. That wouldn't have killed most people but he died right there real close to me."

"Cushion was a little guy from Pennsylvania. He got killed. It seemed like everybody was getting killed. It seemed like everybody who wasn't killed, got shot up. When I got taken back to the camp, there was guys laying everywhere. It was just behind the lines a little ways. Mendel was a good little friend of mine from California. He was shot up pretty good and he was thirsty, of course. You had to watch and not give anybody too much water but he was just dying of thirst. He wasn't shot except through the thighs and the legs in different places. I could hop around so I got him a little bit of water. That day and the next day just everybody came in there. I saw almost everybody in our outfit who wasn't already dead. They was just gone, that was just the way it was. I went back up to help Jack on the 16th of May."

In January of 1946 , a year and five months after the battle for Dakeshi, Jack received the Bronze Star Medal and a temporary citation failing to state the additional award of the "V" for valor. In April of 1948 he received the following, permanent, citation from the Secretary of the Navy:

The President of the United States takes pleasure in
presenting the BRONZE STAR MEDAL to
PRIVATE FIRST CLASS MORRIS D. DOLAN,
UNITED STATES MARINE CORPS RESERVE,
for service as set forth in the following CITATION:
    "For heroic achievement while serving with the Second
    Battalion, Seventh Marines, First Marine Division, in ac-
    tion against enemy Japanese forces on Okinawa, Ryuky Is-
    lands, 13 May 1945. While leading his squad in an attack
    upon the strongly defended village of Dakeshi, Private First
    Class Dolan repeatedly exposed himself to intense and ac-
    curate enemy rifle and machine-gun fire in order to bring
    the full firepower of his squad upon the Japanese and, at
    the same time, give supporting tanks protection. By his
    leadership and courageous devotion to duty, he served as an
    inspiration to his men, and was directly responsible for the
    seizing of the objective. His conduct throughout was in keeping
    with the highest traditions of the United States Naval Service"
    Private First Class Dolan is authorized to wear the Combat "V"

When Jack received the medal, along with the citation, the tiny "V" that he was authorized was missing. More than fifty years passed before the Marine Corps would send him the "V" that denoted the medal was awarded for valor. With the little "V," the Corps sent him five more medals they had neglected to issue at the time he had earned them.

The 6th Marine Division spent another full day searching for the best place to attack the Sugar Loaf Hill complex. No weaknesses could be found, anywhere. The Division Commander, Major General Shepard, decided to proceed with an all out assault on the hill mass. He felt this was the best way and he expected that his Marines would be on the other side of Sugar Loaf by nightfall. He gave the order and the men were moved into place before daylight. One company that had probed the hill was reduced from two hundred fifteen men to seventy-five and some of them had minor wounds. Several tanks had also been knocked out.

The 7th Army Division stayed in their rest area, resupplied, rearmed and processed in more of the poorly trained replacements.

The generals were surprised at the rapid advance of the 96th Division. By evening, one regiment was dug in on one of the north ridge jutting out from Conical Hill. Orders were issued that an attack was to be made the next day on the north face of the hill, itself.

The 77th Division kept moving forward but their movement could barely be measured. There was their natural tendency to move slow, the atrocious rain and mud, the casualties and equipment breakdowns and now a new problem. The Marines on their right and the Army Division on their left were held up at Japanese strongholds. To advance too far would put enemy positions on their flanks. This could not be permitted and movement by friendly troops on both sides was closely monitored before the 77th Division would advance.

Kamikazes hit the large aircraft carrier *Enterprise* and the destroyers *Bache* and *Bright*. One hundred forty-six sailors were killed or wounded. The damage to the three vessels was serious enough to cause their removal from any further action. The loss of the big carrier was a major blow to the Navy. The attrition loss rate of the fleet's various planes was also shocking and the Admirals started wondering how much more they could take. At some point, their ability to support the land battle would be impaired. About all they could do was hope that the Japanese would soon run out of planes and pilots to send against them. They knew that the Japanese had to hold back a sizeable stock of planes to protect the Home Islands. It seemed very likely, therefore, that the enemy couldn't sustain their air attacks in force much longer.

May 14, 1945. The 7th Regiment had been ordered to continue their attack and capture Wana Ridge which ran the entire the length of Wana Draw. The 5th Marines had been tasked with advancing up the side of the draw opposite the ridge and where a sizeable stream ran. This drew was a long ravine that ran easterly up to Shuri, very close to Shuri Castle. The mouth of Wana Draw where the Marines entered was four hundred yards wide and it was eight hundred yards long. It narrowed dramatically as it began to reach the Shuri Heights. Both sides of the draw were heavily fortified. Hundreds of openings appeared, after days of onerous American bombardment. Explosions and fire had denuded the slopes of all vegetation and had blown away other man made concealment of the holes. The Marines would find that each and every position would have to be taken before moving on. This was because connecting tunnels would allow Japanese soldiers to come out behind the Marines, if any openings were bypassed. At night, Japanese came out of the unsecured openings and attacked the Marines however they could. These attackers were small forces, not infiltrators, and there was bayonet and even bare hand fighting throughout the night.

There was great pressure on the Marines to take the ridge and draw. Not only did it guard the way into Shuri, the guns on the ridge, and in it, were firing on the 6th Marine Division to the west. To the 1st Marine Division, the 6th Marine Division may as well have been on the other side of the world. Actually, the 6th and Sugar Loaf Hill were less than a mile from Wana Ridge and that was close range for the Japanese gunners. The 7th Regiment again sent the 2nd Battalion forward and held the 1st and 3rd Battalions in reserve. The Battalion met a virtual curtain of fire when they moved toward the ridge and the draw. Easy Company went through Dakeshi Town and about two hundred yards into Wana Draw. There they found themselves in the open and under fire from three sides. They couldn't bring tanks forward with them until the holes in the road through Dakeshi Town were repaired. The two tanks that had gone into the town the day before were out of fuel and ammunition and damaged from enemy fire.

George Company, followed by Fox Company, swung around the town to the right and moved to within a hundred yards of Wana Ridge. The excessive Japanese fire pinned them down. Colonel Snedeker sent his Able Company from the 1st Regiment to affect a relief but they were stopped before they could even get close. By four in the afternoon they had not advanced and the

1st Battalion was ordered to pass through the 2nd and press the attack. The heavy fire stopped them also, and the 1st Battalion was withdrawn. They were forced to dig in for the night in the same place they had started from that morning. The whole 2nd Battalion had to find cover where they stood. That was less dangerous than withdrawing back across the open ground. One hundred thirty-three Marines were killed or wounded and Wana Draw and Wana Ridge hadn't even been breached, let alone captured.

The 6th Marine Division's advance was completely stalled until they could get past Sugar Loaf so the Division sent a tank supported regiment against the hill. The Marines had to cross about two hundred yards of open land before reaching the hill's base. This approach was covered by mortars, antitank guns and machine guns from Sugar Loaf and artillery from the Shuri Heights. Once the base of the hill was reached, Japanese fire became even more concentrated. It was covering a much smaller area and the base was in hand grenade range. The assault battalion started out with tanks, expecting to be on top of Sugar Loaf well before evening. The highly effective Japanese antitank fire knocked out the Marine tanks almost at will. The tanks could not get close enough to really help the infantry. By late afternoon, the battalion reached and destroyed the hill outposts. Severe casualties resulted very quickly, but General Shepard had ordered the hill taken before dark, so the depleted units pressed on. Near nightfall, no Marine was even on the slope, let alone the top of the hill. Units had been up the hill a few times but were driven off by fire and small counterattacks. The Marines left alive at the base of the hill reassembled and made one more desperate effort to reach the top just at sundown. The Japanese simply went inside the hill and waited while fire from Horseshoe and Crescent blanketed the crest of Sugar Loaf. Then they rushed from their tunnel opening and counterattacked the Marines. Most of the Marines were killed or wounded. Only a few made it off the hill.

The soldiers of the 7th Division remained in reserve near the lines but still weren't needed in the battle.

Senior officers of the 96th Division were convinced that the only way to attack Conical Hill was from the north. The east side was protected by a maze of high ridges that would have to fall before the hill could be reached from that direction. The Japanese felt that their hill was only approachable from the north and that was where their major defenses were concentrated. After a barrage of artillery fire the Americans started up the hill slopes. They faced the same classical Japanese defenses and began reducing the enemy positions one at a time.

The 77th Division "inched," as the Marines called it, forward. Japanese were being killed but so were American soldiers.

An "all clear" day opened for the fleet. There would not be any more ships hit for another three days.

May 15, 1945. The 7th Regiment knew they couldn't continue the attack using the mauled 2nd Battalion as the spearhead, so they sent the 1st Battalion forward again. This time they fought their way through to George and Fox Companies and relieved them. Planners now knew that the ridge facing them was even more heavily defended than they had even imagined. Infantry and tanks were ordered to stay in place for the day and Wana Ridge was plastered with artillery, Naval gunfire and air strikes. Like always, the Japanese went into their deep tunnels and waited for the barrage to end, so they could take up their positions again.

The 2nd Battalion was sent into a bivouac near Dakeshi Ridge. They were kept close to the fighting in case they were suddenly needed. The battalion was seriously depleted of men but spirits were high and these Marines were still ready to fight. The battalion had started May with nine hundred Marines. Now, they could only muster two hundred forty-five men. The regiment wasn't about to use this battalion again until it could be resupplied and reorganize. Replacements were requested as soon as possible to get the battalion back into the fight. The Battalion's rest area was only three or four hundred yards from the Wana Ridge. Incredibly, a lot of Marines went AWOL from the battalion and joined other units in the line so they could keep fighting. Officers and NCOs understood the mind set that prevailed in these men and made no effort to stop them. They just ignored it. In addition to running off to the battle, the resting Marines had numerous snipers and hidden Japanese soldiers in the area that had to be dug out. There was also periodic enemy artillery fire dumped on them.

Jack's battalion to this point in the general southern offensive had accounted for the deaths of at least one thousand four hundred eighty-four Japanese soldiers.

"They was a group from Easy Company crossing the railroad track over on the east side. They had got pinned down and was about out of ammunition. They asked for volunteers to carry ammunition down to them. I grabbed about eight bandoleers of .30 caliber and took off. I didn't get back till the next day. I got down there and they was on the other side of the tracks. It was just about bare around the track bed. You didn't have any cover to get over the track. I wanted to see what was going on and there was a patch of asparagus, growing up on the slope, so I crawled up there. There, in the asparagus patch, was Slitz laying there. That asparagus was grown up to about five feet tall and laying over so it made pretty good concealment. We could see over the railroad track and we could see a steep hill coming down to where the guys was pinned down at. Slitz was looking at my Tommy gun and he asked me if I had plenty of ammunition. I did and he said to look up on the hill over there. Here come an old Japanese and he had a wooden crate with three artillery shells in it. He was on his hands and knees pushing this crate. I remembered that we had taken a gun, over there, a day or two before. He must of not gotten the word and was pushing those shells down to that gun. Slitz asked me for my Tommy gun and I told him the guy was out of range for it. He said that he wanted to have some fun with it anyway. Slitz would shoot a few rounds on the old boy's right and he would turn left and keep on pushing. Then he would shoot on his left and he would turn to his right. He was like a snake coming down that slope. After he got a ways down the slope, Slitz would shoot in front of him and he would turn around and go back up the slope. We was laughing like crazy but I told Slitz that he was running me out of ammunition. I had to get going with that ammunition, for those guys that was pinned down. Slitz covered me and I ran across the railroad track. That was the last time I saw that old Japanese. I don't what Slitz did with him, shot him I guess."

"I delivered the ammunition and started back just as it was starting to get dark. I seen that they had brought in them mobile guns to Dakeshi Ridge and had started firing on Wana Ridge and into Shuri. Well, all hell broke loose. The Japanese fired everything they had right back. A lot of it was falling on Dakeshi Ridge where most of our guys was. I decided that was not the place to be."

"When I had left to take that ammunition, there was a guy named Kaffman digging a hole on the front slope of Dakeshi Ridge. He was digging right between two big pine trees. It was tough digging and I told him that I would have looked for a softer place. He said the pine trees would give him better cover."

"I decided that I wasn't going back up to Dakeshi Ridge until the next morning. I found a big old shell hole in a sweet potato patch. It was big. It must have been a bomb creator. I crawled down in it, and put my poncho down. It was muddy down in there and I got on that poncho and Goddamn it stunk, terrible. Jesus Christ, it smelled bad. There was another poncho there and I pulled down and got it under me too, so I wouldn't get wetter. I just, kind of, slept fitfully. The air corps was going over all night and the artillery would start up ever little bit. It was so cold and wet in that hole. In the wee hours of the morning, I woke up and there was something crawling on me. It was up my sleeve. I shook my arm and it stopped so it must have got throwed out. I woke up when it started to get light and there was something up my sleeve again. I shook it out and it was maggots. I picked up that poncho and rolled it over and here come a fellow's hand out. That was the scaredest I ever was in the whole war. I don't know why that fellow's hand scared me so bad. I found nobody, just a man's hand. It had a ring of some kind on it and it was kind of squished. I put his hand back in the poncho and rolled it up and laid it back down. I just shook and shook all over and then headed back to my outfit."

This day, in May, was a carbon copy of the previous day for the 6th Marines at Sugar Loaf. While an assault battalion headed up the hill, other Division units tried to flank the three hills on each of their sides. All the Marine units were pushed back. The flanks were just as well protected as the hill slopes and were in direct sight of the Japanese big guns on the Shuri Heights. The entire assault regiment had lost 40 percent of their men in two days. The battalion that had tried to go up the slope of Sugar Loaf had six hundred sixty-eight casualties. They were finished as a fighting unit. More than twenty tanks had been lost and the Marines were no closer to getting through these little hills than when they started. General Shepherd's Marines were also suffering from the lack of movement of the 1st Marine Division still at Dakeshi. If that Division would only advance then some of the big guns on Wana Ridge and Shuri would have to refocus on them. This would give Shepherd's men some much needed relief.

Replacements were still pouring into the 7th Division and they were about ready to return to the front lines.

Two lieutenant platoon leaders of the 96th Division eased their platoons around Conical Hill to the rugged high ground on the east side of the hill and found that it was only lightly defended. They moved up the hill and came in behind the Japanese. This movement made the hill untenable for the Japanese and they began a withdraw to the south.

The 77th Division had put a large number of green replacements in the two attack regiments. Because of their inexperience, they were killed and wounded at a much higher rate than the combat veterans. By this time in the four days of fighting, the 305th had suffered seventy-five casualties.

The only ship damaged in the fleet was the escort carrier *Shipley Bay* and that was by collision not enemy attack.

May 16, 1945. The 7th Marines sent the 1st Battalion forward against Wana Ridge with tank support. By late afternoon they had advanced over half a mile and actually had obtained a foothold on the ridge. Then the Japanese threw three counterattacks at them and drove them back to the northeastern tip where they could take cover. The Regiment ordered 2nd Battalion's Easy Company to join them so they could ensure that they held their position for the night. Easy Company's rest was over because they had taken the least number of casualties. In three days, the Marines had only managed to move two hundred yards up the eight hundred yard-long Wana Draw and casualties mounted.

"When I got back after sleeping on that hand, there wasn't no outfit. There was those two big pine trees knocked down and a big shell hole. I though, my God, that was where Kaffman was, they got him. But when the shelling got real bad they had pulled back off the ridge and he was OK. I don't know why the maggots and that hand scared me so much. I just stood there and shook all over. Some nights I just see a big old blue hand with maggots crawling out of the wrist."

" I went out with the burial detail. We went around the first corner where you went into town, that was where a lot of burial tombs was. There was a man laying up on top of the first burial tomb. He had his helmet on and was like he was sighting down the sights of his rifle. I pulled his helmet off and it was Recursion, Frank's buddy. He had been shot right between the eyes. I took his dog tags and turned them in and never thought no more about it. Years later, I was out at Frank's and we was talking. He said Recursion had been listed as missing in action, presumed dead, nobody knowed what had happened to him. I told Frank how I had found him and Frank said his folks lived in Texas. We called them and I told them what happened to their son. They was sad but they was glad to finally know what had happened to him.

That was about twenty or twenty-five years later"

The 2nd Battalion sent Easy Company back off to war by attaching them to the 3rd Battalion. Fox and George continued ridding the area of snipers and the ever persistent infiltrators. Marine Engineers worked the area, sealing caves and tunnels to stop the hidden enemy soldiers from coming out at night. They provided stretcher bearers for the fighting battalions and scoured the battle areas for dead comrades.

"The smell of that place was awful. They used human excrement to fertilize the fields and there was bodies rotting everyplace. I just turned my smeller off. I could sit down and eat right beside a dead body that had been there awhile, it didn't bother me anymore. I could turn my smeller back on whenever I wanted to. The Japanese was always burning incense in their caves. I could smell them when the wind was in the right direction. They smelled like incense, we called it 'foo foo' powder."

"You knew your buddies with you. You can't quite place it in your mind. You'll see a fellow today and you'll say, 'I'll see you tonight,' and you pick him up later and they pour his bones and maggots in a seabag and you watch the burial detail throw him on a truck. That ain't the way you remembered him the last time you saw him. You just can't quite grasp that. You go, well that couldn't be him but there's a dog tag with his name on it. You turn him over and get his stinky billfold and it's got his picture and home address and stuff in it. You realize that he is gone but you want to remember him like he was. You don't want to remember him as a mess of maggots but you do."

"A lot of times we would go out with the burial details and there would be a lot of bodies that had been there for awhile, like several days. The only way you could tell some of our guys from the Japanese dead was by the shoes. You would take the personal effects back to the sergeants and they would see that they got sent home. The burial people would throw them on a truck and take them back to a cemetery and bury them. When they got around to it, they would bulldoze the dead Japanese in a big hole and cover it over."

Frank Moody went AWOL from the battalion field hospital. "I went back up to help Jack and got my foot broken. I don't even know how it happened. Jack said there was some engineers blowing up caves to seal them, in our area. He said they threw a big satchel charge in an opening and didn't holler 'fire in the hole' the way they are supposed to and a rock hit my foot. I never could remember what happened except that I had a broken foot. When it happened, I was trying to get back in the lines. That was the last time that I saw Jack. I was laying back there and guys would come in, I would ask them about Jack and so I knew he was still going. At least I knew it until I got sent to a hospital on Guam. It just kind of depended where you was at, what happened to you. The fighting was real bad where we was at. I was about three years old when the Depression started. People just had to help each other out. That was why I was trying to get back to Jack that day, to help him out. People, now, are just a different breed of people than we were. I would have crawled to help him out. That was just the way it was back then."

Jack Dolan. "Captain Norton came over and told me that I was gonna get a whole pocket full of medals for Dakeshi. Now, I throughly enjoyed knowing that I was gonna get a medal. But it wasn't really the medal, it was that my officers thought enough about me to put me in for one. They was good guys."

"You don't never feel like a hero. You're just doing the same job that everybody had to do. It's just circumstances makes lots of heros. What would anybody do if you were short of ammunition and a guy got hit? You would grab him up and get him back behind the line, behind something and get your ammunition and go on. That doesn't happen just once it happened all the time. There were other guys around with medals and you respected them for it. You seen guys do the same thing or more and they didn't get a metal. Guys like Frank done a lot, probably more than I ever done, and he didn't get decorated for any of it."

"There was one older guy with us that had a Navy Cross and a Silver Star and he was the last guy in the world you would ever think to be a hero. He was an old farmer. He was one of them guys that never expected to go home. I was sent back to the hospital to bring some guys back up to the lines. The medics had released them for duty. An officer at Battalion stopped me and give me Russell's papers to go home. He told me to go get him off the line, even if I had to hog tie him. He said to get him off the line right now and get him off alive. Well we didn't get back up there before dark. We had to spend the night about halfway between the line and the hospital. The next morning we got back up there. They had already told Russell that he was leaving and so they had him waiting in a place that wasn't too dangerous. I give him his papers. He said that last night was as scared as he had ever been, knowing that he was going home. He said that he never expected to go home, that he had been over here for over three years. When he found out, last night, that he was going home he got so scared that he wouldn't make it till the next day and that scared him more than anything in the war. He had a wife and kids at home. I looked at him as a hero but he didn't look like one. He was a little gaunt looking fellow. He had been in every invasion and I had only been in one. Everybody was doing the same things, it mostly just depended on if somebody saw you and wanted to bother with the paperwork. People don't really understand that if everybody is doing the same things then there ain't no heros."

"We was getting a lot of replacements right around this time. Most of our casualties even the battle fatigue guys was not from the veterans, the old timers, it was from the new comers. They hadn't been trained very long and they brought a lot of them in there after Dakeshi and Wanna Draw. A lot of them flew in and you go from six weeks training in boot camp and they sit you down right in the middle of the dead and wounded, it's hard to take."

"Another problem we had, was that we lost a lot of them from bunching up. You didn't bunch up, especially toward the last. The Japanese wouldn't waste ammunition, they wanted you to bunch up. Of course, when things get rough that's human nature to go together not scatter. We just couldn't get the new guys not to bunch up. When one of them guys got hit, usually, you count on there being three or four more. I was lucky that I had got to train with the outfit for months before seeing combat. That eight weeks of sniper school had taught me a lot that most of the guys didn't know. A lot of guys couldn't even read a compass and hardly any of them could read a map. That eight weeks of extra training was a tremendous help. I learned more there that has stayed with me than I learned in four years of high school."

"I think having an outdoor background, growing up on a farm and hunting and trapping, made some of us better able to deal with killing, than the other guys. We killed animals for food and trapped them for money and then you saw some of your neighbors when they died. They weren't all taken to funeral homes like they are now. In a bad winter you couldn't dig a grave, so the family stored them till spring. There was just a lot of death in the rural areas. I think growing up with all that helped me in combat."

General Shepherd, CO of the 6th Division, replaced as many Marines in the shattered 22nd Regiment as he could round up and added several units from his fresher 29th Regiment. Then he sent them straight up the hill and around both flanks of Sugar Loaf. Casualties were again tremendous and all the survivors were pushed back to their starting point. They would try again the next day.

The 7th Division, at their rest area, continued making preparation to rejoin the battle.

Conical Hill fell to the 96th Division. The coastal plain was now open to the Americans for an advance south of Shuri. The Division protected the west side of the flat land and Route 13 from Conical Hill. Navy ships setting closely offshore, protected the east side. The troops on Conical Hill could now provide better protection of the east flank of the 77th Division moving down the center of the island.

The 77th Division was being shot to pieces by the Japanese. So, they tried a tactic that had seen little use by any of the Army units. They began using night attacks. The Japanese were not used to this. They knew the Americans attacked only in the daylight and the night belonged to them. The tactic worked for a while, until some of the Japanese stopped letting themselves be surprised. They prepared themselves for night movements by the Americans. Part of the enemy never did catch on and did nothing to prevent night attacks.

The Navy didn't have any ships damaged. The few enemy planes that went after the fleet were shot down.

May 17, 1945. The fighting was now so intense that the 7th Regiment decided to rotate the battalions again and so they sent the 3rd Battalion to relieve the 1st. The new battalion faced the same awesome fire and was able to move forward only a few yards during the entire day. The 2nd Battalion just kept doing the same things they had started doing, when they were pulled back into reserve to rest. The Japanese did send a little more artillery fire their way. Otherwise, they kept going about their business. The Marines seemed to like their resting units to be close to the lines and therefore they attracted fire. They would frequently move the men from one rest area to another one to keep the Japanese from zeroing in too much. Rest in a rest area was not really an option. They were too busy.

"I was pretty shook up after going in Dakeshi and then that hand thing. Captain Norton come up and said our squad didn't have to go in Wana Draw but I was needed to show the new tanks how to get in there. Then he said that I could just sit up on the slope with my sniper rifle and shoot guys attacking our tanks. He sent another squad run by a guy named Knutsen to provide that protection. Knutsen was a nervous wreck. He got hit at Peleliu with white phosphorus. He was from Newton Iowa. The medics had been told over and over to get rid of him and they would take him back to the hospital. The doctors there would declare him fit and send him back up. You just knew that he was gonna get somebody killed. He wasn't even coherent at times, he would go clear off. We said he was 'Asiatic' but what he had was battle fatigue. He was just a nervous wreck. He was terribly scarred, both him and Marques from white phosphorus at Peleliu. So Knutsen was out there."

" There was a foundation of a house out in the draw and here come our two tanks going by it. We knew there was heavy stuff up there but we didn't know where it was at. Two or three of our guys went down, you could hear the reports but you couldn't tell where they was coming from. I was sitting up there watching through the scope of my rifle. I seen a Japanese raise up over the foundation of that house and shoot at the boys escorting them tanks. He hit somebody. He was way out of range so I took off and ran down there. Doherty's BAR man, Dahl, ran down there too. The guy wasn't inside the foundation. We knew that he was around there some place. There was a dirty old mat laying there. We raised it up and there was a hole that ran under the foundation and went out. Outside there was a piece of corrugated metal roofing laying there. We figured that was his hole so Dahl crawled out there and rolled a hand grenade under there. That was that. We supposed that we got him but we didn't stay around to look. We made a run back to the hill and the tanks went on up."

"Well, after we got back out of there a big gun come out of Wana Ridge and started shooting at the tanks. It was just to the left front of them and they was hitting right in front of the tanks. Through my scope, I saw Knutsen jump up out of the grass and run for the tanks. He was way too far away to hear me but I just started yelling, 'NO, NO, NO, don't go for the tank.' You could tell from where the gun was shooting that soon he would hit the lead tank. KABOOM! Knutsen went down. A piece of that shell had hit him right in his middle. I ran down there. He was just flat in the middle. It was just like his insides was all gone. His middle just looked like hamburger. I pulled his dungaree jacket closed over his middle. He was looking me right in the eye. I told him he would be all right that we would get him out of there. He knew he was not all right and asked me to call his parents when I got home and tell them how he died. I told him that I would go get a corpsman. He said that I ought to know better than to bring a corpsman out there and get him killed too. Then he died, I took his dog tag and his personal effects and I ran back up the slope When I got home, I called his parents and told them how he died. That was really a sad thing to have to do."

General Shepherd requested and received heavy gunfire and bomb runs from the Navy on Sugar Loaf. Battleships moved in and carrier planes arrived to plaster the three hills and the flanks before he attacked them again. The Japanese went deep underground and waited out the bombardment. When the Marines moved forward, they came under the same fire and counterattacks that they had each previous attack. They were routed off the slope and from the flanks, just as happened every other time, with shocking numbers of casualties. The Marine Division had sent almost all of their combat troops forward as replacements for the assault battalions. It was now a concern that the Division might not be able to continue for more than a day or two. The Division combat efficiency had dropped so low as to nearly ruin the entire Division for further combat. A halt at this position could jeopardize the whole American offensive.

Then, just as dark was settling in, the Marines noticed movement on their target area. The Japanese had suffered great losses in men as well as the Marines. The Japanese commander did not think he had enough men left to withstand another assault on Sugar Loaf so he began transferring reserves who had been hidden in deep tunnels inside Half Moon and Horseshoe Hills. The Marine spotters waited until the Japanese reserves moved into the open and then called in fire from all of the division's artillery. The mass of fire killed almost all of the Japanese reserves. The small hill complex was now vulnerable to an attack that could be successful. In addition, the 1st Marine Division had made it to Wanna Ridge about three thousand yards to the northeast of Sugar Loaf. This action put an end to the gun emplacements at Wanna Ridge firing on the Marines at Sugar Loaf. The guns on Wana Ridge were now focusing all of their fire on the Marines attacking them. An attack against Sugar Loaf, with some renewed spirit, would jump off the next morning from the 6th Division lines.

Planners notified the 7th Division that they would be moving back into the lines in a day or two. This was not welcome news for the veterans but a lot of replacements showed enthusiasm to experience combat. The replacements died so fast in battle that it was rare when veterans even bothered to find out their names. The replacements were generally just known as, "Hey you."

The 77th Division pushed on slowly up the west side of their valley. The two regiments on the east were moving toward a three-hill Japanese stronghold clearing the enemy outposts as they went.

Mopping up operations continued around Conical Hill for the 96th

Division. The Division had been notified that the 7th Division was being readied to move down the flats to their east for a run to get behind Shuri.

The destroyer *Douglas H. Fox* was hit by a Kamikaze. She had only arrived on radar picket duty May 7. The ship was attacked by eleven planes and shot down seven of them before being hit. Burning gasoline set her decks afire and killed and wounded forty-two men. Her crew was able to control the fires and she left for repairs under her own power but was not able to return to combat duty.

May 18, 1945. The 2nd Battalion stayed in reserve while the 3rd Battalion went back to work with tank infantry teams trying to clear Wana Ridge. The attack proceeded very slowly with all movement bringing machine gun, rifle and mortar fire. The tanks had to contend with the deadly Japanese 47mm antitank guns and the suicide bombers throwing themselves at the tanks. A few yards were taken at the cost of seventy-nine Marines.

"We was helping the engineers investigate and seal off tunnels and caves around Dakeshi. The place was almost hollow there was so many of them. We had to check them out before we blew them or dozed them. Sometimes they was civilians inside and the higher ups wanted us to look for anything the Japanese might have left behind that might help us. Maps and documents and stuff. I went into one tunnel that had been used as a field hospital. There was a big room and it was full of wounded Japanese but they was all dead, they had committed suicide. Most of them had exploded themselves with grenades. You can imagine what it was like in there. There was one fellow who was still alive. You could tell he was alive because his eyes would follow you around the room. He was a young Japanese officer and you couldn't see anything wrong with him. The flies was eating his face off and he wouldn't even move. He was laying near the entrance of the room. He didn't have any blood or any bandages on him but he wouldn't move. We just turned around and left and they blew the tunnel entrance. I could never understand why he just laid there. You saw a lot of stuff like that. You couldn't make heads or tails out of it."

"A lot of men started cracking up around this time. One of our guys named Edwards did. We went to close a hole in a cave. We was waiting for dark to come so we could get to it without being seen. We was sitting behind a terrace on a side hill out of sight of the cave. There was a mortar crew down below us, not very far, firing toward the front. We was facing them, just watching. Edwards had an old school chum down there firing a mortar. A Japanese mortar shell come back over the hill, hit the base plate and just obliterated his friend. He just went berserk. He jumped up and just started screaming and running. Somebody tripped him up and we had to use straps off our gear to restrain him. We had to carry him out. He didn't come back but about six months later, I saw him. He had been with me all the way through. Back in the states I had been at his wedding before we went overseas. He was one of the trigger happy guys."

"When I got back to the states I was at Camp Lejeune, North Carolina and I went into the enlisted men's bar and there he sat. He was a private but he had been a PFC when I knew him. I asked him what had happened to him. He acted like he didn't know what I meant so I asked him what he was doing there in Camp Lejeune. He said he got sent there and was on his way to Panama. I asked him where his wife was and he said that he didn't have no wife. I asked him if he knew who he was talking to and he didn't. I named off a whole bunch of guys he was with over there and he didn't remember any of them, except one named White. I don't really think he remembered any of us. I still don't know what he was doing still in the Corps, why he didn't have a wife or why he would be going to Panama. I did know that he cracked up on Okinawa. They called it battle fatigue."

The 6th Division attacked Sugar Loaf for what they hoped would be the last time. Tanks and infantry attacked the right flank of the hill complex. When they were fully engaged with the Japanese, the Marines sent another tank/infantry team to attack on the left flank and an assault straight up the hill. The first flanking movement took heavy casualties but some made it around the hill as did the second flank attack. The Japanese simply did not have enough men left to respond, in the force needed, to drive the Marines back. Once the hills were flanked the tanks and infantry poured fire onto the reverse slopes destroying the mortar emplacements. The Japanese left their underground positions in suicide attacks on the tanks and infantry. While these suicide attacks killed and wounded a lot of Marines, they cost the Japanese too many men. They lost the ability to sustain the fight and to hold the hill any longer. Marines had finally captured Sugar Loaf, Horseshoe and Half Moon. By nightfall they were firmly dug in on the crests.

"You would dig-in on what we called the military crest, not right on top. Marines dug in on the side of the crest toward the enemy, down about ten or fifteen yards from the real crest. We did this to keep them from getting back on top and to protect ourselves from fire on the top. The Army guys dug in for the same reason but they always dug in on the back side of the slope so they could shoot at the real crest."

The 6th Division lost two thousand six hundred sixty-two Marines killed and wounded and one thousand two-hundred non-battle casualties for a total of nearly four thousand in the attack on Sugar loaf. They lost more than thirty tanks and a wealth of other arms and equipment. Whole platoons and even companies had just ceased to exist.

Units of the 7th Army Division begin moving from their rest area to a position near the coast north of Conical Hill to advance up the corridor behind the Japanese defenders.

The 77th inched up their valley killing the Japanese but adding a lot of casualties to their list. Two of the regiments working the east side of the valley cleared out the final outposts opposing them and arrived at the base of the first of three hills. The hill complex was a typical Japanese stronghold. A hill that was called Chocolate Drop lay to the north of two other hills, Flattop Hill and Dick Hill. The latter two features were actually a part of the Shuri inner defense perimeter. Like always, the hills were honeycombed with connecting caves and tunnels. The guns on each hill covered the approaches to the other two hills. The greatest problem of all was the low land around each hill. Rain had turned the area into a marshy lake. Neither tanks nor self-propelled guns could help the infantry.

The 96th Division prepared to continue their advance as soon as the 7th was in place and could start down the wide path opened for them by the capture of Conical Hill.

Landing Ship Tank *808* was hit by a Kamikaze and sank with twenty-two crewmen killed and wounded. The destroyer *Longshaw* had been working in close to shore to provide gunfire support to the infantry ashore for four days. After the gunfire assignment, she was slowly returning to her patrol station further offshore. She grounded on a reef just south of the Naha Airfield and could not refloat herself. Tugs were sent to help and were working hard to refloat the vessel. After several hours without much success, a coastal battery whose existence had remained undiscovered, was pulled from a cave and blasted the *Longshaw*. She quickly sank. The Japanese surprise fire killed eighty-six men and wounded another ninety-seven. The destroyer had the unwelcome distinction of being the only ship sunk by coastal guns during the battle. *Longshaw* had been participating in combat operations for a year and a half and had been at Okinawa since before the start of the battle. The captain was killed but a junior officer who survived, said later that the ship was about two miles off course. He claimed that the officers and crew were so exhausted, that they could not remain alert enough to sail the ship with any efficiency, at all. The *Sims,* a destroyer escort, converted to a high speed transport and *LST 808* suffered some damage but kept operating.

May 19, 1945. The 3rd Battalion attacked the ridge again while the 1st and 2nd Battalions stayed in reserve in the Dakeshi area. No progress at all was made. By the end of the day, the Division sent a battalion from the 1st Marine Regiment forward as relief. All three of the battalions of the 7th Marine Regiment were now assembled in the Dakeshi area for rest and to act as the Division reserve. Since relieving 2nd Battalion, the other two battalions of the 7th Regiment had lost five hundred twenty-seven men. They too, badly needed replacements and some time off the lines. Wana Ridge was proving to be difficult beyond belief and the 7th Marines couldn't take any more casualties lest they become too ineffective to ever be able to continue fighting. It was well known that the Japanese had to hold the ridge to be able to hold Shuri, but no one even dreamed the Japanese would be able to hold the ridge this long. No weak points could be found. Heavy guns and air strikes seemed wasted. Tank and infantry teams had to take out each enemy position as they came to them, and they were always under murderous fire from other positions. Replacements began to arrive for the 2nd Battalion and the wounded began to trickle back from the regimental field hospital to rejoin their units. Far too many of them had no business leaving the medical facilities, but they did.

"We was supposed to be in a rest area but they wasn't no rest. They, the Navy, was getting a lot of opposition from a big gun they couldn't spot. It was just giving the Navy fits. The commanding officer called for me and we took two more men out to find the big gun. They thought it was some kind of coastal gun that the Japanese had captured at Singapore or Hong Kong and then brought to Okinawa. They couldn't spot her so they sent me and two helpers out. We traveled all day. It was raining cats and dogs. Our orders was not to fight with anybody, just find the gun. So, we took out to find the gun and we never got anything, only sniper fire. We just bypassed them and kept going. Along late in the evening, the first evening, we followed a little stream out to the coast. Before we got to where we was heading it got dark on us. The little stream passed by a little village that just had four or five little houses in it. The end house faced out on the street and on to the little stream. They was an escarpment hanging over the house, an overhanging cliff. We couldn't really see what was going on above us. So, our little trick was to go in the little house and in front of the door take up the flooring and dig a hole. Then we would put one fellow in the hole and if there was three of us, which they was, then we would put two of us in the hole and put one guy out in the yard in a hole. You would dig in behind the door sill. Tearing up the floor and digging a hole was a trick we had been using for a long time. To go in a house, you didn't sleep on the floor you dug a hole in front of the door and slept in the hole. If a guy opened the door to step in, he stepped on you. You was completely covered by dirt. They could shoot through the little old walls but they couldn't shoot you through that much dirt. So, we used the door sill for a gun rest. You just pushed the door open and you was eye level with the street. That's what we done there that night."

"Boy, it was just raining cats and dogs right after dark and the house began running full of water. It was a small four room house so I went into another room to try to find something dry to sit on. You got to understand that the Japanese had hardly any furniture. It was all mats on the floor. You sat on the floor, you slept on the floor. I was feeling around in there for something dry. I felt something that felt like a bucket. It was one of their eight inch shells. We knew we was close to the gun! There was half a room of them, about a hundred of them. I slipped back in the other room and told the other guy and passed the word out to the boy out in the yard. I told them, 'We're on top of that gun because we got the shells.' He said, 'What's in the other room?' I said, 'Hell, I don't know.' So, I went to the other room and crawled into it in the dark. I used a pen light and it was ten pound powder bags, in silken bags. So now we had both the powder and the shells but we still didn't know where the gun was. We knew we was on top of it, someplace. They wouldn't be transporting those shells very far."

"Along about midnight, everything had been quiet. Down along the line they was fighting but we were clean away from it. The Navy was close in firing on the Japanese. We radioed the Navy and told them we had found the shells but hadn't found the gun. We told them we would tell them what happened the next morning. It was about midnight and we was just changing the watch when we heard a noise. We asked the Navy for a flare. They was really nice about it. They always fired a flare every twenty minutes, anyway. So a destroyer fired us a flare. We saw there was a fellow crawling down the hill opposite the stream. Coming down this big hill. A few minutes later, we called for a second flare. The boy out in the yard come in and said, 'Say, that guy's got a Marine uniform on.' Well, that wasn't nothing new for the Japanese to take a uniform off of one of our dead and use it. I had a thermite grenade (This is an incendiary device that burns at about three thousand degrees C.) and a signal grenade that the Army give to me. All it done was jump up in the air and go boom and throw out a little parachute with a little flare on it. We kept calling for flares about every ten minutes. This fellow just kept crawling on down the hill. He crawled out in the little stream. He got out to about the middle of it. I raised up, out of the house and threw this grenade about as high in the air as I could. He heard the spoon fly off and knew it was one of ours. He jumped up and said, 'Oh God! No, no, no, oh God, I'm a Marine, I'm a Marine, I'm a Marine, I'm a Marine.' Just about that time the little grenade went off and there came a parachute a floating down with a flare on it. He came running in to us. I said, 'What the hell are you doing out there and where do you come from?' He said, 'I've been wondering around no man's land for four days. I got pinned down and cut off from my troops. They evidently abandoned me, thinking me dead. I played like a Japanese up here. I didn't even know what direction I was going for the last four days. I just crawled into you guys by accident.' So, we got him in. We was glad to see him because we thought we might need help."

"The next morning we got up and crept out of there before daylight and stationed ourselves up along the edge of the cliff. When it broke daylight we was staring up in the muzzle of the big eight-incher. She was camouflaged over but the barrel was bulging out from out of the camouflage net. It was on a rail car with about a 2 per cent grade. All they had to do was, they just rolled it out of the door, pulled back the net and let her fire. When they got done firing they just pulled the blocks out from under the wheels. She rolled herself back into the cave from the recoil of the last shot. There was just one man there on the gun. We had surprised him. He was in ceremonial robes, he was gonna commit suicide, I guess, if somebody pushed him to it. But we captured him and disarmed the gun. I put the thermite grenade in the barrel, that melted the barrel down some. The Navy was really happy with us. We captured a hell of a big gun with no opposition. An interpreter, told me later, that the guy we captured said the crew abandoned the gun in the middle of the night, while he was asleep. He didn't even know they was gone. So, when he woke up the next morning, we was the ones that woke him up. We patted ourselves on the back and headed back to the line. I turned myself back into my commanding officer and we headed toward the south end of the island again."

General Shepherd notified his boss, General Buckner, that Sugar Loaf had been captured. The problem with his notification was that the hill complex still contained some Japanese die-hards deep in their tunnels. These soldiers, of course, would not surrender and made the three hills a very dangerous place to live for several more days. Small groups of Japanese infiltrated back through the tunnels. They would pop out of an opening that had already been secured, and counterattack Marines from the rear. Marines, revealing themselves too much, would draw fire from distant hills still occupied by the Japanese.

The 7th Division, in a rare night move, passed through Yonabaru and headed around Conical Hill on the coast side and began to turn west. This route would take them behind Shuri and turn the Japanese east flank. The Japanese were surprised at the 7th Division's move because it had been raining hard for several days and the flats were deep with mud. Besides, the Japanese were always surprised when the American units moved at night. They just couldn't accept it. The "book" on the Americans was that they never moved at night. No matter how many night movements were made by the Army and Marines, the Japanese would not change their minds let alone their tactics. They were always surprised.

Regiments of the 77th Division began attacking Chocolate Drop Hill. It was obvious that it was a difficult job because the armor units could not get through the mud to support them. Commanders did the next best thing they could and moved strong elements of the 96th Division over to attack the hill complex, at the same time.

The 96th Division commenced attacking Dick Hill, which was the southeast anchor, of the Chocolate Drop, Flattop, Dick Hill complex. They had the same trouble the other divisions had, no armor due to the weather.

The American ships and planes knocked down the few Japanese planes sent against them and no ships were hit. A destroyer received some minor damage after colliding with another vessel and a fleet oiler ran aground requiring a tug to tow it free.

May 20, 1945. The 7th Regiment would spend the next week in reserve. They reorganized, and prepared themselves for the combat they knew they would be sent back to. Some of them couldn't stay away from the Wana Draw, though. The draw and the penetration of Shuri had now been assigned to the 1st and 5th Marine Regiments. Now that the 7th Marines had been pulled out of combat for several days, a lot them had breakdowns. Apparently they had held themselves together while fighting in order not to let their buddies down. Now that no one's life depended on them, they could let go. In one week, a hundred twenty-six Marines were evacuated with psychiatric wounds.

"The 7th Marines was on one side of Wana Draw and the 5th Marines was on the other side. We was supposed to be in reserve but a lot of us got sent up there. To my right as you went into the town there was an irrigation or a drainage ditch. It was V shaped and rocked up. The captain told me to take some men out. There was a hole in the line and they wanted us to plug it. He said the hole was at the end of the drainage ditch. We started up the drainage ditch in the mire. There was several inches of water in it. We got up to where a little drainage ditch come into the bigger ditch. I crawled up to it and looked over the edge and a machine gun opened up on me. It didn't bother me but there was a ricochet off a rock and a little piece of copper hit me just above the eyebrow. I passed the word back for nobody to try the little ditch. Well, the last two guys went up it and they both got hit. I don't even remember which ones they was, we had so many new guys. We went on up the big ditch. I thought we was in the right spot so I stripped off all my gear except for my sniper rifle. I told the guys not to move until I give the word. I crawled out to see what the situation was and got pinned down. I heard a tank behind me. It was a dozer tank and he pushed the ditch in about two hundred yards back down the ditch from me. I was pinned down in the grass about ten yards out from the ditch. I was facing a horseshoe-shaped hill. There was fire coming down the hill facing me and everywhere else. I decided to face the fire and crawled backwards toward the ditch. The first thing I knew, .50 calibers began to come my way from a tank. I kept waving at him to show that I was friendly. I waved my hat at him. Well, he just kept firing right at me, so it seemed. When I backed over the edge of the bank, the ditch was full of water. That dozer tank had dammed it up down below where he was making a crossing. My men was gone and my gear was gone. I had been out there for about an hour and was out far enough that my men couldn't see me. They took off before the water got too high. There wasn't no other cover. I heard something gurgling and there was a Japanese hanging over the edge on the other side of the bank. He had raised up out of a hole behind me. He

146

had caught me in the back and I didn't know it. That tank had seen him and that was what they was firing at. And they got him. I had been backing right backwards to him."

"It hadn't rained that day that I remember and I don't know where all that water come from. It had to have had something to do with what that dozer tank was doing. I didn't have any gear left and I started down the ditch and the water just got deeper. I put my cigarettes and my billfold in my hat and just floated down the ditch. I don't know where they come from but I kept seeing something coming at me on top. Pretty soon one came up and it was eels coming up the ditch. I don't like snakes and they're a lot like snakes to me, so I hugged the bank and let them go pass me. I don't know where they come from but it had something to do with that dozer guy flooding the ditch. I come up on that dozer tank backing out and I got behind it and used it for protection the rest of the way out."

"What made me mad about that whole thing was what they didn't tell me. They told me, we was gonna plug a hole in the line. What they really sent us out for was to draw fire so they could plug the hole in the line. We was a diversion. They just sent us out to draw fire. We probably wouldn't have had two casualties if they had told me to just go out there and draw fire. We was fixing to all crawl out of that ditch to plug a hole. If we had, we would have crawled right into the Japanese. It come through Captain Norton but it was somebody above him. I think, if Norton had known he would have told me because he was a hell of a nice guy."

"When I got back, I reported to the command post and they was laughing about it. They said I had done a good job. Well, we hadn't even got close to the hole to plug it. They said we had done exactly what they wanted. While we was drawing fire, they had gone up there with tanks. I didn't think it was funny because we had lost two guys."

"The dozer tank guy who escorted me out of there was the outfit's tank commander. I had about three encounters with him already. He was the one I had gone into Dakeshi with and he was the one who decided he could get tanks in there. Those tanks had saved our lives. If we had to go in there again without tanks, probably none of us would have made it. Now he had saved my life again. As a scout, I got to a lot of places first and could have about all the souvenirs I wanted. I had three Japanese pistols I had taken off downed pilots. I give him those three pistols. I didn't want to carry them anymore, anyway. They made my gear too heavy. I was already carrying my sniper rifle and it was heavy. Then I had my Tommy gun and my pistol and ammunition for all of them and everything else you had to carry. I was glad to get rid of the pistols and you couldn't have found a better guy to give them to."

Elements of the 6th Marine Division were still taking losses on Sugar Loaf Hill and the surrounding area. They couldn't advance and leave the small number of Japanese at the rear, so the Marines kept sending more men on and in the hill's tunnels to kill the enemy soldiers. The 6th Marine Division added a lot more casualties to the list before continuing their advance toward Shuri.

The Japanese recognized that their loss of Sugar Loaf would greatly shorten the time they could maintain a defense of Okinawa. They began examining plans for the best way to continue their defense of the island. All the capture of Sugar Loaf meant to the Americans was that another enemy stronghold had been taken. There were a great deal more in front of them. In the meantime General Ushijima sent all of the troops he could find, even Naval personnel untrained in infantry combat, to join and reinforce his men facing the 6th Marine Division. They fell back and formed new defenses between the Marines and Shuri in the Kokuba River Valley. If the Marines breached this new, and relatively weak, line they would be behind Shuri and Ushijima's defenses. The battle would then be over sooner than the General or any other Japanese wanted.

The 7th Division's 184th Infantry Regiment spearheaded a surprise advance to almost a mile south through the Japanese lines on the east coast. They left the 184th Infantry where they planned to turn west, to guard their flank, and sent the 32nd Infantry west to take positions directly behind the Shuri defenses. In order to succeed in this flanking movement, speed was necessary, even essential. They could not give the Japanese time to reorganize and strengthen the defenses in their path. Speed didn't work because the weather became worse and the tanks and armored vehicles were trapped and unable to move anywhere in the mud.

Chocolate Drop Hill fell to the combined efforts of the 77th and the 96th Division's infantrymen. The position had to be taken without any tank support. Adding to the difficulty of the battle, the Japanese had mined a large area of the flats preventing the infantry from using several approaches to the slopes of the hill. Casualties had been heavy but the divisions were still strong enough to advance to the next two hills. The capture of Flattop and Dick Hills would put the two American Divisions right on the edge of General

Ushijimi's Headquarters. The two American Divisions would fight for Dick Hill and the broken terrain west and south for days. Most of the fighting had to done without tank support and often without air support. Many days it rained and visibility was so limited that the American planes had to stay on the ground or on the carriers' decks. There was a road that passed south of the hill complex that tanks could move on if supported strongly enough by infantry. Elements of the 96th Division began working to clear the road of mines and Japanese outposts.

Three destroyers were hit by Kamikazes. The *John C. Butler* received only minor damage and had no casualties. She remained on the picket line and continued carrying out her duties. The *Thacher* and *Chase* were hit so hard that they were removed from the line and sent to the rear to be scrapped. The *Chase* splashed the plane attacking her but the damaged plane struck the water within yards of the *Chase* and split the hull open. The ship just barely escaped sinking and was towed to a rear area. The high speed transport *Register* was damaged badly enough to have to be withdrawn for repairs. She returned to duty in a few weeks. These ships added another one hundred two casualties to the Navy's ever growing casualty list.

May 21, 1945. It began to rain again. It could and did rain as much as five inches a day during Okinawa's Spring season. The 7th Marines stayed in their rest area without shelter. The other two infantry regiments of the 1st Division continued fighting up Wana Ridge and Wana Draw, slowly moving up to the Shuri Heights, just east of what was left of Shuri Castle.

"The regiment keeps your records. We was sent over to help two half-track drivers that was stuck in the mud and under fire. When we got there, there wasn't no drivers. There was the half-track sitting out there in a big bare field between two or three hills. It had an 88-shell hole behind the driver's seat. No Blood, no nothing. There laid some of the 7th Marine's records in seabags. They had got in the mud and had got stuck. They was using the seabags to try to get out, after they come under fire, I suppose. They had laid a lot of the seabags under the tracks, trying to get out. They had just ground them down in the mud and water. Some of the bags had come open and I looked at some of them. They was from George Company. They did retrieve them later but they had laid there for quite a while. I never did know what happened there but I did know what happened to my records, when they couldn't find them later. They caused me lots of trouble after I got home, especially not having any pay records."

The 6th Marine Division pushed south between Naha and Shuri. They could not turn east and advance directly toward Shuri. There were Japanese to their east, south and west. They would have to hold until the 1st Marine Division broke through Shuri and came up to protect their east flank. They would then continue south and southwest past Naha and begin cleaning out the Japanese on the Oroku peninsula. This area jutted out northwest from the south edge of Naha. The Naha Airfield was located on the west end of the peninsula. The Japanese had posted four thousand troops in the area to protect the airfield and deny the American Navy the use of the Naha seaport.

The 77th and 96th Army Divisions continued fighting the water, mud and the Japanese. The enemy was firmly entrenched in and on the Flattop and Dick Hills complex. By nightfall they had captured Chocolate Drop and Flattop and were ready to move even further south. They would not have succeeded, if they had not managed to get tanks on the road, south of the hills. These tanks blew and burned enough positions on the reverse slopes to allow the infantry to take both positions. The division's assault regiments, then swarmed over and captured the mass of small hills known as Dick Hill.

All ships escaped damage from the few Kamikazes roaming about the air around Okinawa. Sometimes, it was difficult to understand just how badly some of the Kamikaze pilots flew. It became clear, though, when it was learned that many of them were taught nothing but how to take off.

May 22, 1945. It kept raining. The 1st Marine Division kept the attack going up the Wana Draw and its ridge system.

Rain, mud and the inability of the 1st Marine Division to crack Shuri's defenses and move south, kept the 6th Marine Division fixed in place. They could not advance but they could and did take casualties, from the nearly continuous Japanese fire.

The 7th Division flanking movement just ground to a halt, as did all of the other divisions' movements. The rainwater and mud were too deep for men to move. When they tried, they just became slow-moving targets for the Japanese gunners and snipers. Ravines that would have provided cover, were full of water and the small streams and dry washes were flooded and impassable. Supplies had to be hand carried and air dropped. The wounded suffered more and often died because of the difficulty of moving them to the rear.

The other two Army divisions, the 77th and the 96th operated mopping up actions on the dwindling but still powerful Japanese defenders around and inside Flattop and Dick Hills. The Army commanders could see what the lonely, tired, sick at heart, riflemen could not. The all out advance that had started on May 11 had bogged down to a halt, but the American units were still fighting and the Shuri Defense position was shrinking daily.

The American military leaders believed that the Japanese would simply fight to the death, at their Shuri positions. They knew there was a possibility, the Japanese might try a withdrawal and set up a new defense in the south but they didn't give it much thought. So, as far as the American leaders were concerned, each enemy solder killed and each position taken weakened the enemy and shortened the combat. The end of the battle for Okinawa was in sight or so they thought. It would prove out that they were still underestimating the Japanese resolve to keep the Americans fighting forces here, instead of on the beaches of Japan.

For another day, no ships were hit by any bombs or Kamikazes. The ship's crews had been functioning in a state of exhaustion for a long time. It was a relief to the Admirals when a day would pass that they did not have to read new casualty lists.

Just after midnight, General Ushijima called his officers together. It was obvious to everyone that the Shuri defenses were on the verge of being breached. The question was whether to stay in Shuri and fight to the death or withdraw to the south. There were strong southern defenses already prepared, identified as the Yaeju Dake to Yuza Dake escarpment. There were still about fifty thousand troops left who could fight but they were being squeezed into an ever smaller area. No one on the Japanese staff felt it was the best use of manpower to stay at Shuri. There were roads going south that would make movement easy and the escarpments down there were natural defenses. The area was also honeycombed with natural and man-made caves. Supplies, weapons and ammunition had been stored there as well. The simple answer to their question of how best to continue the battle, hinged on the best way to kill more Americans. Moving south was considered the best way to do that.

The move started at once, while it was still the dark and could not be observed by the Americans. Work parties began transporting the wounded and the ammunition. The move would take several days and could not always be covered by night. Luck was on the Japanese side for once. Rain and low clouds covered most of the withdrawing soldiers. When columns were spotted by the Americans, air strikes and Naval gunfire was brought to bear and killed thousands of the Japanese soldiers and the civilians traveling with them.

Surprisingly, none of the reports that the Japanese were withdrawing from Shuri alarmed American intelligence units. They thought the troop movements that they did spot were support troops moving about. They were convinced that General Ushijima was defending Shuri as strongly as ever. They interpreted the Japanese movements to mean that the Japanese general was sending civilians, his wounded and troops that needed rest to the south. General Ushijima was sending troops south, all right, carrying supplies and having them return for more loads. American intelligence thought this to mean he was bringing fresh troops into the Shuri defenses. This further convinced American commanders that the last fight for Okinawa would be at Shuri.

CHAPTER EIGHT
MOVING PAST SHURI

May 23, 1945. Rain continued. The 1st Division did not know that the Japanese had begun to withdraw from Shuri. It was assumed that the battle would continue into and through the Japanese defenses. Plans were for the 7th Marines, as soon as they were ready, to relieve one or both of the two regiments fighting up Wana Draw. These plans would be changed and the 7th would be moved to the 6th Marine Division zone when events permitted. The 1st Division was ordered to fill in an area that the 6th Division was withdrawing from. Since the 5th Regiment was on the west flank of the 1st Division and closest to the new area, it was chosen to take up the positions being abandoned there. The 5th Marines moved into their new area and found a scene that shocked the hardest of veterans. This land had been fought over for days by large forces of Marines and Japanese. The fierce ten day fight and the mud had kept both sides from removing their dead. Marines of the 5th would live and fight in a surreal world of the dead that defied comprehension. They just put up with it and continued with the job at hand.

The 6th Marine Division was mud and water stalled, but they began to reorganize their lines anyway. This movement was creating a gap between the two Marine divisions and the 1st Division shifted its zone west and took up the territory abandoned due to organizational withdrawal. Another troop withdrawal, this one by the Japanese at Shuri, went unnoticed by the 6th Division. It really didn't matter because these Marines were turning to attack the Japanese on the Oroku Peninsula. The Japanese had no intention of withdrawing any more men from Oroku and actually had started sending some of them back.

The Army Divisions were ready to push forward again. This time the push would put them into the last of the Shuri defenses and a breakthrough would end the Japanese hold on Okinawa, or so they thought. The mud and water kept them from being able to move. Supply and other logistic problems were acute. Men instead of vehicles carried ammo, water and food. It required a major effort to get the wounded to medical treatment and the dead had to stay on the battlefield, both American and Japanese.

Kamikazes would not score any hits this day. Bad weather kept most of them on the ground.

May 24, 1945. Heavy rain still fell. The 1st Marine Division, less the 7th Marines advanced up the Wana Draw.

The 6th Marine Division still could not move. Mud kept the tanks, other guns and vehicles from moving or going anywhere. The 1st Division's failure to reach Shuri and protect the 6th Division's flank kept the infantry pinned down.

The 7th Division had brought up fresh troops to get the stalled Division moving west to get behind Shuri. They thought they could move tanks and armored vehicles on the road that passed south of Shuri. Tanks and mobile guns would be able to bring fire on the reverse slopes of the surrounding hills and ridges they had come through on their mile long penetration of the enemy lines. The plan failed because all of their vehicles were mired in the mud. The road was nothing more than a gridlock of stuck trucks and other vehicles. The Division could not move.

The other two Army divisions were in the same situation as the 7th Division.

American fast carrier strike planes struck airfields in southern Japan but the Japanese still sent numerous planes against the fleet. The destroyer *Guest* was grazed by a plane and continued her duties until normally relieved in July. Other ships weren't so fortunate. The destroyer escort *O'Neill* was hit and while damage was light, nineteen of her sailors were killed or wounded. The minesweeper *Spectacle*, the type of vessel used to patrol the harbors and bays in search of Japanese suicide boats, was hit by a plane and damaged so badly she was knocked out of the war. Much worse than the damage, was the fact that twenty-nine of her small crew were killed and another six were wounded. A Kamikaze struck the destroyer escort *Barry* and set her ablaze.

The crew and their twenty-nine wounded was forced to abandon the ship when they could not flood the forward magazine which was threatened by the fire. Before the magazine exploded, the water level rose in the ship enough to extinguish the fire near it. A skeleton crew went back aboard and put out the rest of the fires. The ship was stripped and decommissioned a few weeks later. The Navy decided to tow her to one of the radar picket stations and use her as a decoy for the Kamikazes. On the way, a Kamikaze sank her.

The Japanese had been planning another counterattack. This one would bring two new divisions from Japan for a landing on Okinawa. Japanese planners knew the Americans were vulnerable to attack because the weather had negated the American fire power superiority. The landings would be coordinated with a push from the Shuri Heights defenses and an airborne raid on Kadena and Yomitan Airfields. It was planned for the first day that weather would permit. The weather cleared enough and the attack began. Problems doomed the plan and the attack. The two Division landing attempts had been scrubbed. They didn't have enough fuel to ferry the troops to Okinawa and there were not enough planes to protect the convoy. The High Command wanted the two divisions kept in Japan in case the Americans invaded. Without the landings, the Japanese could not afford to send any forces out of the defensive positions at Shuri.

The Japanese did continue with the two other parts of their counterattack. They sent Kamikazes against the fleet and sent some of their airborne troops against the two airfields to destroy American planes on the ground. There were twelve planes involved in the airfield attack, but only one plane made it through the American anti-aircraft defense. Twelve solders and three crewmen ran from the plane that had made it to the ground at Yonton. They dispersed and threw grenades and charges at the planes parked along the runway. All fifteen were killed by airfield ground personnel, but not before they had damaged twenty planes and destroyed seven others. They killed one American officer and wounded several men before the fight ended. The counterattack was over.

May 25, 1945. Another day of torrential rain. The 7th regiment sat in their rest area living in total misery due to the mud and water. The only consolation was that they were not in the close combat like the other regiments in Wana Draw.

The bogged down 6th Marine Division didn't even know that the Japanese had tried a counterattack. The Marines could only sit or lie in the mud and wait.

All three Army Divisions stayed in place in a muddy and watery world. They had no shelter and rest did not exist. They stood, sat and lay in mud with rain pouring down on them and snipers shooting at them. Japanese artillery still pounded them every day. Supplies could only arrive on the backs of men and occasional air drops when possible. They were short of everything and out of most things.

This would prove to be another bad day for the fleet, especially for the radar picket vessels. The former destroyer and now high speed transport *Bates* was sunk. She had been patrolling near Ie Shima when three planes attacked her, one dropped a bomb that tore her starboard hull open, a second bomb crashed into her pilot house and the third dropped a bomb that ruptured her port hull. Even with help, the crew could not save her and she sank in a few hours. The destroyer *Stormes* and the high speed transport *Roper* were damaged so far beyond repair that they were never returned to action. A medium landing ship transport, the *William B. Allison* was also sunk. Another two hundred twenty names went into the Navy's casualty reports.

May 26, 1945. Rain continued without any let up. 2nd Battalion had received two hundred twenty-two replacements and a lot of their wounded had returned. They were not at a full compliment but their ranks were filled enough to make them a tough combat unit again. It was now decided that the 7th Marines would not go into Shuri. They were not needed there any longer and it would have been a wasted movement. They were to be sent south to relieve the 6th Marine Division in order for that Division to be able to proceed with it's new objective on the Oroku Peninsula. This movement, however, couldn't begin until the weather cleared some. The other infantry regiments were still in Wana Draw and still fighting.

The 6th Marine Division was ready to push southwest past Naha and begin attacking the defenders on Oroku Peninsula as soon as the weather cleared and the 1st Marine Division could move south and relieve them at their current location. This move would protect the 6th Division's flank and the 1st Division could continue down the west side of the center of the island.

The three Army Divisions were, literally, stuck in place. This situation provided the Japanese infantry with an unexpected reprieve in which they could rest and resupply. Their artillery continued to hammer the American positions and the American artillery tried to keep fire going on the enemy positions. It was a struggle for the Americans, however. They had trouble moving shells up to the guns and many of the guns had sunk so far into the mud that they became useless.

The destroyers *Anthony* and *Braine* were damaged by Kamikazes. The former only slightly but the latter was struck by two planes and had most of her amidship's superstructure demolished. She was saved but didn't see any more action during the rest of the war. One hundred forty-four of her crewmen were killed and wounded. The fast minesweeper *Forrest* had started her career as a destroyer and operated in the Atlantic Theater. In 1944, due to need, she was converted to a minesweeper and was present when the invasion of Okinawa began. Vessels like her were highly prized by the Navy because they could carry out the duties of both destroyer and minesweeper. *Forrest's* career ended when a Kamikaze hit her at the waterline. Her crew saved her but repairs were not completed quickly enough for her to return to action. Another surveying vessel, the *Dutton*, was hit by a plane but not badly damaged.

May 27, 1945. The 7th Marines stayed in place waiting for movement orders. Wana Draw was still a deadly battlefield for the sister regiments.

The 6th Marine Division was still sitting in the same place, also. It was still raining and the Japanese were rapidly withdrawing from the Shuri defenses. The Marines were supposed to have pinched in on Shuri enough by now, to have helped prevent any withdrawing. They didn't even know that the Japanese were on the move and couldn't have done anything about if they had known.

None of the Army division's could move yet. The troops had to just endure the mud and rain as best they could.

Kamikazes pilots scored extremely well on this day. Kamikazes hit the destroyer *Drexter*. The ship had only been in commission for six months and this was her first combat assignment. She suffered heavy damage from the first plane but kept firing on other planes that were after her and the other picket duty ships. The second plane crashed into the superstructure. The combination of plane fuel and bombs exploded with such force that the ship rolled on her side and sank in less than a minute. It happened so quickly that most of her crew went down with her. One hundred sixty-eight men died and fifty-one of the rescued were wounded. The few survivors were stunned by the fate of their friends, shipmates and the sudden disappearance of their ship.

The *Gilligan*, a destroyer escort had been severely damaged in January by a suicide plane but was repaired quickly enough to take part in the Okinawa invasion. She seemed to attract air attacks and shot down numerous planes but a torpedo bomber finally made a square hit on her beam. Luckily, the torpedo did not explode but she had to be withdrawn to repair the hole in her side. A five hundred pound bomb just missed the minesweeper *Gayety* but caused enough damage that she had to be sent to the rear for repairs. She had taken damage and casualties from a "Baka" bomb earlier in the month. A landing craft, *LCS(L)-119*, and the transport *Rednour* were damaged enough that they had to be pulled out of combat and neither would return to the war. The high speed transport *Loy*, and the minesweeper *Southard* were slightly damaged by suicide planes and had casualties. The attack transport *Sandoval* was hit for the second time during the battle. Her casualties were light (thirty-four) but the structural damage took her out of the battle, for good this time. All tolled, another two hundred fourteen sailors were killed or wounded.

May 28, 1945. The rain stopped but the deep mud was still an impassable obstacle. The American offensive would begin again in two days even though the tanks would not be able to move through the mud for several more days. The 7th Marines were ready to move but couldn't due to the mud. Almost incredible was the fact that, although the Regiment had not been in combat, the last seven days had produced one hundred thirty-one casualties of which one hundred twenty-six were psychiatric evacuations. Wana Draw had nearly been "processed" but Marine casualties were still mounting in the 1st Regiment and the 5th Regiment.

The 6th Marine Division was ready to move but they couldn't. The mud was still too deep and the 1st Division couldn't get to their positions to relieve them.

The weather had improved but all three of the Army divisions were still stuck in the mud where they had been for days.

The destroyer *Shubrick* was the only ship in the fleet damaged on this day. She had seen a lot of combat in the Atlantic Theater and had been badly damaged by a German bomb. *Shubrick* was transferred to the Pacific in the spring of 1945 and arrived on station at Okinawa for radar picket duty in early May. A Kamikaze crashed into her starboard side and the bomb the plane carried tore a thirty foot hole in the ship. The explosion managed to set off one of the ship's depth charges and it was expected that the vessel could do nothing except sink. Unbelievably, her crew extinguished the fires and stopped the flooding and she was towed from the area to a repair facility. Sixty of her crew were killed and wounded in the attack.

May 29, 1945. The 7th Marines stayed in their rest area except for Easy Company. The 1st Battalion of the 1st Marine Regiment had allowed a gap to develop in their lines in Wana Draw. They had to request assistance or risk allowing the Japanese to exploit the gap and get behind them. Easy Company with Jack's squad attached was sent up the draw and into the gap. A company from the 5th Regiment found an opening to Shuri and walked right into the Shuri Castle grounds. They didn't find anything except rubble. The Japanese had stayed under ground while tens of thousands of bombs, and shells had fallen on Shuri for more than six months. And the Japanese themselves were gone except for a small rear guard and the ever present snipers.

The 6th Marine Division was advised that they would be relieved on June 2. They began planning their Oroku campaign which was going to include a limited amphibious operation. Originally it was intended to seal the east side of the peninsula and send the 6th Division south with the 1st Division. Planners reconsidered their decision about leaving an enemy force in the rear and assigned the 6th Division the task of clearing the enemy from Oroku. Also, the Navy wanted access to the Naha Port and the Naha Airfield was a valuable piece of land for both Navy and Marine flyers. The Commanders decided to organize an amphibious landing with a regiment on the west end and turn their regiment, now awaiting relief from the 1st Division, west toward the peninsula. The Japanese defenders would be attacked from their front and their rear at the same time.

Patrols from the three Army divisions began to probe forward from where the weather had stopped them. It was immediately apparent that something had happened. The vicious defense put on by the Japanese was gone. Patrols faced an abundance of snipers and small pockets of die-hards, but the real defense just wasn't there. Units began moving onto and into the Shuri Heights themselves.

The only vessel falling pray to the Kamikaze flights was the high speed transport *Tatum.* Her damage was slight and she kept to her duties on a radar picket station.

May 30, 1945. Easy Company stayed in the Wana Draw moving on and protecting the 1st Regiment's right flank. The other two companies mopped up.

The 6th Marine Division sat waiting to be relieved from their positions so they could get on with attacking Oroku. There had originally been about ten thousand Japanese Naval troops on the peninsula but most had gone to Shuri over time as replacements for the Shuri defenders. When General Ushijimi withdrew from Shuri all but about two thousand of the Japanese on Oroku had moved south also. Once in their new positions, it was noted that there were very few weapons left for their use and they had left most of theirs in their old defenses. Their Commander, Admiral Ota, requested that they be allowed to return to the positions on Oroku and die. They wanted to die together instead of scattered about in the Army's lines. Permission was granted and some made it back. Enough made it to present a force of about four thousand to the Marines. The Japanese converted the anti-aircraft guns surrounding Naha Airfield into ground artillery and dug them into the hills where they chose to make their stand.

Army patrols reported the reduced resistance and the American divisions began to move forward again. Their tanks could not go with the infantry because they were still mud bound and would be for a while. No one was sure of it yet but all that was left in the Japanese defenses was a strong rear guard force, probably exceeding no more than five thousand men. These men knew there would be no escape for them and they prepared themselves to die. The rest of the Japanese forces were busy completing their new defenses near the south tip of the island. At least thirty thousand Japanese soldiers were waiting in the southern escarpments. They were waiting for nothing except the chance to kill Americans.

The Navy carried out their duties without any ships sustaining damages.

May 31, 1945. The 7th Regiment pulled what was left of Easy Company back to the regimental area. They had taken thirty-four casualties in the deadly Wana Draw in one night and a day. The Regiment completed preparations to move south to new positions that would allow them to relieve elements of the 6th Marine Division. The 5th Regiment would complete the mop up of the Draw and enter an empty Shuri Castle. Empty except for snipers and some rear guard units.

"We didn't even get to see Shuri. We had fought for it for over a month but got pulled out before we could even see what we was fighting to take."

The 6th Marine Division was ready to commence their campaign against Oroku, but they didn't know yet they were only facing a rear guard and they wouldn't move until relieved. The arrival of the 1st Division would release them and protect their rear. Amphibious tractors were being rounded up for the 4th Regiment's scaled down amphibious landing. That would release them and they didn't know that most of the Japanese on their east flank had moved south to new defenses. They noticed that fire from the Shuri defenses had dropped, but they didn't attach any importance to it. They relied on the intelligence reports like the other divisions had done. So they waited for the 1st Marine Division who wouldn't arrive until June 2. These Marines didn't know it, but they were destined to fight on Oroku Peninsula almost until the end of the whole battle.

All of the Army divisions wiped out the pockets of resistance still facing them and cracked through the Shuri Defense Line. They had taken the Shuri Heights on the last day of May. It had been hoped that when Shuri fell all that would be left was for the Marines to clean out Oroku. But they now knew that the bulk of the Japanese were gone. Instead of winning the battle for Okinawa, it had just moved to a new location and would continue. No one knew how much longer it would take. They did know, by now, that planners estimated there were at least thirty thousand Japanese down south just waiting for them to catch up. Commanders, but not the men yet, knew the escarpments in the south would be the most incredible terrain yet faced.

The Navy carried out their routine battle assignments without any ships being hit by Kamikazes.

At the end of May the Americans took stock of the cost of the battle. Leaders had expected the battle to have ended long before now. Since it hadn't, they had reconsidered and expected the fall of Shuri to turn the fight into nothing more than a mop up actions. This had not happened either and the battle and its cost in lives would continue.

The Americans, to date, had killed at least sixty-two thousand Japanese and Okinawan soldiers. They estimated they might have killed another ten thousand that could not be accounted for. They had only two hundred Japanese prisoners that had been taken. None of the enemy soldiers had actually surrendered except Home Guards who were a native part of the Army but were not Japanese. The bulk of the real Japanese captives had been taken when wounded or unconscious from near-by explosions.

American losses, so far, were appalling and they would continue for almost another month. The Army and Marines had lost twenty-six thousand men dead and wounded! What was just as alarming was that, due to the type and length of close combat, there were already fourteen thousand psychiatric casualties.

CHAPTER NINE
THE MARINES CHASE THE RETREATING JAPANESE

Except for a rear guard of a few thousand soldiers the Shuri Defenses were empty. At first, General Buckner thought the battle was over except for mop up operations. He thought the Japanese had fled out of Shuri and scattered south. He did not believe they could reorganize and set up a new defensive line. His own difficulty in moving divisions through the rain and mud led him to the conclusion that the Japanese couldn't withdraw large units with their guns and equipment intact.

American intelligence had recovered from their earlier misunderstanding of the troop movement they had observed between Shuri and the southern Okinawa coastal escarpments. It was now known that the Japanese had a new defense line manned by thirty thousand soldiers with supplies and artillery. They were in and on the escarpments which appeared to be the most hostile land feature yet encountered. For an effective defensive position, what was left of the Japanese Army was crammed into a much too small of an area to be really effective. The defense line stretched across a three-mile line of high ground that consisted of cliffs, step-like plateaus and more cliffs. Both of the flanks were covered by the sea. The north side of the escarpments was flat and open land that any attackers would have to cross. General Ushijimi had concentrated his forces in this manner for a purpose. He knew he was fighting on borrowed time and his sole mission was to kill as many Americans as possible before the Japanese Army was completely wiped out. There was no place left to withdraw. Instead of trying to defend Okinawa any longer, the general just wanted a kill rate as high as possible. Concentrating his forces would work to his advantage in accomplishing his deadly goal. His main problem was that most of his troops were support and service personnel and had little infantry training. He had three major strongholds in his line; Yaeju-Dake, Yuza-Dake and Kinishi Ridge. He put what was left of his trained infantry in these positions with his best troops from the 24th Division installed at Kinishi Ridge. He knew that the Marines would be coming down the west side toward Kinishi Ridge and he had more concern for their fighting abilities than he had for the American Army. Placed between the strongholds were most of his untrained service troops with some veteran units to help guide them.

General Buckner was forced to come up with a new plan for continuing the battle for Okinawa. He would leave the Army's 77th Division in the Shuri area to clean it out and to protect the rear of the divisions going south. His 96th Division would advance down the center of the island and the two Marine divisions would proceed down the west side. All of the forces would converge on the enemy held escarpments, eliminate the Japanese and secure the island. It wasn't expected to take too much time because the final defenses were only four miles south of Shuri. Actually it would take nearly another month.

June 1, 1945. The 1st Marine Division sent the 7th Regiment further southwest to an assembly area in preparation of taking over the 6th Marine Division positions. They moved over captured land but the area was so dangerous that they managed to lose nineteen Marines in the maneuver.

"Tracy was a new first lieutenant that come in when we was about half way down the island. Later on, he got shot in the head. They flew him in, he was clean shaven, had a G. I. haircut and clean clothes. He carried a new M2 carbine. We had never seen one of them yet. They fired full automatic. The captain brought him down where I was squatting in the road. I was melting chocolate in my canteen cup over a piece of C2 composition and dipping them dog biscuits, they give you, in it and eating them. I had several weeks growth of beard and hair. My clothes was worn out and I had blood all over me, especially on my hands. It wasn't mine though, a couple of my guys had got hit earlier in the day. The captain told him that I was the most senior man in the squad right then. He said he wanted me to show Tracy around for a few days. Norton said that if I could keep Tracy alive that he was gonna make him company executive officer."

"The captain left and I offered Tracy the cup of chocolate and some dog biscuits but he wouldn't take them. He had seen me breaking off pieces of that hard chocolate with my bloody hands. Little flakes of blood was dropping in there but I didn't care. Tracy said that I was the direst, filthiest, Marine that he had ever seen and he wasn't about to eat any chocolate that I had made. We didn't have any water to wash in and I told him that some dried blood had fell in there but it wouldn't hurt him. We just laughed about it. He was a real nice guy. He showed me his new carbine and asked me what I thought about it. I told him that it was a nice light little thing to walk around with but it wasn't too good when you got into opposition with it. It didn't have no stopping power."

The 6th Marine Division's 29th Regiment was preparing to turn over their positions to the 1st Marine Division. The relief was scheduled for the next day. The 4th Regiment was making preparations for an amphibious landing on the seaward side of Oroku Peninsula. The 29th Marines and the 4th Marines would execute a pincher maneuver that would trap the Japanese between them.

The Army's 7th Division's infantry regiments headed directly south to cut off any Japanese forces trying to get out on the Chinen Peninsula. This was a mountainous land mass that jutted out to the east a few miles south of Shuri. The peninsula curved back north and formed the southern shore of Buckner Bay. No American force wanted to have to go in these mountains after the Japanese. Fortunately, Chinen Peninsula was not the area the Japanese were interested in defending.

The other two Army Divisions began to advance in a generally southern direction cleaning out small pockets of rear guard units as they went. Resistance was still there but it was very light compared to what the Army was used to and they made long gains.

Little damage occurred to ships in the fleet except for a few groundings. Machines, and men were worn out, the machines could be repaired the men just had to endure. Most sailors just adapted to a life of exhaustion and fear that seemed to have no end. Replacements saw veterans who acted more like robots than men.

June 2, 1945. In accordance with orders, the 1st Marine Division's 7th Regiment relieved the units of the 6th Marine Division's 22nd and 29th Regiments. The 1st Division lead units were now in the Kobakura area southwest of the abandoned Shuri defenses. The 7th Regiment had arrived about noon and without any delay they sent the 2nd Battalion to advance and seize the high ground south of the Naha Estuary. The battalion had to cross the Kokuba River that helped form the estuary. Easy Company was sent across first and came under fire. George Company moved over the river just behind Easy who had already made contact with a Japanese force. By late afternoon both companies had taken up positions in support of each other and both were attacked by a force of one hundred enemy soldiers. The Japanese attacked the line exactly where the Marines had set up a machine gun section and most of them were killed. By evening Fox Company had crossed the river and the battalion held the ridges south of Naha. They were in a perfect position to protect the 6th Division's rear and still move south after the retreating Japanese.

"One of the other squads had a squad leader named Shepherd. He got relieved of his command. He disobeyed orders. We had so many casualties there. Norton would come out and say there was a hill that we had to take. He would tell us to take it the best way we knew how. We had got a new lieutenant named Mason as our platoon leader. He was a by-the-book guy and he would send us straight up the hill. We got repulsed three times. Shepherd had got a lot of his men killed. The next morning Mason told Shepherd to go right up the hill again but Shepherd wouldn't do it. He said we would take the hill but he was gonna do it his way. He said going straight up the hill was nothing but murder and he wasn't gonna do it. Lt. Mason ordered him again to go up the hill and Shepherd wouldn't do it, so they relieved him from his command. We never saw him again and I don't know what they done to him. Mason got killed himself crossing the river at Naha. When he came up to us he brought a new platoon sergeant with him and he was worthless. When the fighting started he run and hid. I found him twice. Once, around Sugar Loaf, Norton told me to go find him and I did. He was over a mile away hiding in a cave, all the guys wanted to shoot him."

"Before Mason got himself killed, he got the Miller boys killed. They was cousins and a machine gun crew and everybody liked them. We was somewhere down around Sugar Loaf where the 6th had got clobbered. Norton always let us figure out where the best place was to dig a hole. He would just tell you to get your line set up. Mason come up there and told the Miller boys where to set up their machine gun. The Japanese counterattacked and we wasn't in position to cover the machine gun crew. The Miller boys just mowed them down but they was both killed. He put them in an exposed place and they was killed. Most of the guys wanted to hang or shoot Mason right on the spot. The thing that stops you from doing that is you just don't want to kill your own people."

"Somebody had to volunteer to find the dead. Somebody like me was always there when we took a hill and so I knew where the dead was. So, who better than me to go? The burial detail guys didn't know where everybody was and they was scared. They was, usually, drawing sniper fire. You had to have somebody to protect the burial detail and they just couldn't find everybody on their own. Like once I was scouting around by myself and I was near a little village the 6th Division had taken. It was raining and had been for a while. I spotted five or six dead Marines laying in a little ditch. Somebody had stuck a rifle up to mark the spot but it had fallen over. The mud had already covered up two or three of them. I stuck the rifle back up and had to go on. I bet that nobody ever found them. I believe I could still find that spot today. I bet they was listed as missing in action. You could see that mud was gonna cover over all of them. That old red mud just ran like gravy and we caused a lot of it by tearing everything up."

"When we was running maneuvers back on Guadalcanal we had run across some graves back in the jungle. They must have been buried by their buddies. They was already all grown over and you know that nobody ever went back and found them."

"Ever so often a Catholic chaplain would come up on the lines, I never seen a Protestant chaplain up on the lines, and he'd ask you if you was killed did you want to be buried on the island or be sent home? Those of us who knowed how they done it always said that if we was killed, we wanted to be buried on the island. When a guy got killed they would take one of his dog tags and his personal effects. They sent the personal effects back to his home. They kept his dog tag to put on his grave so they could either identify it or find him to send home if that was what he had wanted. They would gather all the bodies at a cemetery and bury them but they would get the dog tags all mixed up. You might be buried in grave three but your name might be on grave twenty. So even if you wanted to be buried back home, they might send your relatives somebody else's body. Why go through all of that."

"We went down to relieve the 6th Division and this was where General Shepherd just got the crap beat out of him. The 6th Division had just been made up before Okinawa. They was made up of the old raider guys and other old timers and a bunch of misfits. They were just busted up in these hills outside of Naha. They just got the crap beat out of them. The big joke was that they kept taking this hill but they couldn't hold it. They said the Japanese was short on ammunition and they would fall back till the 6th guys got on top of the hill, then they would really let them have it. They had the top of the hill zeroed in from about everywhere. They had guns cut into the cliffs and our artillery and bombs couldn't get them. You had to get something close enough that would shoot a flat trajectory. The Weapons Company guys and the tank's guns would do that but the trick was to get close enough. You had to fire right into the caves to get them."

The 6th Marine Division welcomed the arrival of the lead elements of the 7th Regiment and immediately began turning their positions over and moving to an assembly area to begin the attack on the Oroku Peninsula.

All of the Army Divisions continued a rapid advance to the south. They would have moved even faster except for the rain and mud and the presence of the many caves and tombs. Every one of these places had to be checked, cleared and sealed. Not to do so would have put small forces of hidden Japanese soldiers in the rear areas. There was also the ever present problem with supplies during the rainy weather.

A large Naval task group had moved north and the carrier planes had pounded and strafed the airfields in southern Kyshusu. Every enemy plane destroyed on the ground was one less for the Kamikaze pilots to hurl at a ship.

June 3, 1945. Orders for the 7th Regiment were for them to advance south and destroy all of the Japanese in their path. Between the Marines and the new Japanese defense line in the south were forces of Japanese left to delay the Marines. All of the rear guard knew their job was to die before letting any Marines get by them. They were not permitted nor did they want to seek the concealment and food waiting in the south. There would not be any further withdraw for these soldiers.

The 2nd Battalion began moving South against light resistance, at first. The bridge the engineers built over the river was the only way to receive supplies and the only way to evacuate the wounded. The Japanese knew this also and moved guns and mortars into place to bring fire on the bridge. Some of the fire was even coming from the west where the 6th Marine Division was operating. It became the 2nd Battalion's task to stop moving south and hunt down and eliminate all of the left over Japanese gun and infantry emplacements.

"We started running across Okinawan women nurses wearing Japanese uniforms. Some of our guys got killed playing with those pretty native girls. Some of them carried Bobbie traps in their rice baskets."

"In the afternoon we was in some Goddamned little town down close to Naha. We was supposed to cross a river but only one little outfit made it across. Real late in the day a Japanese plane come over and a Marine fighter plane shot him down. I was looking at it and a chute opened up. You could see motors and stuff falling but you never seen the man till his chute opened. So here he come, floating down on the other side of the town from us. We was in a yard in that little town. The yards was always walled and they had a pigpen in one corner. You could never see into one of these yards without going in it. It would have an opening but out in front would be a false door like a wall built out in front of the opening a little ways. They was put there to keep monsoons out or evil sprits or something. Anyway, they kept you from seeing in. We had went in there for the night and was in the pigpen. The wall was too high for me to see over. So I had to stick one arm up on the wall and raise myself to see over it. Every once in a while in the night you'd raise up to take a look. Late, I was on watch and I heard something. The Navy fired flares every twenty minutes all night long. When a flare went off, I raised myself up to look. I was looking right down the street but what I saw was a hand on top of the wall right by my face. There was a guy there and he had his head turned looking toward the street. He had a helmet on. I was hanging on the wall with one arm and holding that Tommy gun in my other hand. I raised my Tommy gun over the wall and put it about six inches from his head and pulled the trigger. Burrrrrrrrrrrrrrrrrrr, the Tommy gun went up and I fired all the way down the street before I could stop. I fell off the wall, I had fired a full thirty round magazine and the bullets went down the street hitting the tile roofs. You ought to have heard the racket that made. I had shot right down our own line. Roof tiles was falling off everywhere. All of the guys just started cussing. I know I got that old boy because I started firing just four inches from his head. Later on I found out that I had just wounded him. He crawled off and got captured by our guys the next day or so."

"You could hear someone moaning across the street all the rest of the night. Doherty was down the street and that loud moaning was bothering the guys. He shot into a doorway of a building and that moaning stopped. The next morning we went to look and it was a Japanese nurse. She had a grenade in her medical pouch so Doherty said it was too bad but she did have a grenade and she shouldn't have. My firing down the street had hit her and started her moaning. I had shot her accidently that night."

The 29th Regiment of the 6th Division started moving toward the land side of Oroku, while the 4th Regiment was loaded aboard landing craft with their tanks. The landing would commence the next day at daylight. The 4th Regiment discovered that the landing craft were large enough to have galleys and well-stocked food supplies. They had a fresh, hot Navy meal for the first and last time of the island battle.

The Army Divisions kept pushing south but had considerably slowed. The rain and mud created serious supply problems again. It also slowed and stopped the armor and heavy guns.

The *Allegan* an attack cargo vessel was struck by a Kamikaze but damage was only slight and did not even interrupt her duties.

June 4, 1945. The 2nd Battalion moved south again, encountering resistance from the Japanese rear guard. The Marines crossed the bridge built across the inlet under fire from hills in the 6th Division's area of operations. There were caves and tombs all along their southern route and progress was slow. Each cave had to be checked, blown and sealed. Even with these efforts, Japanese soldiers kept showing up in the rear. The regiment held back one whole battalion to deal with these determined enemy soldiers who kept popping up directly behind the advance battalion. It was a serious chore to protect the back of the 2nd Battalion as well as the supply line.

"The first platoon was the only one that had crossed the river when we got there and crossed over. We lost Caughman that day. A sniper got him. There was this new lieutenant that crossed just behind us and he got his leg blowed off. He was a real rum dumb. He had gotten a lot of people killed before so we didn't miss him."

"We was just in the left-hand corner of Naha moving south. We was gaining a lot of ground because the Japanese was falling back."

It was time for Oroku and the 6th Division Marines to go on the move. The 4th Regiment landed just north of the Asato Inlet on the muddy flats. By midmorning they had a battalion ashore with supporting tanks and self-propelled guns. The 29th Regiment was loaded in landing craft but was supposed to be held in reserve of the spearheading 4th Marines. Resistance was so light against the 4th Marines that the 29th Marines were ordered to land, also. They came ashore on the tip of the peninsula in the inlet that separated Naha from the peninsula. They started to build a bridge across the inlet that would take them to the high ground south of Naha and put them in position to advance inland. The engineers worked on the bridge under constant long range heavy machine gun fire. The 22nd Marines, located at the east end of Oroku where they had been fighting toward Shuri, had been fully relieved. They had turned to face the peninsula and now began to advance toward their sister regiments.

The Japanese they faced were the remnants of the Okinawa Base Force, all Naval personnel. Originally they had numbered ten thousand but after the earlier general withdraw there were only two thousand left. Most of the elite troops among the original force had been drained away as replacements at the Shuri defenses. Very few of them had any combat training, in fact, most of them were service troops. Even so, their leadership was superb and they possessed a great willingness to die while killing as many Marines as they could. There would be no retreating for them.

The Japanese had destroyed most of their own heavy guns when the May withdrawal had occurred but the troops had dismantled anti-aircraft guns and stripped the heavy machine guns and 40mm cannon from the destroyed plane at the Naha Airfield. They converted the guns to artillery and positioned them in the cave and tunnel system in the ridges and hills in the Northeast area of Oroku Peninsula, near Naha Harbor. There they waited for the Marines to come through their outposts.

The Army Divisions kept moving south hampered by the weather and its attendant supply problems. The Japanese new defense line in the Army's area of operations presented both divisions with a wall of coral that stretched across the southern tip of the island. The east side of General Ushijima's line was anchored by two strongholds called Hill 95 and Yaeju Dake. These positions were in the 7th Divisions path and it was their duty to attack these positions when they could finally get there. There was a rocky and broken coral valley near the right side of the 7th Division's area that was a natural path onto the Japanese held escarpments covered on both sides by Japanese heavy guns. It was a virtual "death valley" for the American soldiers.

The stronghold anchoring the west of the valley was still a part of Yaeju Dake. Here, this was a most formidable feature that was in the 96th Division's zone. It presented a one hundred seventy-foot cliff to the soldiers, then Yaeju Dake itself was located another sixty feet above the escarpment rim. The escarpment then sagged westward to another stronghold known as Yuza Dake then sloped further west all the way to the sea along Kunishi Ridge. This western feature was in front of and assigned to the Marines.

The fleet had few enemy planes to deal with and there was no damage but they were kept busy preparing their ships for the storm they knew was coming.

June 5, 1945. Jack and the 2nd Battalion continued south. Mud kept all of their vehicles grounded. Most were still north of the inlet. The Marines had to again resort to air drops for emergency supplies such as water, food and ammunition. Work parties had to hand carry other supplies miles back and forth through the muck. The wounded were carried up to five miles for treatment. Snipers shot at them and their carriers the whole length of the trails back. High ground in the 6th Division's zone kept pouring fire on the 2nd Battalion until they had to take some action. Tanks could move where the fire was coming from so the 2nd Battalion with tank and gun support crossed into the other division's zone and attacked the high ground. Before nightfall several Japanese positions and heavy guns had been eliminated.

"Before night we always withdrew back to a ridge, if they was one, and dug in. Two men in a foxhole. If there was a odd number then I dug in and stayed in a hole by myself. It was always better to have two men. You didn't sleep much. There was fire going on all night and the Navy fired flares over your head. Then there was your buddies. You had to know how responsible they was. You didn't know if he was gonna stay awake on his hour of watch or fall asleep, till you got to know him and trust him you just stayed awake all of the time. On top of that you had to bail the hole out when it was raining. The water run in around you all night, through the sides and come up from the bottom. It was hot in the day but of a night it got cool and it was cold when you was wet or laying in water trying to sleep. You just froze. There was a bathroom problem too. Nobody dared to get out of his hole at night, if a Japanese didn't get you, your own guys would shoot you. A lot of new guys didn't pay attention and got out of their holes to go to the bathroom. Well, a lot of them got killed doing that. The Japanese got some of them and some was shot by our own guys. We wasn't supposed to shoot at night because it would give your position away. You didn't even dare stick your head up or somebody would shoot. You could never get guys to stop doing that, shooting or getting out of their holes. They was just too many trigger happy guys. So you just had to deal with that nasty stuff down in your hole, it was better than getting shot."

"We just got used to being tired all of the time. The bad thing about it was that it worked on your kidneys. That cold, wet, hole made you ache and hurt like you had arthritis real bad all of the time. There was this old sergeant who came in late. He laughed at us because of the way we looked and acted in the mornings. After about four or five days we had to pull him out of his hole and prop him up against a tree, till the sun could shine on him. We couldn't hardly straighten him out till the sun shined on him for two or three hours. He was in his thirties, quite a bit older than the rest of us."

"You just stayed cold and wet, ponchos didn't work because you was laying in water so they didn't help, much. It bothered your kidneys, terrible. You had white feet because you didn't have any dry socks. Everybody had it. The skin would just come off. You just got accustomed to living like that. We learned one thing. The Japanese wore belly bands. We was told that they did that to keep their kidneys warm. If they was warm, it helped keep you warmer. Some of us cut up those old Navy blankets and made belly bands. Wool, when it stays wet, will still keep you warm. Other material won't do that. Everybody just lived like that, laying in that cold mud. You just kind of got use to it after awhile. We really didn't have any food, just those old nasty C Rations and sometimes we didn't even have them. I went from a hundred forty to a hundred twelve but I never felt bad at all from having hardly any food."

All three infantry regiments of the 6th Marine Division moved toward the enemy positions. Units of the 4th Regiment took Naha Airfield and turned it over to service units to repair and then use. The two regiments kept a study pace toward the Japanese defensive positions, taking out pockets and outposts as they went.

The two Army Divisions kept a slow pace too, moving southward toward their objectives in the new Japanese line. On the way they had to deal with a lot of "lost" Japanese soldiers who were still bent on killing Americans. These were individuals or groups of twos and threes who had become separated from their units and didn't know what to do. One thing that none of them would do was surrender. The Army had to clear and seal all of the caves and tombs along their route.

The battleship *Mississippi* was hit in the side by a Kamikaze. There was some damage to a few of her starboard five inch gun mounts but she stayed on station delivering gunfire in support of the ground forces. This ship's guns, probably more than anything else, had reduced Shuri to rubble when she had pounded the Shuri Heights defenses. The heavy cruiser *Louisville* had been hit and badly damaged by two Kamikazes in the battle for the Phillippines. She had to return to the States for repairs and arrived on the firing line at Okinawa just in time to be hit by another Kamikaze. This time her damages were minor enough that, although she initially retired, she was back on the line in a couple of weeks. The worst problem for the fleet was not the Kamikazes, though. A typhoon hit the Okinawa area and thirty-eight major vessels sustained storm damage. This was another reason for the Admirals to be even further irritated at the slow process of the ground operation. Storm damage to the fleet ran from minor to severe enough for several ships to have to be retired to the States for repairs. For example, the heavy cruiser *Pittsburgh* faced winds of seventy knots and a hundred foot waves. Her second deck buckled and her bow structure pushed up and then tore free. The captain and the crew used incredible seamanship in maneuvering the ship to seal off and strengthen the forward bulkheads with shoring. The crew battled the storm for seven hours and when it subsided the *Pittsburgh* was still afloat. This gallant vessel was repaired in the States, and later served during the Korean war.

June 6, 1945. The 6th Marine Division was supposed to keep pace with the advance of the 1st Division to protect their west flank. The former Division had gotten caught up in the battle for Oruko and failed their duty to their sister division. The 2nd Battalion turned west and attacked a fortified hill to protect their own flank. They were near the top when 22nd Marines from the 6th Division showed up. The 7th Regiment was determined to keep it's flank protected. So, instead of recalling their 2nd Battalion they sent them against another hill that was still in the 6th Division's zone but further south.

"We had two guys that wasn't even supposed to have been there, Slitz and Marques. They was both originals in the regiment. They started out in Samoa and had been through all the campaigns. Captain Norton had come in there somewhere and they was all buddies. Marques and Slitz had been through Guadalcanal, Cape Glouster and Peleliu. They was supposed to have gone home before Okinawa but they wouldn't go. Marques was a little guy that probably didn't weigh more than a hundred pounds. He was Norton's runner. He was his right-hand man. He was fast on his feet. For a while he got assigned to another company commander named Captain Beardsly. The company CO and his runner always shared a hole. Marques didn't have a watch so when he stood watch he had Beardsley's. He would wait till Beardsley fell asleep and turn the watch ahead and wake up Beardsley to stand to take his turn standing watch. In about a week or so Beardsley got to feeling real bad. He was just dead on his feet and didn't know what was the matter with him. After a while, Marques went back to Norton and Beardsley got better. Marques finally got hit and before he got evacuated he told us what he had done to Beardsley. When he found out about what Marques had done to him he just laughed. He was a hell of a nice guy and everybody was pulling dirty tricks on one and other. He just kept telling that story on himself."

The infantry regiments of the 6th Division with tank and Naval gunfire support closed in on the main Japanese defense positions west of Oroku town. This area was a jumbled mess of hills and ridges. It was, by now, the classic standard of the Japanese defensive positions on Okinawa. Every hill and ridge was fortified in a manner that allowed fire to be brought on every other hill and ridge. The whole area was criss-crossed with connecting caves and tunnels that created a powerful defensive complex. The Japanese problem that would be their downfall was the lack of manpower needed to fully hold the area for more than a few days.

The Army had slogged it's way south in the mud to within a thousand yards of the enemy positions. However, they were out of supplies and without armor. The attack on the final Japanese line could not begin until supplies, especially ammunition could be brought up. The soldiers could see the cliffs before them and they appeared invincible. What bothered them most was the sight of the flat open ground they would have to cross before they could get to the Japanese.

The fleet was facing ever decreasing flights of Kamikazes, but ships were sill being damaged by them. The escort carrier *Natoma Bay* was conducting flight operations when a Kamikaze got through the screen, came over her stern and crushed through the flight deck near the bridge. There was damage below decks and a twelve by twenty foot hole in the flight deck. Her crew repaired the flight deck and flight operations continued. She later withdrew for repairs. For so much damage, there were only twelve casualties. The minelayer *J. William Ditter* was credited with shooting down at least seven aircraft but a Kamikaze finally got to her and she was knocked out of the war, deemed not reparable and sold for scrap. The minelayer *Harry F. Bauer* had taken a torpedo back in May but it had not exploded. This time her luck would hold. She was operating with the *Ditter* and shot down several planes but took a hit close aboard that flooded two of her compartments. She had to withdraw for repairs and towed the *Ditter* to safety with her. She was repaired and returned to battle. Her crew was a little shocked to learn that during repairs there was an unexploded bomb found in one of the flooded compartments. The *Ditter* had thirty-seven crewmen killed and wounded but no one was even injured in the *Bauer*.

CHAPTER TEN
THE ITOMAN AREA

June 7, 1945. Hill 108 was now the target of the 2nd Battalion. It was plastered with artillery and Naval guns then assaulted and captured by George Company. Hill 108 was far enough south that it commanded the more level ground that ran to Kunishi Ridge. Small groups of Japanese ranging from ten to twenty ran from caves and tunnels into the open in an attempt to get to the west coast near Itoman. This area was still controlled by the Japanese. Artillery and machine guns cut most of them down. The rest were pursued by the Marines. The end of the day found the Marines in control of all of the coastal ground south of the Oroku Peninsula to Itoman. They were at the door of the new and final Japanese defense line.

"Somewhere around this time they hauled me out and put me in a little piper, an L5, to go up and observe and take pictures of Kunishi Ridge. We flew down there. There was a little valley and a long bare ground just as bare as it could be and not too close to any high ground. We didn't get any opposition, so we landed and I got out and took pictures of the escarpments and then we just flew back."

Eight battalions of the 6th Marine Division virtually surrounded the shrinking Japanese defenses on three sides. The fourth side was the mud flats of the Naha Inlet and the Japanese would be out in the open if they went there. There was a battalion of tanks with the regiments. They and infantry began the slow deadly process of clearing each opening and emplacement. One at a time. Sometimes, because of the lack of Japanese manpower the Marines ran through the tunnels and attacked the defenders from behind. Then they would move on the next strong point. Marine casualties were once again appalling for their efforts to overcome a much smaller force. The Japanese resolve to die killing Marines made up somewhat for the lack of men.

The American infantry waited and watched the enemy held escarpment a half mile to their front. Supplies were slowly making their way to the Army but there were still not enough to permit an assault. The armor was still having trouble with the mud and flooded streams that had to be bridged in order to cross.

The fleet's aircraft attacked, in force, airfields in southern Japan and a task force with some "borrowed" cruisers and destroyers from the Okinawa fleet brought fire on the Japanese in Brunei Bay, Borneo. The destroyer *Anthony* had been damaged by a Kamikaze on May 26 but had stayed on station and was now hit by another plane. This one also caused only minor damage and again the ship stayed on station.

June 8, 1945. During the previous night Japanese infiltrators had placed eight cases of demolition charges within the Fox Company Command Post without anyone noticing them. It was presumed they were meant for a pocket of about seventy-five Japanese who were holding a position near-by. Now, Fox Company busied itself with the elimination of the pocket. George and Easy Companies began an advance on Itoman.

"Somewhere around Itoman there was a road that went down and turned and ran into the escarpment. The Japanese was using that road. They decided to put me down there in a spider hole, on the curve so I could shoot some of them. They sent some guys down there to dig me a spider hole. When I went down there they had built a real good one too. Instead of building it up on the slope a ways they had built it right on the road turn so I was level with the road. It had a box to sit on and they had built a lid and put back the sod over the roof. I got in it in the night and the Japanese was using the road. I was out in front of the line about a quarter of a mile. When it got light, I opened it a little and saw that I was level with the road and right on the turn. Guys could see me coming down the road from any direction. No matter which way they was going when they came to the turn they was looking straight at me. I couldn't shoot, I couldn't even raise the lid except to peep out."

"They was moving troops on the road all right but they had them spaced out about twenty yards. I had a 'Walkie Talkie' and called them and told them there wasn't no use in shelling or bombing that road because they wasn't moving more than about forty troops an hour. I didn't want no barrage coming down on top of me, neither. They said for me to stay there, they was pushing down the road toward me."

"When my outfit came by, I got out and joined them. They was a knocked down house just down pass my hole but they was a rock wall still standing. There was a boy about eleven to sixteen years old sitting up against that wall. I don't know how come, apparently he had been armed and somebody had disarmed him. He was just sitting against that wall and he wanted somebody to shoot him. He was a great big heavy boy. He was calling out, 'Shoot me', because he didn't want to be captured. Nobody would shoot him, everybody just laughed at him and walked on pass him. I was walking right behind Doherty. The kid looked right at Doherty and said, 'Shoot me.' Well, Doherty walked over to him and shot him five times right in the face with his .45. I can still see them five holes in his face. He just kept sitting there with them holes in his face. He had shot him point-blank. My God, I thought, is he ever gonna fall over? Doherty said that he wanted to go be with his ancestors so he sent him on his way. Nobody else would do it."

For the first time in weeks, supplies began to pour into the 1st Division's infantry regiments. Capturing access to the sea gave the Navy a way to bring in supplies via the use of amphibious boats and vehicles. The seriously wounded could now be taken directly to hospital facilities on nearby ships. The 1st Division personnel, who do these things, credited the 2nd Battalion with one thousand nine hundred twenty-five actually counted enemy killed on the trek south from the Shuri Lines. Untold numbers of dead Japanese had been sealed in caves and could not and would not ever be counted. Thousands of civilians were likewise killed and sealed in caves. The number of civilians killed on their island would forever be a guess.

The 6th Division closed in further on the Japanese pocket on Oroku taking and making casualties. The Japanese lines were pulled ever closer to each other. As the defensive area diminished the ferocity increased. Suicide bombers charged the tanks over and over again with satchel charges. When the Japanese saw any Marines bunch up, they countercharged in small force with the motive of killing or dying. They would not retreat. Nighttime infiltrators plagued the Marines and cost more lives.

Supplies were now pouring into the Army's assault regiments. Armor had moved up and the men prepared themselves for crossing the open ground in the morning and going at the cliffs.

There wasn't any damage to the fleet, except for a few accidents that are always expected when so many ships operate in such a confined area. Refueling and replenishment of ships is highly dangerous to man and ship even in peacetime.

June 9, 1945. The 7th Marines were at the north edge of the coastal town of Itoman working through the ever present enemy outposts that were between them and Kunishi Ridge.The 2nd Battalion thought that the coastal town was on the north side of an area stream but it turned out to be on the south bank. A patrol was sent across the stream to scout the area. The Japanese let the Marines cross then opened fire on them. When this firing started, other Japanese who were hiding on the north shore opened up also. The Battalion spent the rest of the day wiping out the hundred or so enemy soldiers on the north stream side.

"They ordered us out up against a little escarpment. They wasn't no way to climb it and we just got clobbered. Norton got his radioman killed there. I think we was just ordered out there to draw fire so they could do something else down the line. Norton never said but I'm sure that's what they done. I went back to the Captain to tell him that we couldn't get up there. He said that we had been ordered out of there as fast as possible. He said it was ever man for himself. The other platoons came running by and we took off after them. We had started running back and a machine gun over in the valley opened up on us. I think it was one of the Army's guns. We had to run back through these rice paddies. They was full of water but they had rock terraces that you could walk on, about a foot wide. I was behind Norton about two or three guys back. There was a mango tree ever once in a while and a Japanese soldier stepped out from behind one right in front of Norton. Norton just stiff armed him. He didn't even slow down he just kept running. That Japanese just flew out into the paddy and landed on his ass. When I come by, there he sat stuck in the mud. He was just sitting there with his mouth hanging open. His rifle was stuck in the mud with the barrel down. Everybody that ran pass him just left him alone. Nobody ever even bothered him."

"The Navy had lost the town of Itoman. Me and Carson had to go find it for them. The Navy couldn't get very close to shore along here because of the reef. They was supposed to shell the town of Itoman before our guys got there. They shelled the town they thought was Itoman but it was a mock-up town. They had mock-up tanks built out of wood. They had a mock-up airport with planes made out of water reeds, all fixed up to look like Zeros."

"Later in the day they sent me and Carson out to scout the real town. We was just outside the "lost town" watching the ridge about a quarter of a mile to the east of us. We seen a guy through our spotting scope come out and go up a tree. We knew he was a sniper. We decided to go get him. We wasn't too brave so we moved slow. One of us would work forward a ways while the other would cover him. We took turns doing that and every once in a while we'd put the scope on him to see if he was still there. It was right at the edge of town and it was about five o'clock. That was about the time we wanted to get in that town so we snuck up on the guy as close as we dared but then we couldn't see him. It wasn't a very big tree, only about five inches but it was real tall. We knew that he hadn't seen us otherwise he would have fired. We was close and we decided to capture him instead of killing him. Carson went around behind him and I went around in front of him. Carson got up to him and saw he didn't have a weapon. He was an Okinawan boy and we tried to get him to come down. He wouldn't come down so Carson went up the tree and sawed off the limb he was on with his big knife. He fell out of the tree and we captured him. He was a twelve year old boy. He wasn't a sniper, he was a lookout. We had scared him to death by sneaking up on him. He could speak English."

The 6th Division pressed on against the ever smaller pocket of Japanese still holding on. The Marine tankers lost thirty of their massive machines, mostly due to suicide bombers and their powerful satchel charges. The Japanese liked to throw themselves into or under the tank's track. That would guarantee a disabling of the tank but even when they missed, the forty pound charges could make a mess.

The 7th Army Division moved forward to attack the Japanese stronghold of Hill 95. The attack had to be head on. The cliffs at the sea edge prevented any kind of flanking attempt. The spearheading companies had to go up a slope of broken and cluttered coral to get to the cliffs of the hill. This odd area was eight hundred yards long, artillery did very little damage to the coral and the whole length was pocked with cavities that hid enemy soldiers. There was no progress made in penetrating the hidden Japanese positions and the Americans had to withdraw.

The other regiment of the 7th Division advanced into the Japanese lines at the east side of Yaeju Dake and in the cluttered and tangled valley between

Yaeju Dake and Hill 95. Japanese fire at the exposed soldiers killed or drove back all but a few who managed to crawl through the fire to the base of the cliff and even grabbed some high ground.

The 96th Army Division was in attack position before the escarpment in front of Yaeju Dake. This was the heaviest fortification in the Japanese's final defensive line. Just west of here across a sagging area in the coral and rocks was the Yuza Dake. This whole part of the defense line was the responsibility of the 96th Division. To match pace with the Division on their east flank they would attack the next morning.

Some ships of the fleet were engaged in support of Marine landings on some of the smaller and until now ignored Islands. Resistance was light to none. The destroyer escort *Grendreau* was working close in to Okinawa giving gunfire support to the Marines ashore when she was hit by fire from a hidden shore battery. Damage wasn't too bad and her crew effected repairs while she continued her gunfire support missions.

June 10, 1945. The 2nd Battalion along with the rest of the 7th Marines had pretty well cleared the north side of the Itoman stream and attention was now turned toward the town and remaining high ground to the east and south. Marine artillery, and tanks fired on the town from the north. A cruiser added it's six inch guns from the sea and armed amphibious vehicles came up to the seaside edge of the town and opened fire. Infantry then attacked and swept through the town. After the bombardment, losses were much heaver than expected, due to the heavy mining of the town by the Japanese.

"After we captured that boy we thought was a sniper we dug in for the night and started out again the next morning to find the real town. It was all underground, about. The road that went to the town went around through the hills. There was a real pretty little mountain that the road went through instead of around or over. It was just as smooth and grassy as could be on both sides. Nice pretty green grass growing on it. They had put the road through it. We found the town and pulled back out of it to guide the troops in. The road just went right to it. We had gone back out the road tunnel and found a place to lay down and wait. We hadn't seen anything in the town, just a few Home Guard snipers in there. When you would show up and shoot one of them all the rest would leave. Me and Carson was laying in the ditch on both sides of the road, watching our infantry come up. There was supposed to be tanks but they always showed an hour or two late. They didn't want to get there till the battle already ensued. That way they knew they was gonna have plenty of protection in front of them."

"Suddenly here come a Japanese tank through the tunnel behind us. We never seen him but he had to be hid around that town somewhere. Here he come, clunk, clunk, clunk, down the road. Us and our troops coming up just stared at him, not doing anything. He went up the road a little ways and turned off and went in the brush. Then here come our Shermans down the road, wide helmets on and flags flying. They stopped and a guy in the first one asked us where the town was at. We told him that he had a Japanese tank behind him off down the road a ways in the brush. He said that he didn't see any tank So I walked down there and showed him where it went into the brush. You could see where it mashed down the brush. I told him that was as far as I was willing to go. They buttoned up that Sherman and zoomed down into the brush. He must have been going thirty MPH. That Japanese tank had only gone about thirty or forty yards in the brush and stopped. That Sherman went in there full blast. All he could see with was his power scope. He run right into the back of the Japanese tank. He couldn't even fire because his gun was down underneath the Japanese tank. So he backed up and fired point blank. He just blew that tank all to hell. I always wondered where that Japanese driver thought he was. He was either drunk or he couldn't see too good not to have fired on our guys coming down the road. The 'lost town' was found though."

The 6th Division on Oroku were fighting as they had been for several days. The Japanese they faced were ever closer to annihilation.

The 7th Division's 32nd Regiment jumped off with another attack against the coral ridge, trying to get to Hill 95 the east coast anchor of the Japanese line. Fighting went on all day among the rocks and outcroppings. By evening the slope was in American hands and they discovered that the ridge did not provide a way to the hill. There was a saddle between the ridge and Hill 95 that was covered by murderous fire from the Hill.

The other 7th Division regiment, the 17th Infantry, started forward and at the end of the day had reached the escarpment. The cliffs rose one hundred seventy feet above the men. It was obvious to every one that going up these cliffs was all but impossible in the face of enemy fire. The regiment decided that the only way up would have to be at night.

The 96th Division didn't fair as well. Their two attack regiments ran into stiff opposition out in the flat area away from the escarpment base they were trying to reach. By nightfall the 383rd Regiment was bogged down in a fight in the town of Yuza and did not reach the base of the cliffs. The other regiment, the 381st, managed to get onto high ground level with the base of Yuza Dake. They were taking fire from both flanks but decided to stay there through the night. A heavy smoke screen was laid on the regiment's position so they could dig in without the Japanese being able to register their holes. The Japanese commander thought the smoke was cover for the American's withdrawal and he assembled a company, changed them into civilian clothes for the purpose of going down and infiltrating the American line in mass. They would pose as civilians in order to get close to the American line. Since the Americans weren't leaving they spotted this activity and called fire in on the troop concentration just when they were all out in the open. Most of the Japanese infiltrators were killed. The ones who were left did enough throughout the night to make sleep impossible.

The destroyer *William D. Porter* had been in several battles and had shot down numerous Japanese planes but this time she missed one. The Kamikaze actually missed the ship by a narrow margin but it was laden with explosives which exploded underneath her. The ship was crippled and began to sink but her crew fought for three hours to keep her afloat. They failed and were forced to abandoned her. None of her crew was killed but sixty-one were injured. This destroyer had a fine war record except for one tiny blemish. In 1942 she was escorting the battleship *Iowa* across the Atlantic. The *Iowa* was carrying the President to a war meeting in Africa and along the way the battle group began conducting war exercises. During one of these drills the *William D. Porter* managed to fire a live torpedo at the President's ship. The *Iowa* was able to turn in time and the torpedo missed but some heads did roll.

June 11, 1945. The 2nd Battalion had spent the night dug in, in and around ITOMAN. Now they headed for the nearby Kunishi Ridge. They were met with massive fire from the ridge and withdrew to Itoman, there most Marines spent the day destroying the caves in and around Itoman. Engineers removed the mines and amphibious tractors brought in supplies and evacuated the wounded. Each time patrols set out for Kunishi Ridge they were driven back by Japanese fire from the ridge. Artillery and other guns didn't seem to have any effect in reducing the enemy fire.

" Itoman was a pitiful town. They had a field hospital at the edge of the town. Our shells had torn all the windows out of it. For cover they had taken up the floor and they was about four feet beneath the top of the foundation. These ones that was in there had to have been their worst patients because they hadn't taken them with them when they moved out. They was just lying there on stretchers and the flies had just about eat them up. All you could hear was them begging to be shot. There was a guy lying there that had a fresh wound in his kneecap. His hands was all buggered up and he couldn't move them. The flies had eat all the skin off his lips and had started eating the skin on his face. He begged to be shot because of his dishonor of being captured. Well, nobody would shoot any of them it was just too pitiful. They saved all of them that they could. I seen that guy the next morning, they had cleaned him up and he was looking pretty good. It looked like he had even gotten over his dishonor. Boy, was it ever pitiful. All of their medics had just abandoned them. Usually when they done that they made sure all the patients that got left behind was dead. None of these guys was mobile. Some of them was Koreans that the Japanese had brought over there. They had brought a lot of people over there from countries they had captured."

"They was caves all over this area and things got pretty nasty on both sides. The Japanese had taken all the women and children with them when they went south. We found that ever single cave that had Japanese in it, had women and children in it too. When you blew a cave you knew you was killing women and children. There was no way to avoid it. Nobody could figure out any other way of doing it. You couldn't go in there without being killed. Sometimes our guys would talk them out and then the Japanese would kill them, or the Japanese would hide among them and come out to kill you. Sometimes the Japanese would dress like women and come out with booby traps under their clothes. It was safer for us to just blow the cave with everybody still in it. Our guys just got hardened to that"

"One fellow carried two canteens. You could hear the one on the left rattle. He had it full of Japanese gold teeth. It had got pretty rough for both sides. The ones who done that would shoot the dead Japanese in the back of head. That would loosen the teeth and make it easier to pick them out with a pair of pliers. It seemed pretty sadistic to me. I had heard, but I don't know that it really happened, that some even pulled the gold teeth out of our dead. If I had seen that happen I'd have shot the guy on the spot. I hope that didn't happen and it was just a story."

"When I got wounded I had one gold tooth hanging around my neck on a chain.

The medics stole it. I had picked it up out of an old skull. I didn't go in for it but you had to fit in, be one of the guys so they would trust you. If you had done it you couldn't point the finger at anybody else. So I hung that one around my neck so everybody could see it. Most of the guys who done that was from big cities."

The fighting battalions of the 6th Marine Division had advanced all the way to the cave system headquarters of Admiral Ota, the commander of the Japanese force on Oroku Peninsula.

The commander of the 32nd Infantry, a regiment of the 7th Division, happened to observe a group of civilians making their way down the cliff face of Hill 95. They were on a narrow path that wound it's way up the hill. The men of the regiment worked a flamethrower tank to the bottom of the cliff. Army engineers had come up with a flame hose that attached to a tank and could be carried far beyond the tank's flame throwing range. Infantrymen attached the hose to the tank and carried the nozzle with two hundred feet of hose up the path. Artillery barrages were poured on the hill to mask the movement up the path. When enough riflemen were strung out along the path to press the attack the nozzle man, a tank officer, sprayed the hill as far as his flame could reach. The infantry rushed forward and the eastern most two hundred yards of the Japanese defenses had fallen. More than enough soldiers came up on the hill to ensure that the Japanese could not dislodge them.

Their sister regiment was at the bottom of the cliffs at Yaeju Dake planning a night assault. It would take great coordination because once they reached the top they would not be able to stay there without pinpoint artillery accuracy. They would have only a toehold on the top rim of the escarpment and their position would be perilous.

The regiments of the 96th Division could not move. The 383rd was stuck at Yuza town trying to clear the determined enemy out and resistance was too strong for the 381st to get any higher on the cliffs. Units from both regiments worked hard to clear and seal all of the caves and tombs in the areas they held. The Japanese were quite concentrated in the area and fought to the death.

The Kamikazes only managed to hit a small infantry landing craft. Unfortunately the craft was loaded and eleven men died and another twenty-nine were wounded.

CHAPTER ELEVEN
KUNISHI RIDGE AND JACK IS WOUNDED

June 12, 1945. The 7th Regiment commander decided the only way possible to get across the open ground to Kunishi Ridge was to cross by night. To do otherwise would likely put an end to the regiment. The 1st and 2nd Battalions were chosen to cross. Fox Company of 2nd Battalion was sent out in the lead at 0300 and by 0500 were in a position actually on the ridge. George Company was caught in the open and had to pull back. Fox Company could not be left alone on the ridge and George tried to come to their aid three times that day. All attempts to cross failed. After dark, George along with Easy made it over the open ground to the base of the ridge. Night attacks fooled the Japanese once again.

"We were at the south end, about two miles left to the end of the island. It was all escarpments, they even hung over the ocean, four or five hundred foot escarpments. The Japanese had backed up in there. I don't know how many thousands of troops they had in a little two mile area. Our problem was we was bunched up too. We was getting a lot of casualties from our own fire, because they had an 'L' shaped line. It was even dangerous for a mile from our own small arms fire. Somebody would shoot across the apex and right into our own line. We dropped leaflets asking them to surrender and some old Japanese commander sent word to the captain that they would never surrender. The captain said he didn't want them to surrender, that we was going after them. So that's what we done."

The Marines of the 6th Division pushed up and onto the last hill of the Japanese defenses, before them were the mud flats on the Naha Harbor. There were a lot of enemy soldiers just milling about on the mud flats and Marine riflemen begin to shoot them down. They stopped before killing all of them and one hundred fifty-nine surrendered to the surprise of the Marines. They were native conscripts but it was the largest number to surrender that had taken place on Okinawa.

The Marines spent days mopping up the area and clearing and sealing caves and tombs. They sent search parties in the head quarter's tunnel complex to find the command post. This tunnel system was so complicated that it took them two days to find the Admiral's quarters. He, his staff and two hundred soldiers had committed suicide in the center of the tunnel complex. Two thousand poorly trained Japanese and native soldiers had held off a full Marine Division for ten days. Worse, was that this small unit had killed and wounded one thousand six hundred eight Marines who had out manned and outgunned the Japanese at an almost unbelievable rate.

The tank battalion working against Hill 95 could now get to a road that went along the western base of the hill. The tanks burned out enemy positions as they went and when necessary took their flame hose up the hill to burnout pillboxes. By the end of the day the tanks had gone up on the hill with more infantrymen.

The night attack by the 17th Infantrymen began at 0300. To the delight of the soldiers a heavy fog blanketed the area. Once again the Japanese were surprised because the Americans never moved at night. When dawn came, there were three companies on the escarpment set up in perimeters that were meant to hold when the Japanese counterattacked. When full light came, to the American's surprise, there weren't any Japanese on the escarpment. The Japanese knowing that never attack at night had withdrawn to escape the shelling. The intent was to return to their positions when light came. They came back in groups of fifty and less, expecting nothing. All day long the American soldiers shot the enemy until there weren't any more to shoot.

The 7th Division had breached the Japanese defense line and held the high ground that had once been the east stronghold of the whole line.

The success of the 7th Division provided the 96th with the opening they needed. They sent a company from the 381st up the escarpment being held by units of the 7th Division. This company fought it's way west until they were directly above their own units. There was a road and even a staircase that went up the cliffs where they were now located. Both ways up were covered by intense fire that stopped any movement. Guns were concealed in a chain of caves and the American soldiers spent the day clearing each cave. They worked from the bottom and from the top at the same time. By dark they had a full battalion on top of the escarpment and were ready to attack Yaeju Dake itself the next day.

188

Their sister regiment, the 383rd, and the now committed reserve regiment, the 382nd could not make any headway against Yuza Dake at all. In a flanking movement like they had done on the left going through the 7th Division they pulled right into the 1st Marine Division's zone. This time they failed. They ran into terrain that was so heavily mined that combined with the Japanese fire they were completely stopped. There was a ridge facing them that had five hundred counted cave openings from which poured enemy fire.

The Navy shot down all of the small number of planes sent out by the Japanese.

June 13, 1945. The three Companies of the 2nd Battalion were at Kunishi Ridge. Fox was barely on the ridge and the other two companies were at the base. These already depleted companies had taken eight-six casualties the day before. Reinforcements, water and ammunition were desperately needed or the Marines could not hold their position. Crossing the open space was just next to impossible. Crossing with loads was impossible. The wounded had to be evacuated or many of them would die. The regiment cut the tank crews to a minimum and began hauling ammunition, water and riflemen to the ridge. They returned with the wounded. The Japanese fire knocked out many of the tanks, killing the tankers, the evacuating wounded and the replacements coming in.

"The fighting kept getting worse but we all knew by this time that the battle was almost over. They was jumping off the cliffs, Japanese and civilians. We figured that when this ended we was just going on to fight in Japan so morale wasn't that good"

Regardless of losses, regardless of the heavy fire, regardless of everything, Fox, George and Easy Companies kept fighting to gain ground up the ridge. The replacements brought in by the tanks melted away. One hundred forty Marines went down as casualties. Battleships fired on the Japanese positions as did cruisers, destroyers, Marine artillery, tanks and aircraft. Despite the support fire, when the Marines tried to move the Japanese fire actually increased. They and their guns were dug so deeply into caves that were so strong that all the fire brought to bear on them did little damage.

"I had two men down out in a little rice paddy and none of the tanks would stop for them. A tank was coming back, all buttoned up, and I stepped out from behind the paddy dike in front of the tank. I shot his periscope out with my Tommy gun. He stopped and unbuttoned her because he couldn't see. He asked me what the hell I was doing. I told him I wanted him to pick up the two guys laying in the mud. He said he wouldn't do it because he had been ordered to get out of there as fast as he could. He had a spare periscope, they always carried a couple of spares. I told him I would shoot that one out too if he so much as moved that tank. He could have gone on and there was really no way to stop him if he had. His crew got out and picked our guys up and took them out. I never knew what happened to them. They might of even gotten killed, a lot of guys did, strapped on the sides of those tanks down there."

Except for the Marines of the 22nd Regiment, the 6th Division would remain on Oruko Peninsula in reserve for the remainder of the battle for the island. The 22nd Regiment would be needed in a few days, in the south, to assist the 1st Marine Division.

General Ushijima knew that the 7th Army Division had to be thrown off of the eastern side of his line for his defense to survive. He raised companies of service troops and even turned many of his artillerymen into infantry and sent them against the 7th Division. These were poorly trained and poorly lead demoralized men. They were starving and most didn't have weapons other than grenades and satchel charges but they still fought hard to keep the Americans from advancing on the General's Headquarters. They were no match for the 7th Division but they wouldn't surrender, and the Division had to slow down and dig them out of their positions. They were too dangerous to bypass.

The 96th Division's regiments fought all day without gaining any ground.

The only out of the ordinary event for the fleet was the grounding of the battleship *Idaho* on a reef. In addition to the damage caused by the grounding she was a sitting duck for several hours. There were command sighs of relief when she was towed free. Ship groundings and accidents were always investigated and blame fixed. A lot of senior officer's careers were blemished or ended over these matters regardless of the combat situation.

June 14, 1945. Again, massive fire was laid on Kunishi Ridge and again it failed to slacken the Japanese gunfire. The ground to the ridge was still swept with incredibly accurate fire. Supplies, wounded and replacements could only be moved by tanks. Air drops of supplies were added and helped although many of the drops landed where they could not be recovered because of enemy fire.

2nd Battalion hadn't been able to move, but the 1st Battalion made it up on the ridge and captured the leveled town of Kunishi. Marines were now on the ridge but the defenders continued to fight as hard as always. Adding to the misery of the 2nd Battalion's companies, that night a large force of infiltrators penetrated their lines. Hand to hand combat added to the horror of being a Marine rifleman.

"We had been pounding Kunishi Ridge for days with everything we had, battleships, artillery, rockets, you name it. Then when we started forward they fired more stuff at us then they had before we pounded them."

"I could never comprehend why they pushed us so hard the last few days. The Japanese knew they was whipped and was committing suicide as fast as they could, except for the ones we was fighting. If we had just slowed down or even backed off a little, they would have done themselves in and we wouldn't have lost so many guys."

In the Army's zone, the rag-tag Japanese force sent to try to regain the east end of their line made a concentrated night attack on the front elements of the 7th Army Division. They caused little harm and hundreds were virtually wiped out by the now more spirited American infantry. The end was now in sight. They were coming across a lot of Japanese who had already committed suicide.

The regiments of the 96th Division kept advancing south taking out each and every cave as they went. They overran and captured Yaeju Dake.

The fleet was aware that the ground battle was drawing to a close and plans were being prepared to get ships that wouldn't be needed much longer to repair facilities to ready them for the next invasion. The carriers would soon be able to go further north and use their air power against Japan proper.

June 15, 1945. 2nd Battalion kept up the fight but made little headway. The Japanese positions in their area were the heaviest encountered on the ridge. The Japanese were so concentrated at this point that small counterattacks were a regular tactic. Supporting fire was as heavy as ever and call fire missions brought down hundreds of the Japanese when they came out in the open to attack. The 1st Battalion was fairing better and consolidated their position on the northwestern slope of the ridge. They began to systematically clear and seal the caves and tombs in their area.

"We was glad when they would do those little counterattacks. We just mowed them down. You knowed that when you killed one of them out in the open, there was one less up on the escarpment waiting for you. Mostly though, it seemed like they was never gonna run out of men."

"There was open ground you had to cross to get to the ridge. Most of the battalion had crossed it in the dark but it wasn't dark when we went across. We started across the open ground till we ran out of cover. They had a raised road that went in there across the rice paddies but they had it mined. When we started in there, they was three or four wrecked tanks so you knew you couldn't go down the road. They even had it covered with crossfire. You couldn't move on the road."

"We had crawled through the grass till we got to about the middle of the valley and the grass run out. Machine guns opened up on something out ahead a ways. When it quit, I crawled up there and there was a guy there named Woods. Cpl. Woods. I didn't know who he was with or where he had come from. A ricochet had hit him. I turned him over and looked at him. A bullet had hit his jaw and come out his temple. He spit out a tooth or two and asked me for a cigarette. I give him one. Blood was running out his mouth. I figured he was a goner but I told him that I could bandage him and I would get him a corpsman. He wouldn't let me get him a corpsman. He said a corpsman coming out there would only get killed. I zipped open a 4x4 bandage and put it on the left side of his face. I told him he would have to hold the bandage on the other side while I wrapped it all up. He didn't know till then that the bullet had gone clean through his head. He stopped me and told me to get going, he knew we had to go. I started to crawl back. I thought, 'there goes a dead guy and he don't even know it."

"Later on when I got wounded and was taken out to the hospital ship, I saw a guy leaning against the rail looking at me. He was standing there with two canes just looking down at me. That night when a doctor come around to look at me, I asked him how Woods had survived. Of course, he didn't know who Woods was because he had treated so many guys. I told him it was a guy who had a bullet go clean through his head. He remembered him when I said that. He said that Woods was alright. He had lost some teeth and he would have to have some gristle put back in there and he needed a plate put in his head. I said that I had seen his brain sticking out of that hole. The doctor said that he had lost a little but it only affected his balance. The rest of his brain was supposed to pick that up."

"Woods flew out of Guam with me, on the same plane, so I know he made it. I couldn't believe a guy could get shot like that and not even lose consciousness. He had a pretty good sized hole in his temple."

The Army's 7th Division moved south through the Japanese lines. They were in ground that was made up of large boulders and scattered coral ridges. Even so, tanks were able to operate and for the most part they just burned the earth wherever the infantry wanted to go.

The soldiers of the 96th Division turned their attention to Yuza Dake but could not take it. They had some tank support but not enough because the terrain wouldn't permit it. The Japanese had dug a tunnel over a mile long through the escarpment and kept replacement soldiers pouring into the division's lines.

The fleet suffered only slight damage to a destroyer that had a collision while refueling. An occurrence that had become a little too common due to the utter exhaustion of the sailors.

June 16, 1945. The 1st and 2nd Battalions continued their attacks. The 1st Battalion rapidly captured all Kunishi Ridge that was in their area of operations and commenced mopping up operations. The reserve 3rd Battalion moved forward and went up the ridge behind the 1st Battalion mopping up as they went. By nightfall their section of the ridge was secure.

The 2nd Battalion still experienced a large Japanese force but had fought their way to their first high ground. Japanese fire from even higher ground still raked the flat land in front of the ridge forcing the battalion to continue using tanks as they had every day. The tanks had brought out hundreds of wounded Marines and unloaded them in a protected area but Japanese fire prevented any evacuation. They decided to bring in the spotter planes and evacuate the wounded one at a time.

"We was tail end squad that day. The first squad got clobbered, they didn't make it. Some of them got as far as the base of the cliff. Doherty was next. He had a new medic with him, a brand new guy. The Navy had run out of corpsman, so they grabbed some new Marines and gave them a few days training in the field hospital. Then they give them a medical pack and sent them to the lines as medics. I doubt if he even knowed how to open his medical pack let alone help somebody. We was sitting and waiting behind a rock to see if the first squad made it. That new medic said that he hoped he got a Purple Heart up there real quick so he could go home. He said that he didn't like the looks of this place at all. Doherty and them took off and they didn't make it. Dohery come back with a bullet through his arm. It had gone through his arm and through his BAR man and hit the medic in the hand. It had just blown his hand to pieces. When he come by, I said, 'Well, it looks like you got your Purple Heart,' and he said he wanted to get it but not this bad. His hand was a mess. He left his medical pack with me and went on back. Doherty wasn't hit bad enough to pull out but most of his squad was."

"Norton sent word up that we was next, we was his last resort and we made it. We lost four guys but we made it. I called Norton and told him we was up on the ridge and running out of ammunition and we couldn't hold it. It was pretty late when we got up there. Norton said that we had to hold it and he would get plenty of ammunition to us.

"When we got up on the ridge it was late. The reason that we made it and they didn't was there was a little cliff overhang and they tried to go out around it and got away from the cliff. That didn't work. We hugged that cliff and was under the overhang and they couldn't shoot down on us. All they could do was drop grenades on us and their grenades wasn't nearly as powerful as ours was, so they didn't mean much to us. So there we was, up on the ridge under a overhang. If you moved about ten feet out they would shoot you. Otherwise they couldn't get nothing down on you. The Japanese couldn't get us from the cliff but they could come down the ridge slope and get us and that was what they was gonna do. We was facing a real bushy slope that they would come down."

"I called the Captain and said that about five of us had made it up there but we didn't have much ammunition. He said not to worry about it that they would get us ammunition. I told him we had some but without enough to last through the night we wasn't gonna make it and dark was still several hours away. The Captain said, 'Use your ammunition! By God, I'm gonna guarantee you we're coming in there with tanks loaded with ammunition for you.' The first tank made it, dropped the ammunition and took off. They couldn't stay there. They was under tremendous fire. We backed off and dug in and started shooting. At first we didn't even shoot at Japanese we shot at every bush we seen. You couldn't miss, because, hell, we had thousands of them pushed into them hills. Just before dark, early in the evening, they just sounded like they was cheering a football game. Here they come in just a wave, a counterattack. Bout all of them had shed everything down to a gee string.

Naked as a jaybird except for a jockey strap. All they had was their rifle and bayonet, yelling 'Banzai' all the way down the hill and we mowed them down in heaps. Hell, we had plenty of Tommy gun ammunition and plenty of BAR ammunition by then. There didn't have to be very many of us. We got set up in a crossfire on them. We didn't have no trouble finding them. I didn't know how bad it was till the next morning, really."

"We was holding the bottom of the slope, it was almost a cliff it was so steep, looking up until about dark. As soon as it got twilight we moved up on top where they had been coming at us. As soon as they slacked off we moved up. They had backed up after dark because the Japanese claimed that we never moved at night. The rest of our company and Fox Company come with us. There wasn't too many of us left by then. There was a little box canyon that ran at right angles to the cliff. At the opening they had a ladder in a cave that went up on top. Carson and me went up in the apex of that canyon and dug a hole. Fox Company was across from us about thirty yards and the rest of our company was down the slope a little ways. When the Japanese come running down the hill at Fox or our guys they had to run out a little bit around our little canyon to get down the slope. They couldn't even see us."

The 7th Division had taken all of their assigned area and had turned to the deadly task of mopping up.

There was a small town named Makabe in the 96th Division's area that they had not been able to take. Toward dark, it was noticed that large units of enemy soldiers were being assembled in the town. Artillery was called in and all of the Army and Marine guns in the area fired. The town was completely leveled. All of the Japanese were killed as well as all of the civilians who lived there.

The destroyer *Twiggs* had been hit by a Kamikaze on April 28 and had been out of action for repairs until May 17. She had soon returned and was now on radar picket duty. Just at dark, a torpedo bomber made a successful run on her. The torpedo went in her port side and exploded in a magazine. Before much could be done to deal with the situation the plane circled and crashed on the ship's weather decks. The destroyer was enveloped in fire and sank in less than an hour. A hundred twenty-six men died and thirty-four were wounded but there were, also, one hundred eight-eight sailors rescued.

June 17, 1945. The 1st and 3rd Battalion spent the day continuing to mop up their area. The 2nd Battalion fought but was so decimated that they couldn't be very effective and were in danger of being completely wiped out. The 22nd Regiment of the 6th Marine Division had finally arrived and was sent up the ridge to relieve what was left of the 2nd Battalion. When night fell the 2nd Battalion was pulled off the ridge. Jack was wounded before getting down and George Company could only bring forty-five Marines off of Kunishi Ridge and even some of them had minor wounds.

The following article was printed in the Kansas City Star:

TO REST ON OKINAWA.
Kansas Citian Is Among Marines relieved in Battle
By Vern Haugland
Itoman, Okinawa, June 17
(Delayed, (AP) -- A fresh Marine regiment relieved a tired and battered battalion on Kinishi Ridge early today and by nightfall crushed through stubborn Japanese defenses that had been holding up the American advance on the western Okinawa flank.

A five-day fight had reduced the companies of the 2nd Battalion of the 1st Marine Division (normally about 290 men each) to pitiful compliments of seventy-five, forty-six and forty-eight men.

Sergt. John D. Langley, Greenville, N.Ca. And pvt. Max C. Lowe, Atlantic, Ga., said F Company's three most blood thristy men on Kinishi were Cpl. John Doherty, St. Louis; Pvt. Morris Dolan, Brimson, Mo., and Pvt. Victor J. Dahle, Seattle, Washington.

Doherty, a former St. Louis policeman, killed eleven Japanese. He was so provoked that Dolan nosed him out with thirteen that he wanted to remain on the line for a day or two longer.

Others among the first off the ridge and happy in the knowledge that the Okinawa campaign would almost certainly be over before their services were needed again included Sergt. John D. Routh, St. Joseph, Mo., and Pvt. Donald Chaney, 800 East Forty-fourth street, Kansas City.
(The men were actually from G Company not F Company and Jack's rank was PFC, "Acting Corporal.")

"Vern Haugland was a war correspondent that was around us off and on. I don't remember if he was a Marine, I think he was from the Kansas City Star. There was both kinds of them around. I think Hougland even got hit in the butt with a piece of shrapnel once. Langley was the guy who was brought up with the company that was gonna relieve us. I knew him. Guys transferred back and forth between companies when they was needed and I had worked with all the companies one time or another."

"The day before we had got up on the slope. When it got light planes started coming in and dropping stuff on the slopes. They didn't use napalm they hit them with gasoline. They burned the foliage off all the brush. You could see men behind every bush sometimes more than one. We didn't know if we had shot them or the fire burned them to death."

"There is a lot of difference between cover and concealment. They had concealment but not cover. We had sent a tremendous barrage of small arms fire up that slope. I don't really know how many actual casualties they had or how many we accounted for among them. They was really bunched up there, they was gonna stop us from coming, in mass. They didn't have any other place to go. There was a cliff behind them that only went down to the ocean."

"During the day they had two or three bayonet charges. We slaughtered them, me and Carson, because they had to run pass us every time. When they went down the hill they had to pass our hole and they never saw us. If they had seen us, for them to get us they would have had to bent around a big ditch and they never did. Me and Carson had them every time. That must have been when Langely told that story that said I shot thirteen Japanese, he had come up there by then."

"Well, after the last bayonet charge everything quieted down for us for awhile and Fox company started taking opposition. Our artillery had been laying down their fire fifty yards in front of our lines when we had those bayonet charges. We knew when a charge was gonna come because of all the noise they made before they started. Our artillery would lay down fire at a hundred fifty yards in front of us and then come back fifty yards and then come back another fifty yards. They was shooting from a lot of miles away, they was really too far away. They was shooting proximity fuses. The shell breaks about thirty feet above the deck and throws all shrapnel. It don't touch the ground. It is just tremendous the casualties you can get from that. They was firing in support of Fox Company and they fired short and the shells hit the company. Fox called us on the radio and said, 'God, see if you can stop that! We got twenty-seven casualties from that last barrage.' We had a radio that allowed us to talk to the artillery and we called and told them to knock it off up here. We said their fire was too far left and that they had hit Fox Company and caused twenty-seven casualties. One of my hometown boys was in Fox Company, Dub Miller. The artillery asked us what they had done wrong and we said their fire was too far to the left and to come to the right and raise it a hundred fifty yards."

(Records may indicate that it is possible the shells that exploded over Fox Company were coming from a different battery than the one Jack talked to. It appears that a different Marine unit had called for fire on the ridge pass the one Fox Company was on. The distance at which the guns were firing brought their trajectory too close to the ground where the company was positioned and the shells exploded. Someone corrected this fire because it wasn't going where it was supposed to go and Jack, perhaps, corrected fire that should not have been corrected.)

"The artillery observer asked us if we were having any opposition right then. We told him no but we could hear them and it sounded like they was gonna have another bayonet charge. He said that he would send up two HE shells, these shells explode when they hit the ground, and for us to mark the spot where they hit. We was being relieved and was gonna get out of there, we was already out of our hole. I had set my pack and Tommy gun down against a stump and old Carson set his pack down there with my stuff. The old artillery boy said he would give us a holler when they (the shells) were on their way. I went over and picked up my pack and Carson's pack and my Tommy gun all with one hand, I was holding the radio in my other hand. I came back and was handing Carson his pack but he had to take my Tommy gun to get his pack off my arm. I had the pack through the shoulder straps and I had just reached out to him when the old boy said, 'They are on their way.' Well we could hear them coming and me and Carson knew right where they hit. We just seen two blasts of light like an arc welder."

"We had been up on that cliff and the next time we realized where we was at we was sitting in a rice paddy several feet out from the bottom of the cliff. Clear off the top! It blew us clear off the top. I can never remember falling. I had medical supplies in my pack and I still had the pack. But I didn't know where Carson was. I couldn't see. Couldn't hear. My first thought was that it was getting dark and where the hell was Carson. I tried to turn around, I didn't realize that I was blown clear off the cliff and was in a rice paddy. I was feeling around for him. He was sitting astraddle of me like we was riding a bobsled but he was out. It had popped my right eyeball out and I still had a canteen and I got it out and got a handful of water and pushed my eyeball back in. I could now see out a little with my left eye. I turned around and old Carson, his face was all blood. His right hand was all blood but he was breathing. I got the medical pack out and give us both a shot of morphine and it couldn't have been much longer till the medics come and patched us up. That was the end of our careers as combat Marines. A corpsman tried to wrap a bandage around both my eyes but I stopped him. He said that it was necessary, that if he didn't I might lose the vision in my good eye. I wasn't about to lay out there without being able to see. I wouldn't need any vision if a Japanese crawled up on me in the dark. I don't really know what I would have done, my Tommy gun was smashed and someone had stolen my pistol but I wasn't gonna lay out there blind."

The Army's 96th Division pressed their attack on Yuza Dake the next to the last enemy stronghold. Before dark the hill was captured and only Kunishi Ridge still held out. The Army Division's missions were over, although they would spent several weeks mopping up their areas of Okinawa.

This day was free of Kamikazes, collisions and groundings. A rare day for the Okinawa fleet.

June 18, 1945. "They had a lot of us casualties laying near the base of the cliff. They still had tremendous fire across that valley where the rice paddies was. They had mined the road and there were two disabled tanks out there that they had turned off the road. They had lost their turrets. They was just tremendous fire out there in the flat. The boys who got back under the cliff was safe, once you made it. They had a whole two days pile of guys piled up there under the cliffs. They had decided that the paddies was dry enough to bring tanks across them. Tanks made it but they got a lot of fire coming across. The first tank that I noticed, they backed up and loaded. They could only take two inside and they could strap two to four on the outside. They strapped them on and started out across the rice paddies and the fire got tremendous. They backed back up took the bodies off. The Japanese had killed the wounded that was in the stretchers on top of the tank. I was just kinda coming and going and they come to take me. They was just going down the row. There was a guy beside me that had his leg blown off. I said for them to take him next so they did. They took a load and I don't know how many made it across. The tank came back through that fire and backed up against the cliff. I was next and a guy asked me if I could make it up on this tank. I said that I could crawl up on it but that , by God , I wasn't gonna ride on the outside of that tank! He asked if I could make it inside and I say, yeah, I could. They strapped a few guys on it and I crawled up on top and started down into the turret head first. When I hung my head down in there I passed out and boy he took off. When I come to, my butt and feet was stuck up in the air and my head was in the gunners seat upside down. I passed out a time or two but I made it. I was still upside down when they pulled me out of the tank but I had made it across the valley."

"We was on the other side of the valley out of range. There was about eighty-five people there up on poles (stretcher cases) and no way to get us out. We still had as many Japanese behind us as we had in front. The corpsmen were there but there wasn't no doctors and about all they could do was give you a shot and put a patch on you. I knew that I was hurt but not how bad. If I had just had open wounds I would probably have bled to death but that shrapnel that hit me was so hot that it had seared the holes where it went in. They was just black holes that oozed instead of bled. What really bothered me was my eye. What happened was that shell caused a vacuum and we rode the blast out as she went. Blood had popped out all over both of us just like perspiration . Just little droplets all over us. No holes, just pressure done it. In the same way it had popped my eyeball out. I had put it back in with dirt that was on my hand. We laid there until the next day."

"While I was laying there they brought a little girl in. She was pretty as a picture and shot through both legs. She was just terrified till a corpsman started taking care of her. She knew then that we was gonna help her, not kill her. You could just see her relax."

The 22nd Regiment of the 6th Marine Division was brought south and went into battle again. They replaced the smashed up 7th Marines who hardly seemed to even exist at this point. Jack's battalion's rifle companies could only muster one hundred sixty-nine Marines out of five hundred seventy.

General Buckner was pleased with his Army's success and against strong advice went to the forward observation post of the 1st Marine Division. A Japanese artillery shell killed the General.

"I know that we was only a few hundred yards from Buckner when he got killed. The dates in my mind is not quite right on it. I thought he was killed a day or two before I got hit for the last time. I just know that he didn't get killed on the same day that I got hit or I wouldn't have heard about it. It wasn't that way."

June 19, 1945. "Where I was laying there wounded there was these sugarcane fields around behind where we was. The Japanese infiltrated ever night behind us in those cane fields. There ain't no way you can get a guy out of a cane field. You can't find them. It's four feet tall and it just grows up and curls over. (Sugarcane was the only Okinawan export during the war. The Japanese refined it into fuel for vehicles.) You can just crawl under it. They just tunneled under it. They would get in there and shoot at us from behind. There was bunches of them ever night. Tracy, the officer who wouldn't eat my chocolate, come up there were I was laying. I was waiting to be flown out. He said that he took my squad out and went into the sugarcane to clean out the snipers one morning. He asked me what I thought he ought to get instead of that carbine. He said on the way to the cane he spotted a Japanese. He got behind one tree and the Japanese got behind another one and they started shooting at one another. He said he knew that he had hit him two or three times but he suddenly jumped up and took off. Tracy said he was lucky that he was down behind a little hump because the Japanese bullets was going right through the little tree he was behind, and his bullets wasn't doing anything. I told him that he needed a Tommy gun, it had stopping power. That little hump that he was shooting from was why I carried a bunch of armor piercing bullets for my sniper rifle. It kicked the hell out of you but it would go through almost everything."

"Later on, I was taken out to that hospital ship and sent to Guam. I was there a few days and a nurse come up and asked me again what outfit I was from. She said one of our officers was there, a Lieutenant Tracy. She left and the next morning here come Tracy. I couldn't keep from laughing even though it hurt like hell. His head was as red as a barn and he didn't have a hair on it. He had something in his hand and was grinning from ear to ear. He had something to show me. He said he had taken my guys back in the cane field after I left. They had got seventeen snipers and only had two men hurt. He went back to the Command Post and set down on a C ration crate. Well, nobody ever sat up on nothing at the CP. You mostly laid down against your pack and stayed as low as you could while they gave out the orders. He said he was so proud of himself that he felt like giving himself a medal. So he sat up on the crate and was telling everybody what he had done. He remembered waking up a few days later and finding out he had been shot in the back of the head. They had flown him to Guam because he was partially paralyzed. They had shaved his head and poured methylate all over his head. The doctor come in looked his head over and pulled the bullet out with a tweezer like thing. It had gone under the skin and hit his skull but it hadn't gone all the way through. It just knocked him coo coo for awhile. He had that little bullet there to show me."

"He was a nice guy and he had always called me pops. He'd come around and asked me what I thought he ought to do. One time, I told him that he was in charge and ought to be telling me what we was gonna do. He said he thought that I knew a lot more because I was a lot older. We compared birthdays and it turned out that I was nineteen days older than he was. I had started turning white headed and white whiskered so I guess I looked a lot older. That early turning white haired was in my family but I think living on Okinawa didn't help much."

June 20, 1945. "They had all us wounded guys laying in just about the same place that we had landed in a little L5 spotter plane, some days back, when I was scouting for the regiment. The pilot had landed there and I had got out and taken pictures. He saw me there and told me that, I think it was some lieutenant maybe the Fox Company CO, some guy knew we had landed there before and they had decided they could fly the wounded out. They had done it before up the island a ways. I guess since he knew me he said he would fly me out. There was other guys wounded worse than I was but he wanted me to go with him.

"He could only take one person. The plane had a door that opened on the side and they just stuffed me in there on a stretcher. My head was right behind the pilot. He turned around and asked me if there was anything I wanted to see before I left the damned place. I told him that I'd been eighty days looking for the south end of the island. He said that we'd see it and I'd heard about the Japanese jumping off the cliffs and I kinda wanted to see that too. Those little planes was really souped up, he put the power to us and we had just got out over the cliffs where the Japanese was committing suicide. We was looking down on them jumping when there begin little black puffs above us. You didn't hear anything but you seen little black puffs. They was firing little anti-aircraft guns at us. I told the pilot that I had seen everything on that Goddamned island that I wanted to see and to get us the hell out of there. He just laughed. He was used to that, I guess. So he took me north to Yontan Airport and put me ashore. (The little planes flew at least one hundred twenty wounded out on this one day.) When I got to Yontan Airfield, that was the first time that I had seen a doctor and he repaired my eye. By this time, Carson had come up and they sewed up his head and his hand. That was all they done and then they headed us for a hospital ship. They had two colored guys with a DUK come to get some of us. That's an Army vehicle that went on land and in the water. It had wheels and a propeller. That was the first time that I had any close contact with the Army except every once in a while see a fellow on the line. They said they was gonna take us out to a hospital ship. One of them said that we was kinda skinny. Of course, we hadn't had much to eat for a long time. They said the Navy really feeds good and I liked hearing that. They loaded some of us and took off. We got right at the water when an air raid went off. The Navy started throwing smoke and you could hear the planes. The two Army guys grabbed our stretchers and stuck us under the DUK and took off. About an hour later the smoke cleared and the Navy shut her guns down but no two Army guys. In a while here come a major down the beach doing something. He asked us what we was doing under that damned DUCK. We said that we didn't know but we wasn't going anyplace. He asked us who just left us there and we told him about the Army guys. He said that he would fix things and went back up the beach. Pretty soon here come a Higgins boat. They loaded us in and ran out in the harbor to the hospital ship. They throwed a rope over the side and hooked it on my stretcher and I was aboard the USS Solace. I was finally off that damned island and I knew that I was going home."

June 21, 1945. Military officials declared that the island of Okinawa was secure. The 2nd Battalion of the 7th Marines had started the month of May with 919 men and ended the battle with 816 casualties.

"Toward the end it just seemed like everybody had just kind of melted away. Most of the guys was replacements that I didn't even know who they were. Didn't even know their names. You'd have some guys with you but you didn't even know if they was yours or just lost."

August 14, 1945. Japan agreed to surrender and World War II ended. Celebrations broke out everywhere.

September 2, 1945. Japan signed the surrender documents and the war was officially over.

Frank Moody. "We were glad when the war ended. We knew we had made it. The 1st Division would have gone into Japan. We knew there would have been a million casualties and you knew that you wouldn't make it through that. You couldn't do another invasion like that, it would just be impossible. These people who holler about the atom bomb wouldn't be saying anything about it if they had been on Okinawa, with us. After I was wounded, I was taken to Guam. I heard about it on a radio. I had a walking cast on so I went to tell the other guys they had dropped a bomb on Japan that had killed like a hundred thousand people or so. They laughed about it. The war was over and I had made it. You just can't believe how that feels."

"People ought to know what the Marines did over there. Ernie Ply was there but he got killed. I wish he could have wrote about it. One time they sent me and some guys out on a burial detail. We went around picking up dead guys and stacking them where they was gonna bury them. Some of them was in pretty bad shape and some of them had been dead for a long time. Sometimes we had to dig them up out of the mud where they had been for a long time. We was helping the Graves Registration Service people. We stacked up eighty dead guys and then they made us guard them until the next morning. So we had to sleep and eat right there with them. It was really horrible. I've always wished that civilian Americans would have spent a night like that with us. They would find out what war was really like and everyone should know what it's like. I wish they could have spent just one night like that, then they would know what we went through."

BIBLIOGRAPHY

1st Marine Division, After Action Report (1945)

7th Marine Regiment, After Action Report (1945)

2nd Battalion, 7th Marine Regiment, After Action Report (1945)

2nd Battalion, 7th Marine Regiment, Radio/Phone Logs (1945)

Foster, Simon, *Okinawa 1945, Final Assault on the Empire*, Arms and Armor Press (1994)

Frank Benis M., *Okinawa: The Great Island Battle*, Talisman/Parrish Books, Inc. (1978)

Astor, Gerald, *Operation Iceberg, The Invasion and Conquest of Okinawa in World War II - An Oral History*, Donald I. Find Inc. (1995)

Leckie, Robert, Okinawa, The Last Battle of World War II, Penguin Group (1995)

Sledge, E. B., *With The Old Breed, At Peleliu And Okinawa*, Naval Institute Press (1996)

Marines attacking Dakeshi Ridge. Smoke in the center is from a Japanese mortar round. Photo courtesy of the National Archives

Wana Draw, the gateway to Shuri.
Photo courtesy of the National Archives

Jack Dolan just out of "boot camp" (basic training)
Photo courtesy of Jack Dolan

Photo of Frank Moody on Guam, 1945
Photo courtesy of Jack Dolan

Jack Dolan and his bride, Roberta, at home shortly after his discharge
Photo courtesy of Jack Dolan

Frank Moody during a training exercise
Photo courtesy of Jack Dolan

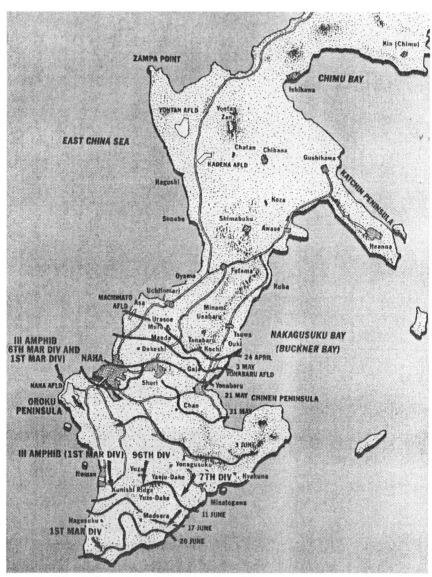

Map of Southern Okinawa showing the American lines on various dates
Photo courtesy of the National Archives

Marines attacking a Japanesse held cave
Photo courtesy of the National Archives

U.S. Soldier examining a tiny destroyed Japanese tank
Photo courtesy of the National Archives

Jack Dolan recovering from severe wounds in the San Francisco Naval Hospital.
Photo courtesy of Jack Dolan

Marines searching for a well-hidden enemy
Photo courtesy of the National Archives

**Jack Dolan's unit advancing on Dakeshi Ridge. Dakeshi Town is
to the right of the photo where the tank is pointing.
Photo courtesy of the National Archives**

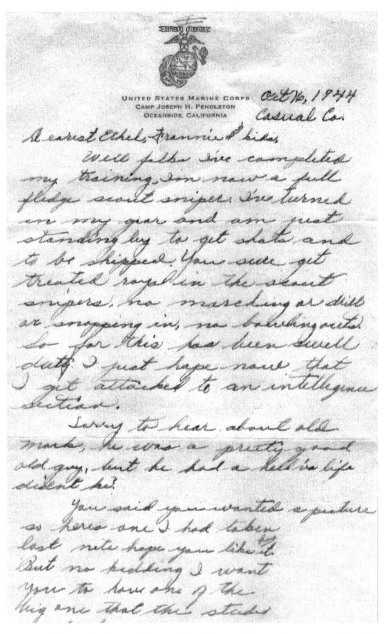

**Letter from Jack to the author's mother about graduating
Scout/Sniper school
Photo courtesy of Ethel Pearl Dolan**

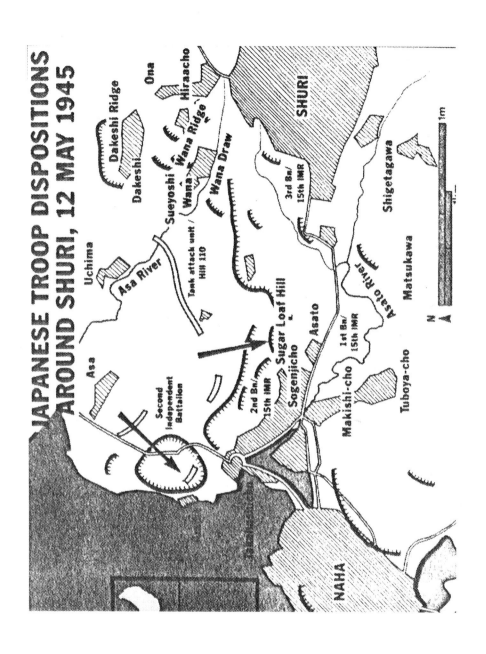

Map showing the relationship of Dakeshi to the Shuri Defenses
Photo courtesy of the National Archives

JAP RESISTANCE IS COLLAPSING on Okinawa
under the multiple assaults of Yank infantrymen and marines, indicated by arrows biting into the fighting front (solid line). Shuri town becomes a trap outflanked by the 96th infantry division on the southeast and under assault by the 1st marine and 77th army divisions. The 6th marine division, mopping up Naha, island capital, is sending an attack spearhead southeastward, with an apparent trap in the making if a junction can be formed with army forces moving westward from the east coast. The fight is becoming a chase as faltering enemy troops pull back. Broken lines indicate the belt across the island where the enemy may make a last stand, but some American officers believe he cannot mount the strength, after severe losses, to continue even suicide fighting more than a week or two—(Wirephoto).

**Kansas City Star article that appeared on June 1, 1945
Jack's mother clipped the article and saved it for him.
Photo courtesy of Jack Dolan**

Printed in the United States
20679LVS00007B/202-204